under the naga tail

A TRUE STORY OF SURVIVAL, BRAVERY, AND ESCAPE
FROM THE CAMBODIAN GENOCIDE

under
the
naga
tail

MAE BUNSENG TAING
WITH JAMES TAING

GREENLEAF
BOOK GROUP PRESS

This book is a memoir reflecting the author's present recollections of experiences over time. Its story and its words are the author's alone. Some details and characteristics may be changed, some events may be compressed, and some dialogue may be recreated. Some names and identifying characteristics of persons referenced in this book, as well as identifying places, have been changed to protect the privacy of the individuals and their families.

Published by Greenleaf Book Group Press
Austin, Texas
www.gbgpress.com

Distributed by Greenleaf Book Group

For ordering information or special discounts for bulk purchases, please contact Greenleaf Book Group at PO Box 91869, Austin, TX 78709, 512.891.6100.

Design and composition by Greenleaf Book Group
Cover design by Greenleaf Book Group
Cover images used under license from
©Shutterstock.com/Ms Moloko; ©Shutterstock.com/SAYASOUK
Interior map used under license from ©Shutterstock.com/Serban Bogdan

Publisher's Cataloging-in-Publication data is available.

Print ISBN: 979-8-88645-018-7

eBook ISBN: 979-8-88645-019-4

To offset the number of trees consumed in the printing of our books, Greenleaf donates a portion of the proceeds from each printing to the Arbor Day Foundation. Greenleaf Book Group has replaced over 50,000 trees since 2007.

Printed in the United States of America on acid-free paper

22 23 24 25 26 27   10 9 8 7 6 5 4 3 2 1

First Edition

To Eng Ngo Taing and Roberta Alice Dow,
the greatest and grandest mothers of all time.

Preface

JAMES TAING

My conviction to write my father's story began after a trip to his former homeland of Cambodia. I was studying abroad in Singapore, but there amid the island's westernized Asian shopping centers and sparkling glass buildings, I felt burdened by my recent experiences in Cambodia, and doubly burdened by the knowledge of what that country used to be. At one time, Cambodia was far ahead of Singapore in its state of advancement.

Then the devastations of civil war began in 1968.

I thought about what my Cambodian father and the country of Cambodia itself could have become if genocide had not consumed the nation. It was perpetrated at the hands of a megalomaniac named Pol Pot, the Cambodian "leader" who inflicted mass murders on his own people. He was especially hard on those who wore eyeglasses; it mattered not whether glasses indicated inferior eyesight or brainy intellectualism, he objected to both conditions. In the name of social transformation, he also targeted students, intellectuals, teachers, writers, artists, businessmen, lawyers, and doctors.

Anyone who might be guilty of independent thought.

My father was a teenager when he was swept up in all this. In the years since his escape, he locked away many traumatic memories. Growing up in his household, I learned small bits and pieces of this story, but it was only enough to spark a deep need to know more about the man who raised me. Finally, after years of pestering from me, he began to tell me how it all happened.

When I shared his stories with friends, they were awestruck by the depth of determination behind his struggle to escape tyranny from that murderous regime. It brought them closer to grasping the sheer scale of senseless brutality, meaningless suffering, and unimaginable death within that country.

However, every time I told of his long journey, I came away dissatisfied. It felt hollow for me to allow such experiences to be confined to a fleeting conversation. I knew the ephemeral nature of memory doomed this story to be forgotten. What if my father or our family members could no longer tell it? After all, I knew the value of the stories to me, my other family members, and close friends who heard them. Forgetting those accounts would have bankrupted me of the ability to be shaped and inspired by them.

That same collective memory is available to many others, if they are given the chance to absorb the knowledge. As Elie Wiesel put it regarding the Jewish Holocaust, giving up the responsibility to remember would be to consign the victims to a second death, this time from the collective memory of society. It would be a denial of reality, as if all those inexcusable crimes never happened. As if the element of human nature which allowed them to occur had left us.

And so, if this pattern of collective forgetting repeated itself, would I be partly responsible because I had been silent? It was a challenge to my personal character.

If I did not care, how could I expect caring from anyone else?

Thus my passion for this story, a deep need to offer something vital to the world. The story provides an inspiration to thrive in our current lives, and to boldly recognize that every one of us bears the power of an indomitable human will. In each of us exists a spirit that can break free from the imprisonment of fear and hurt; a tenacity to overcome whatever hardships are given.

These memories are living things, because the dark side of human nature behind them has not changed. Any look at your daily news will confirm that. The common thread between everyone in this story and the rest of us is our shared human nature, in both its light and dark forms.

This story, told in my father's voice, is an appeal to the better angels of our nature. My desire is for it to strengthen you, as it has me, against the darker demons we all carry and the darker times many of us will face.

Yeay Sek
(family nanny)

Sihong — eldest child and woman of the family. She was a shrewd businesswoman and owned a small delivery service that carried their clients' packages from Thailand to Cambodia.

Sihun — second-eldest child; and married her husband Wensun in 1966. In the early days of their marriage they sold items such as candy and canned goods before they had enough to build a house of their own.

Tai — third born and eldest son. He once saved enough to start a cigarette venture with two of his other friends, and at one point customers made the long trip to Poipet for their cigarette brand.

Choa — younger twin brother of Tai, but resemblance ended there. Unlike Tai, who always kept his eyes out for his next business idea, Choa enjoyed an easier pace of life driving a taxi cab and spending time with friends.

Chiv — the third-eldest son, he had many friends who joined the freedom fighters in the civil war. He sympathized the most with their struggle to restore the king's power and authority, as much of Cambodia did. He sold freshly hatched baby ducks for a living; married his wife in 1970.

Wenqing — the sixth child and third daughter, who fondly enjoyed sewing at home more than anything else.

Luor — the seventh child of the family and fourth son. He worked with Sihong in her parcel-delivery business.

Mae — the youngest of eight and fifth son.

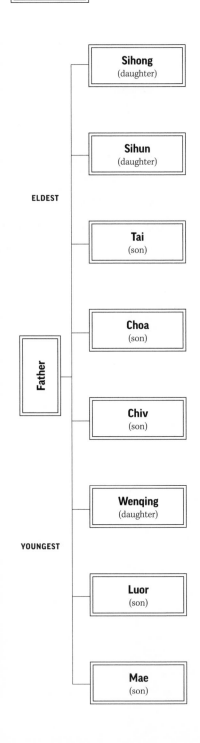

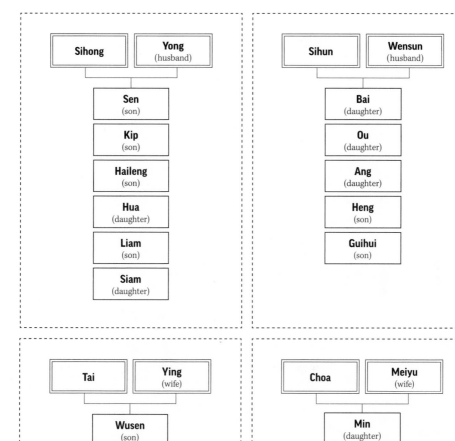

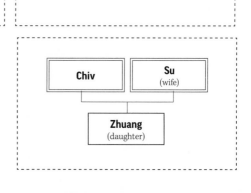

Author's Note

Nagas are legendary multi-headed serpents that control the rains, and therefore are symbolically the guardians of prosperity and treasures in the Kingdom of the Cambodians. Cambodians say that they are "Born from the Naga," descendants of this divine bloodline, tapping into the spirit that irrigates the rivers and seas, alongside the rainbows that bridge earth to heaven. They hold the key to the crossing from the world of man into the abode of the gods.

Nagas mostly live in the deepest underworld, far under the land, and therefore in some tellings if Nagas are not treated with reverence, they are believed to bring about natural catastrophe in the form of floods, famine, and even drought.

This power to bring calamity is depicted in a popular mythology, Samudra Manthana, one of the more central Hindu stories that is carved into the famous ancient Cambodian temples of Angkor Wat and Preah Vihear. According to the legend, a pact is formed at the beginning of the universe between the gods and the demons to obtain the nectar of immortality. In order to do so, Vasuki, the King of the

Nagas, is enlisted to be used as a rope to extract the Water of Life from the seas. However, as the gods pull from the tail and demons pull from his head, mishap occurs that jeopardizes all of creation. The enormously long Vasuki spews forth a terrible choking poison, Halahala, that begins to contaminate the ocean beneath him. If it had not been for the act of a prominent god to valiantly drink up the flood of venom himself, disaster would have engulfed the world of the gods and humans underneath the Naga.

In the aftermath, the gods and demons were able to work together again and use the gigantic Vasuki to retrieve from the cosmic oceans fourteen impressive treasures, including a cow of plenty; celestial dancers called *apsara*; *Kalpavriksha*, the wish-fulfilling tree; and the hard-sought *amrita*, the elixir of immortality. Also born out of this so-called churning primeval ocean was the moon, immediately nearly blinding the gods with his bright, glittering body. This mystical god rode wondrously on his lunar chariot across the night skies.

From this point on, the creation of the moon blessed humanity with magical light to traverse the dark.

PART I

Red Thunder

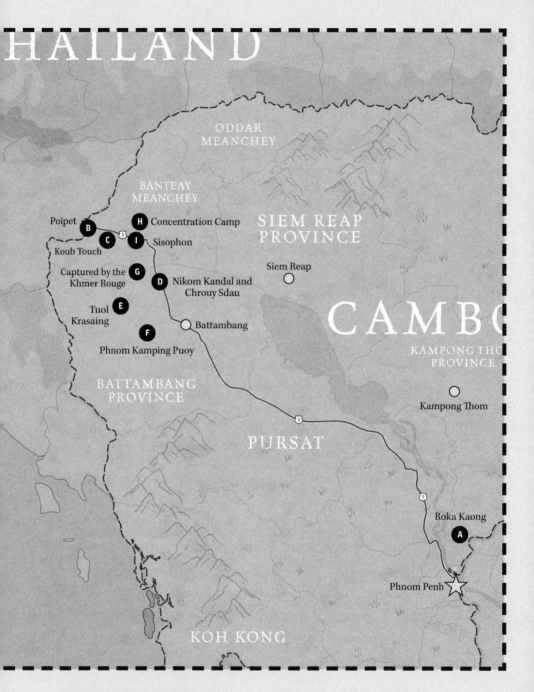

PART I – RED THUNDER

Chapter 1

Apollo

MAE TAING

Apollo was there. I pretended that if I looked closely enough, I could see its wobbling shadow roving on the moon. The moon shone bright like burning silver, and its uneven surface was brittle and speckled. I had a hard time seeing how the moon had been touched by human hands.

It was inconceivable for the Cambodian people, too, as they had long worshipped the moon. In our culture, the moon was Heaven's most adored lantern, largest and brightest, floating high in the black curtain of the skies. Apollo had to be a big bullet, carrying wingless pilots and riders, shot upward in the air—in the riot of lit fireworks.

I was an eleven-year-old Chinese Cambodian boy on the day the Apollo mission successfully landed astronauts on the moon. I had first learned about the Apollo rocket program in class, which was unusual because my schooling was mostly devoted to math and Chinese. Father had enrolled me in Mandarin Language School where there was no science, history, or art; just Mandarin. He was strict in keeping our mother tongue alive in us, and we were not allowed to speak Khmer at home.

At school, the mandatory uniform was knee-length blue trousers, bright white short-sleeved shirts, and Maoist pins, which were prominently displayed on our uniforms.

My teacher was a tall, pretty woman with beautiful black hair and a youthful voice. Yet even as a teacher she was more stuck on her own interests than on caring for the needs of her students.

We students had to stand behind our desks each morning before class to recite from the Red Book, *The Quotations of Mao Zedong*. Our teacher was born of a Chinese family, as I was, but she was also passionate about Mao, requiring us to carry his book anyplace we went. For encouragement, we were assured that if we closely followed Mao's teachings, we could be granted the prestigious privilege of wearing a red band and a red Communist Pioneer tie over our collar. This gave one lucky recipient the responsibility of watching over his classmates during recess and policing the walking lines to and from class.

Teacher protested about the unfairness in America, claiming they enslaved Blacks to labor for the Whites, that the country and its people always trampled on the poor, and that their government allowed for corrupt gambling wagers on whether a person lives or dies. They call it "insurance," she told us, and the rich sell it to the poor.

"The rich live above the ground," she declared. "The poor live underneath the ground. But Mao is fair and just. He wants people to live equally. No rich or poor. No social oppressors or classes. Everyone shall be the same."

She proceeded to ask us to commit everything to Chairman Mao.

"One thousand years! One thousand years for Mao Zedong!!" I rehearsed with the class.

"Be a good soldier!" we sang in Mandarin. "Fight with the

Americans. Devote your mind! Sacrifice your life! Don't be afraid of the Americans! They are only paper tigers!"

Yet in class, when I recited curses and blasphemies against America, my heart did not truly hate the country. I thought, *How can I hate an entire country without even knowing where it is?* I never saw it, or any American people. The fact was, deep down, I admired America. It was the only country to accomplish reaching the moon. And from the day the Americans landed there, my imagination had run wild with wonder and marvel.

For countless generations, the moon was a deity associated with an ample harvest for plants and crops and therefore of high reverence to Cambodians. After news of the Apollo 11 landing was proclaimed with a single radio declaration, Cambodians worshipped the moon with greater intensity, erecting incense shrines outside their huts and placing second offerings of fruits and moon-shaped cakes in the evening fields. The eternal moon was nearer to them. They could almost hold it in their hands and feel it with their hearts.

Vendors began selling white T-shirts with the Apollo 11 spaceship printed on the front—one with Apollo 11, shaped as a bullet, standing upright in flight, and another with a man in a white space suit. The vendors sold out at a record pace with each restock, as every single kid in town wanted Apollo space T-shirts. I wore mine everywhere, even beneath my uniform when I went to school.

* * *

Consumed by wanderlust, I often thought of Apollo and all the other places to visit after the moon. *How long would it take to sail to the edge of the sun?* What would it be like to peer into a diamond star? I even pictured myself riding my own silver bullet to the sun. Life seemed limitless. At the time, I had yet to even experience what it was like to sit in a plane.

At the time of the moon landing, these stirring daydreams lingered even stronger. Apollo seemed to me to signal a certain newness was arriving with this next generation. That intuition became more potent once I heard my family decided to make a move to a new province.

The civil war between Lon Nol's army and the so-called freedom fighters had affected our family business in Roka Kaong, so we moved to be with my eldest sister, Sihong. She lived in Poipet, Cambodia's most northwestern city. Given the distance, Poipet's economy was well outside the fighting.

Cambodia stood in a delicate balance. It was hard to believe how fragile the scales were between peace and war.

Revolution was on its way.

* * *

Although I had known since I was little that I was meant to do business like the rest of my sisters and brothers, there was an incident when I was sixteen in Poipet that taught me that the ways of running a shop would soon change dramatically because of the civil war.

Three weeks into the month of February 1975, someone shouted, "Hurry up! The guards are here!" Border guards were coming to confiscate our merchandise. They did this from time to time, since some of our items were sold without paying border tariffs. Immediately, the entire street was in a frenzy, with shopkeepers taking down their storefront awnings and hiding their wares. I pushed all the full crates into the back of my home and when I came back out, a Lon Nol soldier appeared in front of the store.

He wore the conventional outfit of a soldier: a bill cap, a khaki green jacket with the sleeves rolled up, and an insignia patch on his arm. He looked at me coldly and said, "I need sixty ten-kilo bags of sugar. I cannot take it myself. You will need to bring it to the train for me." It was a wildly large demand, the equivalent of 1,320 pounds of sugar. The most I had ever sold was fifty bags.

"I need sugar, sixty bags," he said again.

"I will only do thirty bags," I countered. Although I would have rather not done any business with him at all, I had a lot of sugar left over. In the past few weeks, the civil war had affected the number of customers who came to Poipet by train, and rats were eating into my sitting inventory.

He looked slighted, but he agreed and reassured me he would pay once I brought it all to the train. He departed toward the station, an M16 assault rifle slung over his back. Since he was armed, I followed through on his demand.

My helper, Kane, drew up his rickshaw, and we loaded the carriage with thirty bags before we drove to the station. There, we turned into the circular entryway and parked right in front of the two-story building, below the station's big wall-mounted clock.

The soldier already stood in the third freight car before the end of the train, and he gave a signal to the both of us. I hauled three bags, heavy as lead, and handed each off to the soldier. Each bag must have been only a few pounds below my weight, which was the most I could carry. Passengers filed past us, piling into rust-colored cars. Kane and I made five trips, back and forth, hefting each bag to the soldier. When the whistle blared, Kane handed me the last of the bags for the soldier.

"Sir, that is all of them," I told him. "Now you have to pay me." The soldier took the bags and turned his back to me, piling and ordering the packages. His strapped pistol jigged up and down with his waist.

"I might not have enough money on me," he said weakly. "I can come tomorrow and pay you."

"Pay me now!" I was furious. "We had an agreement!" The passengers on the roof all looked at me in one motion. "You said you would pay me once I delivered all the bags to the train!"

The whistle blew a final loud shrill, and before faltering and lunging forward, the wheels shivered. At the last moment, the soldier went into his green satchel and handed me a brown bag. I opened the bag and quickly counted the money in it, but it was nothing close to what the sugar cost. Before I looked up, the last of the train's freight cars pulled ahead, gaining speed. That's when I started running.

"You didn't pay me enough!" I shouted as I ran along. The train continued to gain speed, so I had to run faster. The end of the station platform approached, where a stone slab sloped down level to the ground. I raced down the slope and ran hard to reach the freight car he was in.

"Heyy!! Heeyy!! You didn't pay me enough!" I screamed. I felt the eyes of onlookers while he wearily turned around, hands poised on his hips.

"I know where you live. I'll pay you the rest when I come back in a few days."

The train gained speed. Hurriedly, I grabbed the bar of the freight door and leapt onto the steel stirrup steps. I stood halfway on the ledge, my other leg dangling in the air. The train quickened. I was stuck. The car was crammed with people all the way to the door.

A kind Cambodian passenger reached down and put his hand out for me. I grabbed ahold, hopped into the freight car, and wedged myself between the crowd of people and the soldier. The soldier cried out in surprise amid the murmurs and whispers of the other passengers.

Taking some comfort from all the people surrounding me, I pulled my shoulders back to draw a deep breath and hollered, "Pay me now!!"

The soldier's eyes fidgeted back and forth, panning around the passengers, who eyed him disdainfully. Without a word, he reached for his military satchel, opened the flap, and began leafing through his pack. He pulled out a stack of money. I took the stack and counted it right in front of him. It was a heck of a lot of riels and the stack took several more recounts. And still it was not the right amount.

"That's all I have. I will pay you next time I come and see you."

Figures, I thought. *At least I got most of the money*. The train's whistle signaled it was pulling into a station. New passengers at the platform edge forced themselves into the car, pinning me in a crushing wave, pushing me toward the back. I sawed and elbowed my way through the crowd, hugging the stack of money in my arms.

The train whistle gave a cheerless blow, its stacks of smog blemishing the clear blue sky. I was the only passenger who exited. It was a desolate backcountry populated with vendors who seemed like they had no business being there. I grew nervous from carrying all the money on me, so I rolled the brick of cash under my buttoned shirt and tucked it beneath my waistband for security. I did not know where I was, but I could tell my home was far up the highway.

Across the platform, I saw a few vendors selling home-cooked snacks and malted drinks. I went to a stall and interrupted a vendor fanning away flies, more flies than customers. I asked where the closest town was. His hand shot up and pointed somewhere in the vast scrubland. I asked if he could drive me to Poipet and he pointed in the direction where the train had come from, gesturing as a question.

I nodded.

The man dismissed me with a wave of his hand. I wandered to another stall and this time asked how much it was to take me to Poipet.

"No one dares to travel at night," the owner said. "It is too dangerous." But he gave a price that was high, demanding triple the normal rate for traveling there and back at night. I accepted it and he led me to his motorcycle with a triangular rickshaw mounted in the back, while his family stayed to manage his shop.

We were alone in the expanse of the dry countryside. Nothing much else was there except for a few poor hedges, parched bushes, and scraggly trees. The deep throbbing of the motorcycle echoed in the isolated countryside.

Cruising along the straightaway, my eyes fell upon a dark lip blocking the road ahead. It grew larger the closer we got, and then abruptly it appeared to be a deadly hill cutting across the highway.

The brash driver suddenly swerved onto the rough shoulder of the road, causing me to pop from my seat. I gaped at the sight of anti-tank trenches, carved deep enough for anyone to hide in. As the vendor drove back onto the smooth pavement, I stared at the dune while it withdrew farther away and became a speck. A shudder went through me.

Throughout the entire trip, we came upon more black dunes hunched like grave mounds over the roads, forcing the driver to retreat to the loose gravel shoulder. Having never ventured outside of Poipet, this was the first I had seen of the trenches. This was the reason Poipet was cut off from supplies and transportation to the city. The freedom fighters dug up the road and attacked the vehicles that were stuck, stealing their supplies to prevent them from reaching the hands of the Lon Nol government. Even though the freedom fighters were doing noble work to reunify the country for the king, I was still scared because the fighting was getting nearer.

I heaved a sigh of relief when I saw the stark city appear. The sun began to recede; shadows crept up to the sky. On the roadside, a woman poured out a dingy pail of water. Canvas awnings to storefronts were taken down.

When I arrived at my house, it was empty. Father was gone. I saw only a portrait of my late mother on the wall, and a golden altar sitting beneath it on the floor. I went back outside and saw Kane around the corner closing down my shop.

"Your father went to the train station to look for you," Kane told me. "He asked me to clean up."

From afar, the tents in the bazaar were also being taken down. When I walked to the train station, I saw Father standing solemnly outside the closed security grills. He was gazing up at the big station clock and the darkening sky.

Father gave me a long, steady look.

"Mae," he said. "It was dangerous to get on a train with a soldier!" But he was not saying so to scold me. He went on, "It was a very brave thing of you to do." Seldom did Father commend me, and while that was all he said, it was all I needed to hear.

Until that day, I was considered too young and inexperienced to have done such a thing. But I had showed that the business was now mine to run.

In the days since Mother passed away, Father spent more time at the family's ranch, a few miles from Poipet. He was retired now and had decided to hire some workers to help him maintain the property. Half the week was spent there and the other half in Poipet. When he was in Poipet, he spent much of his daily time reading imported *Kung Sheung* newspapers.

I was the youngest in the family and still lived with Father. All my brothers and sisters had married and were in homes of their own in the neighborhood. Originally it was just Mother and me who ran the shop. Mother used to cook sweet buns and Cambodian tapioca-banana pudding for me to put out in the mornings, as well as cut watermelon and other Chinese desserts. Sometimes we took turns and she handled the shop, while I took the sweet goods to the train station and sold them to the people there. Travelers loved her dessert pies and bought them by the dozen. As the last born of eight, I was closest to Mother. I cared about her so much. She was the one who started teaching me how to run a shop. Her greatest desire for me was to start my own business.

When Mother passed away, Father must have felt sorry for me. He gave me one and a half million Cambodian riels and told me, "Here. Go run your business shop."

I had started with space on the side of Sihong's home. All the money I earned was mine to keep, and that was how I got my business going.

Qingming, meaning "Tomb-Sweeping Day," arrived in April, and I planned to bring sweet buns to offer Mother, just like the ones she cooked, so she had enough to eat in the afterlife. This would be the first year we celebrated the Qingming Festival at the ranch. Although she had died the year before, we did not celebrate Qingming for her. People do not worship ancestors who recently passed, in the belief that it will bring bad luck. Only the Chinese people in Cambodia celebrated Qingming.

Everyone in the family planned to go to the ranch to spend a couple of days to visit her, and sweep and pull weeds around the tomb. We would also feed her with pails of water over her grave and then place chopsticks, tea, sweet buns, roast suckling pigs, dumplings, fruits, and pudding dessert on the grave steps. Then gifts of incense, gold foil, and paper money would be burned before the tomb for her to buy comfort in Heaven.

* * *

Two weeks before the Qingming Festival, there was an incident at the shop. The early morning brought new customers lining up at my stall. They all wanted live rabbits, which were a new trend, however, I had no idea how to get them.

Suddenly, the busy peace of the morning was broken by an outburst of weeping and a woman's terrified wail from nearby. The customers looked back at a thin, slovenly woman crying on her knees before my sister, Sihong. The poor-looking woman gripped on to her, clasping her hands and crying inconsolably. I wondered what had happened to her. *Did she lose a loved one?*

Sihong took the woman into her home for the night, where she began pouring out her story, and that of thousands like her. She had lived in a village within a southeastern province of Cambodia, near the border of Vietnam, when it was taken over by the freedom fighters. She urged us not to believe that the freedom fighters had good intentions, nor were these men simply racketeers. They had no leadership and formed no group allegiances, doing as they pleased. These vicious men took people for prisoners to force into harsh labor and exterminated the unwanted ones. "They murder people left and right," she wept, giant tears spilling from her eyes. "They destroy what they can. Even children . . . little boys and girls. Monsters . . . barbaric monsters . . . that's what they are!"

She told of hundreds of people like her, who had been chased into the jungles of Cambodia to hide. They were pursued, and once located, eliminated. She was a runaway and made the perilous trek north, alongside heavy fighting from the war, and lived as a fugitive in Phnom Penh before she reached Poipet. The woman had heard from others in town that Sihong was capable of helping her get out of the country. It was true. Our father had always been willing to help, even if you were not family, and in that regard my sister took after him.

For the next morning, Sihong arranged for one of her workers to take the refugee woman through the forests into Thailand by foot. This path ran through thin game trails that slender foxes appeared from and went panting by. Only smugglers like Sihong's worker knew of it. I went with Sihong in a separate vehicle to Thailand to ensure the woman had safely crossed. Before the woman left ahead of us, we gave her working garments and a shroud to cover her face.

We drove through the customs checkpoint at the border and worked our way to the location where we had agreed to meet. When we arrived, we were pleased to see the woman standing at the precise spot where Sihong's worker said they would come out of the jungle. We gave the refugee woman food items, water, and other provisions to take along and asked her where she would be going. She said she planned to look for her friends in Bangkok, although she had no idea where they were. She was just glad to be out of Cambodia.

She warned us, "Beware, you must leave! Stay at your peril! Please believe me. They are cruel, bad-hearted savages. If you don't leave the country, you will be sorry. They will grab everything you own."

We listened attentively and forced a half smile without a word. We tried our hardest to understand her stories of abduction and imprisonment, but none of us had ever seen behavior like that. It was hard to believe people could do such things. The freedom fighters were defending the honor of the king.

We decided she was desperate for our pity so we would help her get out of the country. She was a good actor who had convinced herself of her own imaginings. We still felt secure, without a desire to sell everything and start from scratch again in a foreign land. We had been in Cambodia for so long, we simply could not believe our lives would be endangered.

"Have a safe journey," we said as she walked on a path that curled through the trees. It seemed as if we were making the right choice, the wise choice.

If we only knew.

Chapter 2

The Last Village

April was a busy month, and signs of life returned to the city. Poipet was actively preparing for another festival: the Cambodian New Year, called Choul Chnam Thmey. Despite the roadblocks to the city, from dawn to dusk the streets filled with people purchasing fattened piglets, new clothes, and ornaments for their altars to welcome in the new spirits. Every family was getting ready, repairing their roofs and giving their houses a proper scrubbing.

On April 13, the holidays started. Candles and incense were lit outside to ask the new spirits to come and partake of the residents' offerings. The city feasted and prayed at the monastery for three days. People danced in the temple, night markets, and streets. Gifts were exchanged. It was a sign of renewal for the New Year. Peace and optimism were promised.

The next day, the radio was the first to usher in what seemed to be that new promise: "The freedom fighters have liberated Phnom Penh!"

It was April 15, 1975, right on the heels of New Year's. We felt the gods smile upon us.

The broadcast went on all day. Then after that, the radio never worked again. Only static and crackles came through when we turned the dial. We wondered why a new government would disrupt the normal order. Everyone relied on the radio broadcasts; there was no television or telephone across the country.

From the day of the announcement saying the freedom fighters took Cambodia's capital, a pervading lawlessness ensued. In Poipet, all the Lon Nol officials and soldiers fled into Thailand in defeat. Looters struck the governor's house, the businesses, the barracks, the locals' homes. Streets were deserted and life stopped short. An ominous atmosphere of quiet settled on the city.

"Should we flee or should we stay?" my brothers and sisters asked Father. There were rumors that the freedom fighters were Communists, and several townspeople had already fled to Thailand.

"Cambodia will never turn Communist," Father said. He pointed at the newspaper. "According to them, they are predicting the new government will be democratic. They will reorganize the government to make this happen."

The newspaper said Cambodia had always had tumultuous transitions: the festering French colonization since the 1800s, the four-year Japanese military occupation during World War II, and the post-war independence as a constitutional monarchy under the beloved King Norodom Sihanouk. For the past five years, Lon Nol had stolen power from the king, but now Lon Nol had finally been defeated. After all these transitions, the newspapers proclaimed the golden years would now be restored once again under King Sihanouk.

Father had lived through much of this before, when he journeyed through Communist China. "Cambodia is a small country with a small population, rich in resources. Nothing can compare," he said. "The people will not starve. This country can grow anything it desires." For Father, Communism in Cambodia could not be as ruinous as it was in other countries.

"I have already prepared well if it came to that," he reassured us. "We have a ranch and can live off the land. There is a pond to raise fish and wells to drink from. It is not a matter of our concern."

He grew up as a farmer in rural China, in a small ancestral village called Xinxi. We could learn how to farm and raise animals from him. He also reminded us that the ranch held a river in the back, with Thailand just across the water. It was simple enough to slip into the country if the situation was not right. It was easy to convince the family to stay in Poipet.

However, the Poipet we hoped to remain in was rapidly dissolving. The town ceased operations. People stopped going to work, shops closed, and trade halted on the borders. Neighbors talked about the old days, bringing back fond memories of when there was peace and stability. And even so, optimism still reigned. We were not conditioned for betrayal by our own government.

"Don't worry. This new government will be even better," people assured me. "The king is coming back and he will learn from the past. He will fix it all and make sure it doesn't happen again. We will have a secure government again and it will be here for a long time." Confidence was high, and with eager anticipation we awaited the arrival of the freedom fighters.

* * *

When they showed up, they resembled peasants and villagers, except for the red-and-white checkered scarves draped over their shirts. Many wore black or green Maoist caps. In a long march down the street, the freedom fighters passed my house, their footsteps clicking and clapping. The soldiers were stone-faced, with dark attitudes far from the people's jubilation.

We clapped and cheered them on, but the passing parade was hardly what I expected. Most of the soldiers were teenagers, some as young as twelve, looking badly fed, scrawny, and pale, like they had been hiding in the forests. Many bent beneath the weight of their old Chinese rifles, appearing on the verge of collapse while trying to hold the gun straight at their sides or sticking out behind them. A number of them were so small, their AK-47 guns stood as tall as they did, dragging trails in the ground at haphazard angles.

"We are independent now," one soldier shouted through a microphone.

The soldiers set up posts along the street, hugging their guns and scrutinizing everyone with hard looks. They did not wander the city publicly celebrating their victory, yet every home in Poipet cooked food offerings for the freedom fighters. We all wanted to believe they were the heroes of our time, the pride of our country, the symbol of dedication to our people. Even monks came to give blessings to the soldiers, stirring more cheers in the town. In the minds of the people, this gave bedrock credibility to the soldiers.

When I walked at night, oil lamps hung on the front of every house, lighting all the way along the streets, just the way it would be for the Cambodian New Year. The light of new justice shining. The townspeople walked along singing folk songs, remarking in joy, "How great is the new government! Long live peace!"

The peace did not live long, and was a strange "peace" indeed.

On the second day after their arrival, the freedom fighters immediately fixed prices. Butchers and fishermen were to sell their products for ninety percent less. As the townspeople flocked to the market shops, the

Chinese store owners told everyone to leave. People angrily swarmed their storefronts, demanding services. The store owners reopened and sold a little bit, then re-closed their shops, telling everyone they had run out of stock. Outraged, people threatened to bring the soldiers. The store owners relented. The fresh meats and fish disappeared first, followed by newly caught prawns, fermented and salted fish, pickled vegetables, imported beer, and rice. The shop owners were losing their shirts, as everyone bought as much as they could.

A soldier came through the streets proclaiming they had caught several Thai thieves who were stealing cows from Poipet in the night, hoping to smuggle them over the border. As the first prisoners of the new government in Poipet, they were going to be executed two miles outside of town as an example and a warning for everyone to see. The townspeople were happy over this because the Lon Nol government never lifted a finger to protect the border or even the people. It felt as if soldiers had indeed arrived to protect the citizens of Poipet.

In a large open area of ground by a river, at least five hundred had turned up for the spectacle. They were packed shoulder to shoulder, obstructing my view. Guards dressed in black stood still and straight, with their backs to the crowds. Other soldiers dug three holes in the dirt and placed wooden poles inside each one. We saw no prisoners, until a vehicle lumbered in, carrying three blindfolded men with their hands clasped behind their backs. The soldiers pulled the men out and led them to their poles. Their wrists were retied behind the wood.

"These people have committed crimes against Angkar. Not only have they been stealing from Angkar, but they are also foreigners who we deem our enemies. All enemies need to be eradicated from our country. Death is the penalty for their crimes."

Abruptly, three soldiers stepped forward in front of each prisoner. Their rifles were raised at the men's heads. I wanted to look, but I was too scared. We were all going to witness the government's commitment to its people, its promises to handle criminals. Then three loud, crisp shots rang out. A shiver shook my frame.

A murmur of admiration ran through the gathering. The crowd whooped and cheered. "Now we have somebody who will protect us! Now we finally have a government that cares for us!"

One high-spirited person cried, "Those people deserved it! These thieves have been stealing from the people for a long time."

Another man declared, "Take this as an example, that you cannot mess with Cambodia anymore. These men will judge you!"

The people saw it as an act of honor for their country, choosing not to recognize the horror of what was truly being done. The human nature of the crowd took the more cheerful course, as wrong as it would prove to be.

The celebrations continued for one more day. Many townsmen gambled and drank away their salaries. As I lay awake that night, I began thinking about my new life under this government. In the distance, pent-up music of overnight partying played. People danced late into the evening. The beat of the sounds got even faster, amid raucous laughter and shouting.

But then the lights went off and the neighborhood was pitched into total darkness.

The music cut out.

Dogs barked.

Silence descended.

* * *

A confused sense of alarm filled the night. The town's electricity generator had run out of oil. The family that supplied the power to the town said that since the border was closed, there would be no businesses open for several days to sell them petrol. It would take time. So we set out candles and kerosene lamps throughout the house.

The battery-powered radio was still useless; just noise on each channel. We did not hear a single dog bark again. It was April 26, 1975. A soundless shiver went through the city.

* * *

One day later, on April 27, a new megaphone announcement blared: "Everyone must evacuate the city immediately!" It was early, before sunrise, and the voice echoed harsh and shrill from down the street.

"Gather your things and leave the city! The Americans are going to bomb this area! Leave the city immediately!"

The disturbance came from a billboard truck used for theatre advertisements. "Everyone must leave for three days. America is going to bomb the city! Leave now! You will return after three days!"

I heard the sound of cars driving up and down, and I snapped out of bed. Everyone in the house was frantically running around, asking questions none of us had an answer to. Noise in the streets drew me to the windows. Outside I saw the soldiers patrolling the street. "Leave now! Leave now!" they kept repeating. "You will be going ten kilos away from the city. Do not take much with you. We will take care of everything until you come back. You'll return in two or three days."

Two or three days.

The family collected our most important valuables: money, gold jewelry, clothes, food supplies, and kitchenware for cooking, throwing it into bags. The house became a heap of wreckage with chairs knocked down and tables turned over.

I opened my drawers and retrieved my watch, a gold necklace, and a handful of Cambodian riels. Impulsively, I dumped out my trash can and took the rest of my savings out of the drawer. I placed it in the trash can, covering it with all the garbage on top. We were going to be back in a few days, but if thieves came during that time, I hoped they would not think to search the trash can. I raced around my room and gathered three days' worth of clothes and remembered to feed my fish. I scooped out a generous amount of mosquito larvae and dumped it into the fish tank.

When I came out of my room, Father asked me to put food on the altar and worship Mother with incense before we left. This was a duty not for the husbands, but permitted only for the children. I lit incense and brought my hands together before her altar and made a prayer for her to protect us. Then I heard honking outside our doors. I called my Pekingese dog, the last one in the house, and went outside.

When I stepped out of the house, I was taken aback. The road hemorrhaged with people: the old, the young, the rich, the poor, the healthy, and the lame. House by house, the human snarl poured out of the city, most toting bundles. Bicycles and motorcycles wiggled through the clogged streets and sidewalks. Amid the sounds of chaos, a monstrously large white dump truck, used to repair the roads and railroad tracks, pulled up and stopped in front of my house.

My brother Choa sat in the driver's seat. He was the only one in the family who knew how to drive, and during the evacuation, he had found the dump truck sitting alongside the railroad fences. There were no keys inside it, so Choa used a flathead screwdriver to turn the ignition and rumbled off with the truck.

The family headed for Father's ranch, three miles away. Most of my family, some forty members, were already huddled together in the truck's dump box—my eldest brother Tai, third brother Chiv, my eldest sister Sihong, and my second sister Sihun, and all their spouses and children. Two of the family's Cambodian maids who did all the chores also came for a ride, as well as a Cambodian nanny named Yeay Sek. She had been the family's nanny for many years, as far back as I could remember.

There was not enough room to hold my family and many other strangers, so I walked behind the truck. My little spotted brown dog with a lolling tongue followed, trying to stay by my side and looking so sad. I had raised her since she was a puppy, when I purchased her from a breeder. I named her Lucky and had wished to breed her myself and sell the puppies.

The dump truck hummed along the street, joining the multitudes. Choa kept his fist on the horn. Those with rickshaws parked in front of their homes to pack the carriages with their families and all their luggage. Roars came from trucks and automobile engines, along with bursts of exhaust and the loud "reep" horns from motorcycles. Mothers clamored for their children to stay by their sides. People walked with bundles in their hands, over their shoulders, or on their heads. Some stacked their bicycles high with loads and wheeled them while walking alongside instead of pedaling. Others pushed overladen little home-made carts. Noise filled the air while Poipet plunged into chaos.

It took us more than three hours to reach the overcrowded roads outside the city. I looked back and saw the sun sinking on the hazy skyline, smog filling the air. The sight of the now-lifeless city hung in the distance, lying in ruin, with the streets and shops emptied of people and goods.

At last the fragility of our existence was revealed.

Confusion dominated everything. I couldn't understand the way we were rushed out. Why would Americans bomb innocent people? Maybe the freedom fighters desired to restore and clean the city for our return? Somehow, I intuitively knew any return home would be different; nothing would be the same. This was the last time I was going to see my home or the city as I remembered it. It made me feel sad.

Long, squiggly lines of people stretched out of the city, filling the wide streets. The lines seemed to extend forever, evaporating into the burnt orange horizon.

Outside the city limits, weary farmers from afar crossed onto the highway, jamming traffic to a stop. They were sun-charred men, glistening with sweat, grunting as they pulled their braying hungry donkeys and aging oxen onto the pavement. Beasts of burden cried out in protest while frenzied men whipped them along the roadsides where dogs fought over scraps. My eyes roamed the tired and listless crowds. I kept a tight watch around me to ensure that I did not lose my family.

The crowds jockeyed forward for position. We moved two steps and put down our bundles, and took them up again after a moment for another step, and another, as if the crowd itself was carrying us along. Choa fought to advance the truck through the jammed traffic, jerking one glacial pace forward at a time. Suddenly, abruptly, he stopped, jamming on the brakes.

Choa had just barely nicked the back of a rickshaw. It was only a tap, but everyone's nerves were on fire and I heard the furious shouts of the driver.

"Chinese pigs!" he cried. "You rich Chinese pigs! You hit me on purpose! You own this big vehicle and now you think you have the right to run us over!"

Choa was confused. The man's vehicle was still in one piece, there was hardly any damage. Without even talking to Choa, the man ran off to find a soldier. A Cambodian boy with a thin, hardened face returned, dragging his gun. The boy wore the same oversize black pajamas, red krama scarf, and a green Maoist cap as the others.

The moment Choa saw the soldier, he ducked behind the truck and escaped alone into the crowd, leaving his wife and children in the dump truck's wagon. He knew he was the one they were looking for.

"Don't move! Where is the driver?!" the boy yelled in an angry, high-pitched voice. "I want to kill the driver. He thinks he can run over the poor people."

"We don't know," we insisted. We feared looking the boy in the eyes. "We do not recognize him, sir. We were just taking a ride, sir."

"I am not to be called SIR! That's a capitalist word. From now on, no more capitalism. We are now all classless—we are part of Angkar now."

Angkar. I had heard the word before, the day they executed the thieves. The word Angkar meant organization or party in the Khmer language. However, if they killed the Thai thieves and now wanted to kill Choa, then no matter what they called themselves they had to be a criminal organization. No government would kill its own people.

The offended Cambodian driver came back and saw that Choa had already fled. He pointed to us and shouted madly, "This is the family of that Chinese man. You should punish them, too!"

"Shhh!" Sihong quickly pulled his arm away. "Be quiet, we can talk." She whispered to him. "That was an accident and you know it was not intentional. You and your family were not hurt. Don't keep screaming. We will give you money." When the man heard the mention of money, he quieted down. She gave the man one million Cambodian riels.

"This is an imperialist machine!" the boy soldier shouted. "Get out! You can all walk! Go another ten kilometers!"

We looked to Father for answers. He was the voice of reason.

"We must continue for the ranch," Father said. "We cannot wait for Choa." I hitched their heavy knapsacks up on my shoulders as the family unloaded off.

The boy took a second long look at my face.

The abandoned truck faced the center of the road as a thick tide of people hustled, yelled, and pushed to get themselves around it.

The empty sky stretched; the summer's rays beat down harshly. The ground baked, dry and parched, singeing my black hair and shoulders. The traffic had fully stopped. No one could move more than a foot each moment. The crowd dragged their feet slower and slower. The air was choked with dust.

By the time daylight had waned, our family was close to the ranch, and we disembarked off the straight highway. I realized then what a privilege we had in having a place to retreat to where we could survive all this chaos. The ranch would make all the difference in the world to us.

The freedom fighters stood at the edge of the grim parade watching the people fill the streets without end. The crowd pressed on to get as far ahead as possible to avoid any confrontations.

From here on, the soldiers went by a more proper name: Khmer Rouge—the "Red Party."

* * *

The ranch stood right on the border of Thailand, with a wooden fence enclosing the twelve-acre perimeter. But as we approached in the deepening twilight, we saw bonfires scattered throughout the fields. Four Khmer Rouge soldiers were walking about with guns under their arms. And inside our ranch house, it appeared the Khmer Rouge soldiers had already set up their station.

Choa was waiting outside and delivered the grim news. "The Khmer Rouge have taken over the ranch. They won't let me in. I've been here a long time."

When we approached the fence gate, the soldiers came out with their guns drawn. "Where do you guys think you are going?"

"This is our ranch," Father said.

"Angkar has abolished all ownership. Keep moving. No one is allowed to stay here."

"This is my ranch. I do not understand."

"You are forbidden to stay here. You must move another ten kilos." They threatened us, brandishing their guns up and down in the air.

Forced to leave, we roamed until sunset, when we came to an open field where we found a ramshackle granary to sleep in for the night. We spent a dark and lonely night there, and our spirits fell.

"These people are thieves and bandits," Father barked in rage. "A band of robbers are living on my land."

Even then, we still clung to the story we had been fed. *The king will make this right*. It was all a misunderstanding. At the end of the third day, the Khmer Rouge would politely undo their actions. This haunting on the people would not last, and it would all be over.

Yet the very next morning soldiers came, crying out: "Move! Move!"

"Faster! Faster!" They screamed bitterly at us, as if we were their enemies. "Forward! March!"

We passed a Chinese graveyard half a mile from the ranch. A Chinese family pushed a funeral hearse along the highway, decorated with white curtains streaming from the top; the Chinese color of death. The family had removed the casket inside and replaced it with their personal belongings. I took it as a sign. An omen.

These Khmer Rouge soldiers were not here to liberate the people. They were here for revenge, representing a government whose purpose was to carry out its rage and punish anyone who opposed it. They regarded all our property and possessions as items to parade to the grave as burnt sacrifices. This was a countrywide procession for one purpose: to mourn the final end of Cambodia's wealthy and urban classes.

Chapter 3

Chinese Crying Fields

Several hours of exposure in a hot, grueling sun made us weary with thirst and exhaustion. Heat waves danced over the roads. I felt like I was in the strange grasp of a powerful dream, waiting to snap me back to reality. The deeper inside the backcountry we went, the farther they commanded us to move. Vehicles that ran out of fuel were abandoned on the roadsides, their doors opened, some overturned.

We observed the unending migration of people up close, while we rested on logs by the side of the road, tired and battered by the journey. The children giddily ran to play in the yellow dirt, scrawling wobbly circles into the clay and stoking angry ants crawling on the ground. They were so cheery, unaware of all that was happening. For them, we were on a long sunny retreat. Most of the thirteen children in our family had hardly ventured out of their homes before, much less beyond Poipet.

Tai sent his maid Chloe to fetch drinking water. She returned with a jug of dirty water because the ponds nearby were brown and murky, disturbed by people also looking for a drink. Chloe was young, in her early twenties, but spoke like an old lady with a slow drawl. She did not understand why the water was not acceptable, as if we thought it was poison.

"This water I got? What is the matter?" she asked. Tai sent her again to go further out for cleaner water. Liam, Sihong's youngest boy, skipped along after her. We were too tired to have the will to call the boy back, and the child slipped from our sight. Liam was quick on his feet, the most active of the children, often curiously nosing around. He always smiled. I never saw him cry.

Later, when Sihong looked for her boy, we assured her that Liam had wandered off with Chloe and was on his way back. Hours passed. The maid returned with a fresh jug of water sitting on her head. The boy was still missing.

"Where is Liam?" Sihong asked, worried. "He followed you. Where is my boy?"

"Liam? There was no boy with me." Chloe's speech was slow and wooden. "You wanted me to get Liam? Not the clean water?"

Panicked, Sihong hurried for the ponds and I trailed after her. Although half a mile is a short walk, it felt like a long time before we reached the pond.

There we saw a mother dangling her baby's feet in the cool water. Children ran amok in the tall grasses, their elders shouting at them to stay near. We searched around the big round pond and scanned the faces of the children. None of them were Liam. I stood motionless, staring into the shallow pond. Surely it was impossible for him to have plunged into the waters.

The family split off in different directions, asking people if they had seen him. I saw a woman holding the hand of a seven-year-old who resembled Liam. I ran up to them convinced it was him, but the boy was a stranger.

I turned in the opposite direction of the crowd and asked those passing by if they had seen a boy of his description. They all shook their head no; they had not seen a missing boy. However, someone said they heard, secondhand, that somebody found a child farther back and were looking for the parents.

I pushed through the crowd, trying to shout his name above the noise while also staying out of the Khmer Rouge's sight. One family said they saw a little boy crying on the street alone, farther down the road. He was still alive! Then a grandmother told me she saw a boy crying who was taken by a Chinese family. She saw them in the back of the crowd, walking very slowly.

None of the other answers I gathered matched up. In addition to the story of a cute little Chinese boy taken by a Cambodian family, another person said they saw a Chinese girl, not a boy, who was taken by the Cambodian family. Or that the crying boy was placed on an oxcart and driven away.

The farther back I went, the more varied the information became. I found my family again at the log site to see if they had come up with anything, but there were no good leads.

Two Khmer Rouge soldiers came up to the circle. "Keep moving forward. Staying here is prohibited."

"Comrade," we wept and pleaded, "please let us search for our lost child. He is just a boy out there."

"Keep going. If we find him, we will return him to you."

"Comrade. How can you find us if we keep moving?"

The Khmer Rouge soldier coldly pointed his finger ahead. "You can find him up the highway. Everyone will be on the same road, to the same place. He will be there. Understand?"

Sihong was inconsolable, but we had no choice but to pack our bundles and move on, slowly falling behind the dusty crowd. The Khmer Rouge maintained a close watch of my family from the back of the masses. The faces streamed past. We searched as we walked, but only encountered more strangers. Sihong sobbed and begged people to go look for him. We offered all that we had. I had asked everyone around me, listened to all the cries of children, called his name any-where I could, but I was losing hope that the boy would be found.

Nightfall. Lantern in hand, we lugged our baggage to a wooden overpass. Two Khmer Rouge soldiers allowed us to stay there until sun-rise because the footbridge had filled up with hundreds of travelers trying to cross to the other side. We kept searching by holding the lantern up, light and shadows flickering on every passing face. They streamed by, one after another, bundles in tow, with never a glance in my direction.

After an hour or two, fewer and fewer people came through, until the last person passed and there was no one to ask, no more faces to study. The boy was gone. The letdown made my heart sink like a stone.

I watched Liam's baby sister, Siam, in her mother's arms. She cried meek little tears, calling out for her brother. "Brother! Are you there? Come, Brother! Brother, I am here!"

* * *

By the third day, we were still not allowed to return home and had no choice but to continue on. We arrived in Phal Tbul, a small town where many foreign Laotians lived, and immediately heard rumors that the Khmer Rouge were planning to eradicate the use of currency within days. Anyone caught using money, especially foreign currency, was to be severely punished. Father fashioned a bamboo stick into a walking cane and discreetly stored his Thai baht, U.S. dollars, and gold pieces in the barrel.

The markets in the town had already been dismantled, leaving only a fat Laotian lady with dark, brooding lips sitting beside her hut frying rice pancakes. After three days of roaming the roads without food, the starving crowds of people were drawn by the aromas of her cooking. She had two metals pans in front and a dried bamboo basket overflowing with paper money. The normal price of a rice flour pancake was ten riels; hers was five hundred riels, and still she could not make the cakes fast enough.

I dug into my pockets for the last of my money and painfully dropped it into the basket for two pancakes. Here was the horror of instant inflation; all the work I put into earning that money over the past year was only good for two pancakes today.

One Laotian family lived in a small but sturdy house on tall stilts; the lower level under the house was used to feed pigs. We had to find someplace we would be allowed to stop and rest. So we exchanged clothing and supplies for the permission to sleep in the pig stable.

The family had no better conditions for us, but they were kind and extremely generous; willing to lend us their tools. The father and son were out fishing in their canoe, and when they returned, they shared their catches of fish with us. The Laotian family had lived there for a long time, and the Khmer Rouge did not seem bothered by them. We thought this might be a place where we could spend our days farming and fishing with the people.

* * *

In the morning stillness of the fourth day, again a rude Khmer Rouge announcement woke the neighborhood. "Everyone out! All people must leave now!"

We got ready to leave, thinking our three days of isolation from our village were finally finished. It was time to return home, was it not? Surely this mistake must be drawing near an end.

One by one the houses emptied and the people carried their rucksacks up the street. The Khmer Rouge followed along with wolfish delight, pushing their flock of sheep into the untamed woods.

Before long, the clumps of trees expanded into forests. The forests reached into the far reaches. The far reaches became the unknown. I looked down at the ground, trodden by countless pairs of feet. The path cut through tall, crisp reeds of elephant grass with thick stalks and sharp, wind-bent leaves. From here on, we slept in the wilderness. All we saw was forest and skies.

The days stretched by as we wandered without seeing a town. Each morning, we pulled ourselves up and resumed the journey.

The forest floor got lighter, the forest silence thinned, and eventually we came out into the open where no trees grew and the broad beaten path shot straight through a vast, dead land. Dry, withered elephant grasses spread over everything.

The wasteland was silent. Not a sound. The quietest place in the world. Wisps of vapor floated, shimmering in an endless rising steam. We were ants in the mouth of a furnace, the shining bitter sun smothering everything inside into heaps of dust and ash. I could feel fire in my bones. It was impossible to breathe normally. I choked for air, my shallow gasps coming up empty.

"Water! Water!" the children cried for a sip. "Mama, water! I am thirsty." But there was not enough for all the children. A strong wind came up, causing the bone-dry grasses to twirl and hiss. We pressed on, exhausted and lost.

* * *

Once the first cold stars turned out with the moon, we silently unrolled our straw and cloth mats atop tufts of dried grass for bedding. I stretched out my legs and gazed at the half moon, thinking about it for a long time. Its bright light was empty and shadowless. I had begun to wish even more for the chance to go to the moon, so far from this sorrowful place. *What kind of things would I find up there?*

Finally, after another day on the move, we saw the distant outline of a small town and made our way toward it.

Two of the Khmer Rouge soldiers who had been shadowing us watched our group enter the town, and one said, "All the Chinese are crying from that field. That is the Chinese Crying Field." They both cackled, and one added, "This is only the beginning."

The village was depleted. The land was barren and empty, with only a few huts and trees. The Khmer Rouge commanded that our family go to the next village, which would supposedly be our final destination.

But the next village had also been plundered. We found nothing but five sour tamarinds to pick, with the green pulp being one of the most bitter and acidic of young fruits. The land had few trees because it always flooded in the rainy season, sweeping the roots from the ground. We knew a family of our size could not survive there.

However, we also heard of another portion of the National Highway 5 where there was a village called Koub Touch. The village had a river to fish and was still close to the Thai border. We would have to double back through the dried, grassy fields to get there.

It was decided among us together we would leave at midnight, before the Khmer Rouge forced us out in the morning. We quickly restocked our supplies and all contributed to buy an ox from a villager. The ox was young, a teenager, thick and muscular. It had a shiny light-brown coat, except for white fur from the legs up to its belly. We harnessed the ox to a wagon and wearily stowed our possessions inside. Under the cover of night, we trundled back into the parched land.

The ox's bell chimed in the hushed moonlight of the Chinese Crying Fields while an unseen lonely fox cried once from afar. Choa handled the ox down the path, flicking the reins and clicking his tongue. But the young bovine protested. When Choa tugged the ox one way, it furiously twisted its head side to side with a loud bellow. When Choa pulled harder, the ox bucked and whined. Then, frightened, as if it had seen a snake, the bull wildly jumped the beaten path and ran in blind terror, mewling across the night fields. The animal and wagon attached to it sliced through the grass like a scythe cutting reeds. The children sitting in the back rocked and screamed.

Choa pulled the reins and then desperately tried whipping up and down while we ran after them. The ox headed for a hillock and one wheel jerked over the mound, tipping the entire wagon on its side. The children and all our possessions spilled out, leaving the children crying on the ground. My dog Lucky was in one of their arms, whimpering.

Choa managed to stay on the ox's back, but the animal remained unaware of what it had done. It continued to romp and kick its hooves, dragging the wagon along behind it.

At last Choa was able to leap off and pull the huge beast to a stop. Fortunately, none of the children were hurt and he began to pet its white underbelly and neck to calm it down. My brothers and I helped to push the wagon back. Choa saddled himself back on the ox, which continued to nervously prick its ears and tussle at the reins. The beast snorted and made several aimless loops around the field, still frightened of something out there.

Cambodian folktales say that when oxen are scared, it is because they see ghosts around them. They have keener senses than humans and can detect delicate movements that are invisible to the human eye.

We looked all about but did not see anything to fear. The ox soon tired itself out and Choa quietly got the animal back on course. One of the two wheels was damaged though, making a clack-clack-clip in each revolution. We had nothing to use for repairs, but since it was still loosely intact, we lightened the load to salvage it for the length of the way.

Even after traveling the entire night under the moon, it was not hard to wake up the young-blooded bull the day after. It opened its eyelids quickly, looked me in the eye, and got up to move. In the daylight, the ox was docile and obedient. We placed a couple of the older children atop its bony back. Their playful attitude was long gone now. They were cheerless, their eyes downcast, no longer excitedly pointing at rasping birds, flying insects, and trees in full bloom. After days of privation and the loss of Liam, their little souls could not bear it.

We came to a river, and the sound of running water was sweet and restorative. We refilled our tin pails along the clear bristling river, flowing calmly beside a Buddhist temple. I stood at the far shore of the river, seeing the golden pavilion's reflection softened on the blurred waters. I was drawn to the mysterious quietness inside and waded the river to the temple.

The illusion of peace was shattered at that moment, when people abruptly began to run out of the temple, screaming. They fled ahead of three black-shirted soldiers hauling a Buddha statue's head, with its customary beatific smile.

"Our Angka does not allow religion!" they screamed. "We don't believe in any superstition!"

They dumped the chopped head into the river, and the painted pink face rapidly sank beneath the rippling waters. Then they tossed the dismembered body in after it, as if it were a human carcass. "Look at Buddha!" they jeered. "If Buddha can help itself, it would be floating. Why is it sinking?"

Once they destroyed the idol, the Khmer Rouge departed, and onlookers darted out of their paths.

I waded close to the tattered god and saw the gold-leafed statue shimmering on the river stones, smiling back up at me. The message of peace still remained.

"We have a grave problem," Father said. "These thieves have no religion. When men no longer believe in God, fear and mercy are lost. Nothing will guide their conscience except their own desires. They will no longer have a God to judge their actions. There is nothing that will stop them."

Chapter 4

The Young Revolution

When we arrived in Koub Touch, a crowd of about a hundred Chinese people had just gathered in a big open lot. We slipped in among them and saw two Khmer Rouge soldiers who were speaking in the middle of the circle. They took no notice of us, having no idea we were even there while they tore the hope from our hands.

"This will be your place," one soldier said. "You are not going back. You will have to find and build a place of your own. You will also have to grow your own food. This will be your home."

We were too stunned to process what he was telling us. He gave instructions of what we should do next and then went around in the circle, assigning families into sections of the estate where they could choose their strip of land.

He finally came to us and took a glance at our ox. "You cannot have this ox!" he shouted. "This ox belongs to Angkar and not the people! You will have to work the land with your hands, instead."

Still, we did not say a word. This news made no sense. It was like listening to a crazy man babble.

He reached down and picked up the ox's reins, then waited while we removed our bundles. "Time to give the ox a rest," he said, as though his heart bled for the animal but not the people suffering all around him. "Time for you to work with your bare hands."

Lucky, my dog, was in the wagon, and when I picked her up the soldier gestured to me to stop. "You must leave the dog. Civilians are not allowed to own any dogs. All animals belong to Angkar. Not just the ox."

The dog was quiet and still in my arms. Lucky looked at me with her black beady eyes. I felt sad and angry inside. I had no time to think or even say much of a goodbye. I wished to refuse, and if they were to take her, to force them to pull her from my hands.

Of course I already knew if I kept Lucky, I would see the same punishment as the Thai thieves who stole the cows. I would be killed for keeping stolen property from the government. With little I could do or say, I stroked her soft fur for the last time and put her gently back into the wagon.

As he led the ox to the other soldier, I heard his comrade say, "Whoa, this is a good ox. We've been looking for one like this."

And just that quickly, our homes were gone, our families fractured, and our livelihoods destroyed.

All it required was a few days' worth of time.

The Khmer Rouge assigned my family to join a portion of land where fifteen other families were also living. Within those grounds, we claimed our own plot. It was several acres wide and two miles from Highway 5. Yeay Sek, our Cambodian nanny, considered herself family and stayed with us, while the other two maids left to find their families.

Soon the Khmer Rouge quickly circulated the information that their patrol brigade had captured a family attempting to cross the border. They were promptly sent for "reeducation." Before long, however, the native villagers began finding these people exterminated in the woods, one body after another, corroborating the threats of the Khmer Rouge.

We were unwilling to risk the escape, and instead we grimly accepted our situation; we were now dirt-poor farmers from Poipet, stripped of our former lives, with nothing but our clothing, bedding, pots, silverware, and some small sums of foreign currency and gold.

Beginning the next day, they had us harvest the land. The only equipment Angkar gave us to get the work done was a single plow. Our schooling never taught us how to grow rice; Father was the only one who knew how to farm. So, he began to teach us how to till the land to prepare the soil bed for seeding. With the ox taken, we had to churn the fields ourselves. In a matter of days, we had been thrust into a dark, primitive existence, as if thousands of years of human progress had never occurred.

My three brothers and I held our arms underneath the yoke and pulled in unison to lurch the sled into motion. We learned to plow straight together, fording across the water-laden fields. Waves of mud brushed heavily to the side. The yoke left marks on our chest and arms. My pants became cardboard-stiff from mud and sweat, ripped and torn by the sharp grasses.

Father found good-hearted Laotians who bartered seed samplings of various vegetables and crops with him. They did not have rice seeds, since the Khmer Rouge had tightly controlled rice seed supplies in the village.

From that point onward, we toiled into each night when the light was no more, planting the seeds in the ground and ignoring the pain in our bodies. From sunrise to sundown, we did this every day. I never thought anyone could reach such lengths of deprivation.

* * *

With his sole tool a machete, Father set to build a tent for the entire family to live under. His own father had passed along these skills to him during his boyhood in the countryside. Father had many hands to help him, but he was the only person with the knowledge of how to do the work. My brothers and sisters knew little of survival in the wild, brought up in a sturdy cement house, with clean well water and latrines, and paved streets.

There was so little building material in the village, we scoured far to find useful materials like bamboo or grass, but we could never get our hands on enough. Father wove the reeds into braids, and together we built a mound-shaped dome that barely offered adequate cover for the forty of us.

Father was old enough now that he needed Choa to support him while he climbed to the top of the hut to cover the roof. Choa lifted a panel of red reeds and Father bound it with vines in crisscrosses to the tent frame, patching together a rough shed for his children and grand-children. It hurt him to have his family sleep on dusty, bare ground.

Soon he was unable to hold himself up anymore. The ladder shook. He came down and sank to the ground. Until now, I had never seen him cry.

"Nowhere on earth, nowhere is there such a place in the world like this." Father was in tears. "Not like the Communists in Cambodia. No one would upheave families from their homes—not even in China. They call themselves heroes and liberators, but they are just a band of jungle thieves. They are only here to rob from the wealthy and poor alike. All their promises are lies. Wicked, cruel lies."

His voice choking bitterly, he wept aloud, his body shaking. The guilt of not leaving when we could have freely departed was too much for him. He condemned himself for not knowing it would come to this.

* * *

Before the day was over, a Khmer Rouge soldier came with a message for everyone living and working in the fields along the highway. We were being ordered to take the next day off.

"There are important people passing by," the soldier said. *Who was so important?* I could only think it was the king. We had not heard of what happened to the royal highness. This must be the moment when he finally returned to reclaim his control of the country. The king would surely be disgusted by what he saw the "liberators" doing. The Khmer Rouge must want us to hide, to save face when the king marched back to the capital. This would be over soon if it truly was him.

The next morning, my third eldest brother, Chiv, gave me a nudge to wake me. He wanted me to come with him to see who was visiting. Without much said, we both went out under the pretense of finding some wood for cooking.

Chiv led the way, shouldering a path through the waving thickets of rice grass, keeping his head low. Another friend joined us, and both he and I closely trailed Chiv. We ran down a gentle dike slope and sidled along a sparse hedge of trees. Crouching close to the tree trunks, we kept up our guard while we slowly crept forward toward a strip of wooden houses lining the paved road.

The half a dozen or so Cambodian-style houses—retaining old charms from better times—were all in varying states of decay. In most houses, only a single beam was left standing, or an empty staircase rose from the piles of rubble; everything else had been stripped for firewood.

A number of houses had collapsed in a heap, with half the roof pieces scattered about the floors.

We slipped through an empty doorframe and saw the walls of the house smudged with moldy residue. Every wall survived except in the back, where instead a large green mound sat overlooking the highway.

A framed Buddha portrait lay on the floor, fully torn through. Strewn about were faded black-and-white stills of the old owners. I picked up a coverless book with the red-and-tan leather binding still intact, the spine stamped in gold-embossed Khmer letters. Black spores, rain spots, and dirt grew thick between the first few pages.

I turned it over in my hands and read, "Those who do good deeds will merit that good will be received back to them. Those who intend evil will not succeed. They will fail because their evil deeds will seek to return back to them." The book was about finding enlightenment and blessings. I took a quick scan and pocketed it in my pants waistband to take for a read later. Then I joined Chiv and our friend, already hunkered behind the grassy mound.

Everything was still while we lay on the cool, grassy earth. I began to have doubts about being here in the first place, and thought to tell Chiv we should go back. But the moment was interrupted by the roar and rattle of diesel engines and axles squeaking on steel springs. A vehicle with jerky movements peaked above the road. We ducked until it drove slowly past, then we cautiously craned our heads around to see one large truckload after another punch cheerlessly through.

In the convoy, young men stood with their shoulders over the guardrails, hundreds of them carried by the five trucks. An armed Khmer Rouge soldier stood at the back of each truck.

The young men wore fancy European clothing, silver and black suits and ties. Some wore big, bold sunglasses, which looked out of place amid the misery. I realized these were children of the privileged and wealthy, sent by their families to study at university abroad in France. Their exceptional lives overseas did little to avoid the snare that we all were caught up in. The pale-faced students stared bleakly out. Many shook and cried. A wave of sadness passed over me while the last of the trucks disappeared. We sat alone in the torn silence.

I wondered, *How could they get so many of them to leave France?* But I already knew the answer: They would have no reason to travel back here unless they were fed lies and promises, some sort of assignment or high position in the new government—the same trickery that had been used on the Lon Nol soldiers. On all of us, in reality.

The following day we returned back to work by the highway. In the afternoon, a man who was tasked with caring for the cows lumbered down the road, pulling along two of them. He had seen something that shook him to the core, and he now trembled, so startled he had nearly forgotten how to speak. Slowly, he told us in stumbling words that while feeding his cows, he accidentally encountered a mass of bodies in the fields.

I was horrified by his descriptions. Their western suits and ties matched that of what the students had been wearing. The local towns-people themselves did not dress that way.

The man said little more before he hurried off, leaving us stunned at the news.

* * *

In the month of August, three months after planting, the first fruits began to form. Dark bok choy, red tomatoes, green beans, leafy taro leaves, and sweet corn protruded upward, ready for harvest. All the villagers began to say that Father grew the best vegetables in the whole village. Yet, there lay a stubbled area where sudden spouts of vines remained twisting and sticking out wildly. I did not see the plant bear any crops, expecting bulbous shapes growing out of the scrubby soil. I asked Father why they looked so different from the rest.

"Those are taro and potatoes," Father said. "They are already fully grown in the ground."

Father pulled out the sprouts, unearthing sweet potatoes underneath. I felt foolish to not realize that crops could grow underground. All the foods I saw in the city were in markets, already plucked and neatly arranged on merchant tables.

Chapter 5

Piggy Bank

The skies were brewing rain clouds over Koub Touch when Sihong came home on an oxcart with a smile on her face. The male driver helped unload three newborn suckling pigs in a bamboo cage, along with their mother, who was fastened to a leash. Sihong had just traded two ounces of gold and several bushels of crops for the animals over in the next village.

Overjoyed, the family stood around the mother pig, examining it from head to toe, salivating while we picked which parts we wanted to eat. The pig was white and round, standing about half a foot above my knees. For the moment, we had begun to settle in Koub Touch with a regained sense of ownership. Eagerly we dreamed we could soon raise her piglets to breed many more pigs. Having counted six months since we had had any morsels of meat, the mother pig's fate was swiftly decided, as we were to cook her that very night.

We stepped from the hut to search for firewood, and immediately big drops of rain fell, followed by a cold, miserable downpour. Then, over the sounds of the rainfall, we heard the static and buzz of a disembodied human voice speaking through a megaphone: "Everybody is to leave now. Gather all your things and evacuate now."

An armed Khmer Rouge soldier patrolled the village to enforce the order, saying, "You must go to the train tracks."

We asked many questions. *Why were they rallying the people again?* But the soldier refused to tell us anything more.

We bound our things together and headed out, abandoning some of the objects we had worked hard to accumulate in the last few months. I took the pig by the leash and sloshed through the sodden earth, following the villagers heading out for National Highway 5.

The ground was repeatedly trampled underfoot by each passing villager, compacting it until it was slick as ice. I had the pig walk in front of me, unable to pull her weight myself. The pig tugged me along, nearly making me lose my balance.

After we marched past the rice fields, we saw people standing in front of empty train tracks, seemingly emotionless in the gloomy rain. They were guarded by nearby soldiers.

While we quietly waited for the train, I found a wooden stick and pierced it into the ground, then tied the pig's leash to the post. I commended myself for securing the animal.

A faint blotch edged out of the rippling rainfall and the train silently came into view. As if to compete with the din of the falling rains, it gave an ear-piercing whistle: *PETEEEEEEEEEEE!*

"Soweeee!" The pig's snare snapped. She was off like a shot, squealing, her hooves clicking over the tracks. "Oeeeeyyyy! Oeeeyyyy!" She splashed through the fluorescent green rice grass. The broken stake bounced along in tow.

My feet seemed to move on their own, hotfooting after the pig—the animal was too valuable to let it escape. She raced into the center of the field. The longer I chased after her, the deeper the mud and waters around me grew. When I pulled the soles of my flat-footed sandals upward, the mud swallowed them like suction cups. My sandals were lost in the mire, so I slogged forth barefoot.

The animal stopped after a couple hundred feet, breathing heavily. When I crept close, she ran straight off again. In another fifty yards she wound up sitting on her hind legs inside a nest of rice grass, her large belly heaving in and out for air.

From nose to tail, she was as long as my entire arm span. I bent forward and grabbed the end of the rope, wrapping it around my wrist. Once I pulled on it, the pig sprung up and turned her head sideways toward me.

The train's horn went off again. The pig whipped around like she had been stung by pinchers and she hurtled across the field once more. The rope pulled tight, and the force of the pig pulled me forward. I landed facedown in the mud. The coil of the rope tore from my wrist, leaving me on my belly staring at the rear of the pig's two-hundred-pound body while it galloped off in the rice grass, wailing in terror.

The pig ran only half the distance of what we had already covered and became caught in deep mud. With low, guttural sounds, the pig flailed, sinking herself further down to her shoulders. She tilted her nose, unable to take in a breath. She could not move. I took my chance and grabbed the leash. She fought back, and I turned to tightly place the rope on my shoulder. I pushed and slipped forward, tracing my mud tracks back.

The rain stopped and the colorless skies left a steamy mist. I looked ahead several field-lengths and saw the train's double cargo doors slung wide open, the cars overflowing with passengers still clamoring to get in. Terrified of being left behind, I tried to call out. The train trundled onward, but I was relieved to see my family still there waiting for me.

The pig dug her hooves into the ground, thwarting my attempts to bring her back, and I lost my footing several times pulling her. When I was close enough to my family, they came into the muddy water to help me rein her in. We tied her legs together and left the pig on her back, with her little hooves squirreling in the air.

The children were distressed. I was soaked. I sloshed off big clods of mud still clinging to my shoulders and wrung my wet, drenched shirt. I worried that my family might have missed the train because of me, but there were a few other remaining families who were also unable to get on. Some went walking on. We watched them disappear, trudging beside the train tracks, miserable gray shapes fading into the foggy haze.

Father looked at the approaching darkness and said, "We will have to stay here tonight and begin walking tomorrow." He was tired and so were his grandchildren.

* * *

A blustery, needling rain fell and then lifted—spreading wet fog over the brown and green fields. Yeay Sek spread a pair of blankets on the bare ground, and she and Sihong started cooking, preparing watery rice soup. Breakfast that morning was a quiet meal; long and restless.

Worrying about the journey we had in store, I got up and walked along the edge of the tracks. Soon my ears picked up a faint hissing, like the far-off wheeze of an animal. I stooped and peered into the thick fog to see a shadow approaching, its outline fading into the fog. Then I saw black plumes escaping from a tall pipe.

"There is the train!" I cried, dancing and waving my arms. "Hurry up!"

At once, without removing the dishes, Yeay Sek pulled the ends of the blanket and tied it into a sack. The rest of the family raced to put away their parcels and get the children organized. The train rolled fast on the tracks and skidded, braking directly in front of us. The freight car in front of us was empty but for a Khmer Rouge soldier who hung on the sides of the door.

"This is the last train. Get on or you will be left behind!"

Without delay, Tai, Chiv, and I lifted the trussed pig by the hooves and hurled her, shrieking, into the back. The train compartment was pleasantly warm and dry; and my single family filled the empty room. Other families not quite as large as mine hobbled into the other cars while the sound of the train whistle echoed across the fields.

The train pushed off with a light clippety-clippety-clip. The slow going through the lifting fog almost sent me to sleep. At fifteen miles per hour, the train shuddered and clanked while it traveled over an earthen dike wall. I stared off into the muddy countryside and saw old and crumbled huts squatting next to the highway. The train bristled past arms of overgrown grass, shaking and bowing backward.

After passing many towns, we saw immense groups of people working in the rice fields. The train slowed down while we glided past the people. They picked up their heads and rested their hands on their hoes for only a moment before resuming their work.

The train's lunging motors and metal wheels ground more slowly, until it settled back with a little jerk and sat immobile. We became dimly aware of voices from the other train cars. Coarse yelling from a man. The noise of two people quarreling.

There was a noise like oil cans rolling over the deck, uneven footsteps, and the sound of something falling. Tai rose without inviting the others to follow him and jumped outside. He returned and shouted, "We have to get out now! Get your belongings! Out!"

The small children cried. Tai, Sihong, and Choa's families were the first to unload, reaching out to find the hands of their children. The three baby pigs in the round bamboo cage were handed to them. Then Sihun climbed down from the car and reached up for her two youngest sons. Her husband, Wensun, handed off the toddler, Guihui, to her, and then the other boy, Heng. Two of their daughters, Bai and Ou, stood idly, waiting for their father to help them off.

I took Father's hand to lead him to the door, but when I looked outside I saw we were passing large clumps of tall grass while the train charged forward. My heart began to palpitate. We had been separated from the rest of the family.

I took stock to see who was with us. Besides myself and Father, there was Wensun and his two girls, Bai and Ou, plus Chiv and his family. "What are we going to do?" Chiv asked the rest of us. We withdrew to the corner to keep out of sight.

* * *

As we crouched in fear, a soldier's loud voice erupted outside the cargo doors—it froze my blood. "WHAT ARE YOU DOING HERE?!"

A Khmer Rouge soldier with intensely red eyes climbed in from around the ledge. He was followed by two other soldiers, who appeared to be just as formidable.

"WHY ARE YOU STILL HERE?!" screamed the one with the burning red eyes. Paralyzed with terror, we did not dare look back at him.

"WHY DIDN'T YOU GET OFF WHEN THE REST DID?!" He moved toward us.

"We tried . . ." Chiv spoke in soft words, his head turned down. "We didn't have enough time. We were separated from—"

"I ought to kill you for not getting off!!" the soldier screamed. Then he saw our pig in the corner. "You are bourgeois people. Capitalist pigs! You didn't get off the train fast enough because you are still holding on to your possessions. You have to get rid of it all."

He wanted us to push the pig off the carriage. "I will be back. If the pig is not gone, I will destroy all your personal attachments." The soldier gestured at Father with his gun.

Long after the soldiers returned to the roof, we trembled with fear. Despite their demands, we had no desire to get rid of the pig, since the fear of a quick death by bullet was not as threatening as a slow death from starvation. We pulled the pig to the other corner and covered it with our bundles, hidden from their eyes.

The train gave a loud, shrill hiss of hot air, clacking and sighing its way into the station at one o'clock in the afternoon, then it stopped with an old and rusty screech. The station was quiet. I peeked out the cargo doors, feeling a strange sense of familiarity.

I realized we had pulled into the city of Battambang. Several soldiers strolled on the concrete platform. Outside the entrance grills in the circular drop-off lot, two soldiers played checkers, listening to Communist music. And at the end of the station was a corrugated ticket building swarming with many black shirts, happily enjoying themselves over lunch. Someone called all the soldiers outside to join the rest in the ticket office. They all looked like city rats, more well-fed than the ones that marched into Poipet.

Once the Khmer Rouge soldiers were gone, the few passengers in the other cabins trickled out. A Khmer Rouge leader appeared. Through his black-stained teeth, he made a terse pronouncement: "The train will not be going back, but will be going forward to Moung. No one is allowed to stay here!" He returned to the ticket building.

I went up to the entrance grills, mournfully gazing into the dusty main street. The city was abandoned, with only a few lone Khmer Rouge patrolling the alleyways, the lanes heaped with litter and rotten food scraps.

Battambang had once been noisy and rowdy, larger than Poipet's marketplace. Now open windows gaped, posters barely clung to walls, animal carts were ditched crookedly on the side of the roads, and empty stall tables and tents were still set up for business. I was struck by the strangeness of it, appearing as it had been left, frozen in time.

As I brooded over our cruel fate, a sudden shout from Chiv caused me to turn my head. "Look! It's Aunt Ding!" He waved his hands in the direction of a woman walking toward us.

I blinked for a second—or two. Aunt Ding was an old friend and frequent customer of ours who lived in Battambang. She made daily trips from the city all the way to Poipet to buy goods from my family.

"What are you guys doing here?" she whispered. "This is the city. No one is allowed in the city."

"We've been separated from our family. The comrades said they are going to ship us forward to Moung."

She leaned in and continued in a lower whisper, "You don't want to go to Moung. Many people are starving and being murdered there. You won't survive. I am here because I am the cook for them." As soon as we heard her say "cook" we quickly told her we had not eaten since morning. "Okay. I will come back with food." She went and disappeared behind the back of the ticket building.

Father quietly whispered, "We should ask if she can help us get back to the family. This could be our only chance. I trust she knows the leader very well."

After forty minutes or so, Aunt Ding appeared at the door with warm rice topped with black preserved soybean sauce, skewered pork, and dried fish, wrapped in large lily leaves. The rice was pure white, polished to fluffiness like cotton. Since the takeover, white rice was a luxury only the Khmer Rouge could have. The fresh scent of the leaves soaked into the rice. Even though it was just leftovers from the Khmer Rouge's lunchtime, she had brought us ample food.

"Will you talk to the leader for us?" Father asked. "We do not want to be shipped to Moung. Can he give us a travel permit to walk back on our own to find our family?"

"I will see what I can do." She quickly gave us the food and took off without allowing us to thank her for her kindness. We ate the leftovers for a quiet hour, huddled in the corner of the freight car.

Shortly after, the leader came out again.

"Attention. The train is going back," he said, speaking through his discolored teeth. "But, this time it is not stopping. Your only option is to jump out when it slows down." We were all gathered around him when he made the announcement and thanked him exceedingly. He gave a cold, still reaction.

No sooner had we boarded than the train chugged to life and lapped around the tracks surrounding the station to turn. Once we rode away from Battambang, we gave a sigh of ease. Chiv and I arranged all of our belongings near the door to prepare for the jump. I pulled the pig by its tied feet, dragged it from the corner and placed it squirming beside the rest of our stuff. Then we patiently waited, leaning against the cargo doors. The sun's rays warmed the inside of the train and the scent of woodland and fields floated into the cabin.

The sun was setting when we returned to the drop-off point. The train trundled around a bend in the track and we spotted our family. The women and children were sitting, watching the train snaking in the distance, and jumped up in exuberance. They waved and ran for the train. The closer the train came, the louder we heard their shouts:

"Tai! Choa! The train came back. Hurry! Hurry! Go help them!"

The train petered to a crawl. Chiv and I pressed our backs against the floor and kicked our feet; the pig shrieked off, rolling down the hill into a brush pile. The simple act made me feel lighter. Then we kicked off the rest of our belongings, which landed with a crash before rolling.

Father inched his way over to the door rails and gripped them, cane in hand, and kneeled down to the floor. He slowly lifted one foot over the ledge of the train car, and then the next. He prepared to jump, his tired body cringing forward, but for a moment he stalled. Tai ran alongside the train and reached up to grab Father's free hand. He opened his body for Father to lean into and together they managed the exit from the train. The two girls, Bai and Ou, were helped off, then Chiv's family. Being the youngest and most nimble, I waited to be the last one out and shouldered our remaining bags before I reached down to my brother's hand and jumped onto solid ground. I was immediately locked in my family's embrace and there was an upswell of tears. We had thought we would never see each other again.

The family led me to their makeshift camp, crossing over a strip of marshland. I was barefoot, and after wading for a few steps I had an eerie thought that something was lurking behind me. I turned around and found several black worms swimming after me, darting for my ankles. Frightened, I sprinted through the water to the dry land on the other side, where Sihong's children, Kip and Siam, were laughing and making fun of their uncle. It was the first time I had ever seen leeches.

The pig was gutted that night and the innards were cleaned in a pond. We gathered firewood and boiled the salted pig. Sihong, the eldest cook, cut off the fatty layers from the pig and slowly stir-fried it to extract the oils for canning.

Before we finished cooking, a loud motor rumbled up the darkening highway, and we whipped around to look. It was a soldier of high rank sitting on a motorcycle. Suddenly, he veered off the highway and wheeled straight over the wetlands toward our camp. The motorcycle braked hard in front of us, and he looked briskly from person to person. He quickly found who he was searching for.

"Ma!" the Khmer Rouge soldier shouted from his seat. "Let's go! You have to come with me!"

We all looked back, confused.

"What do you want?! Haven't I already seen enough of you?" Yeay Sek yelled, surprising us all. "Why are you here?" Yeay Sek approached him, wagging her long fingernails at him.

"Ma. You need to come with me. I can't let you stay here with them."

"Why? Every time you come, you only want something! Every time! It's the same thing. Always needing money. What else are you going to ask from me this time?"

"You're not allowed to stay with these Chinese people. I can't tell you until you come with me. Go get your things. We must leave now."

"Why are you telling me to go? I'm not leaving without them. I've been with them for fifteen years. If you want me to go, then you have to take them all. They are my family too." They withdrew and argued away from us, their loud shouts of outrage and curses heard all over the fields.

Her son went back to his motorcycle, and the engine stirred with a hard, drumming start. He turned on his headlights and rolled toward the highway, and I watched the motorbike's light glide away. Yeay Sek and her son had never gotten along, and she had not spoken to him in years. She assured us he only came to cause trouble for his mother.

That night, we chatted and traded rumors with other families in the area, and shared portions of the cooked pig. Afterward, I took shelter beneath a tree.

When I opened my eyes, I saw a single bloody track trickle along the length of my thigh. I jolted up and hastily examined my shorts to see if it avoided my tender parts. A black toe-sized clump dropped to the ground—fat and squishy—and for a moment it moved like a slug, then it stopped, rooted to the spot. Staring at the blind, bulging thing was enough to make my flesh crawl. It had narrowly missed my groin area.

I collected my nerves and plucked up the slimy, squishy creature between two sticks, and flung it into the blaze of our campfire. I watched and commended myself as it smoldered into a dry raisin. But quickly I realized there were more nasty black leeches, lurking and wriggling around. I shook my head to dispel the image.

Chapter 6

Out with the New, In with the Old

The place where we had camped was soundless. The people in the area had gone their separate ways at daybreak. Some headed to small villages where they knew friends and relatives, while others decided to travel to the closest town. My family was slow to resume traveling; we were just too large, with too many children to watch.

A Chinese person strolled into our campsite. He was another customer of ours back in Poipet, named Juiqui, and was curious about the number of people dropped off the day before by the train. When we told him about the expulsion from our original settlement, he mercifully brought our whole family into his home in Nikom Kandal.

Juiqui owned the town's only mechanical rice-polishing machine, which made him the wealthiest landowner in Nikom Kandal. His home was larger than any of the grass huts around him, fitted with teak walls and floors worn smooth, and columns rising to the ceilings as high as any marvelous temple. There was enough room to hold my entire family and he fed us a feast of rice and poultry bred from his many farming estates.

The next morning the village was required to turn out at the town center. We gave our names to the *Meipum*, the Khmer Rouge chief in charge of the village. They split us into organized groups assigned to different work duties. While some old men and women were required to labor in the fields, Father, luckily, was sent to handweaving to make straw mats, bamboo baskets, and cups for Angkar. My brothers and sisters were assigned to grow rice, irrigate ditches, till the ground, and feed the livestock. I was assigned to build rice dams. None of us found ourselves in the same working group. The soldiers had separated members of families, dividing us at random like human cattle without giving reasons.

Those new arrivals in the village, like my family, were informally called the New People, and the existing villagers were known as the older Base People. The New People compared to the Old were different, spoiled, clean with smooth hands and soft feet. We were regarded by many as corrupt, vile vermin who needed to eliminate the Western contamination that had infected our minds. We were instructed to follow the Revolutionary Spirit of Angkar. And then Angkar would help us purify ourselves through manual labor, thereby destroying any individual attachments. We would be cleansed from the filth of the cities, properly purged of our envy and greed.

Once we gave our all for the sake of Angkar, they pledged the Revolutionary Spirit would teach us to increase crop production and we would be able to double and triple our yields in the next harvest. Together, obeying this most powerful and awesome Angkar meant we could all rebuild the former Kampuchea to its ancient glory.

Within a couple days of arriving in Nikom Kandal, I was called for a ten-person meeting. It was held beneath the cool shade of an apple tree, and we seated ourselves in a circle around it. The tree was thin and rigid, growing large, leathery green fruits.

Soon, a roofless jeep drove in behind the circle. The car doors slammed. Three soldiers walked forward. They circled around us and the tree, and I thought they desired some of the fruits. But they turned their glances to the people in the group. It was clear they were looking for someone, circling like panthers. The men stopped right behind me. My stomach sank in fear. I did not move an inch. They drew their guns at the head of the man sitting next to me.

At once, the bare-chested muscular man in shorts raised his hands up. He was a former Lon Nol striped officer, ranked admirably in the military, and spoke educated and refined Khmer. The strong man tried to ensure his survival by working well, doing his best not to get noticed.

While the soldiers tied his arms tight, with his large chest sticking out, his wife left the circle and ran into the nearby house. She, too, was exceptionally cultivated, an ageless beauty with long, fine black hair, white teeth, and big almond eyes. As they loaded her husband onto the jeep and drove away, the panic-stricken wife reappeared and chased after the vehicle, clutching a white shirt in her hand.

"Wait! Stop! Just let him have his shirt!" she screamed, her outstretched arm carrying the T-shirt in the air. "Stop! Let him have his one shirt!"

She cried loudly, running until she could see them no more. She sank to the ground, her whole body shuddering with sobs, still holding the shirt.

The T-shirt meant more than keeping him warm; everything between them would now disappear. In their deeply held religious beliefs, whatever possessions one held at their time of death, meaning the money in their pockets, their clothes, necklaces, and watches, will all accompany them to the next life. Without anything, the man would step into an emptiness, cut off from the face of the earth. His wife would be forgotten in his next existence. Without so much as a T-shirt to bind them together in the next life, the cherished reality connecting the two had yawned into a deep chasm.

The woman worked in our hectare. One day, when there were no soldiers around, I heard her singing. She cried a mournful melody, singing an unknown song. Her heart was broken. In the fields, her head tipped heavenward, and she sang loudly:

> *From the crossroads, I've been watching,*
> *Always there to see you come home;*
> *Because in my late dream last night,*
> *Just before dawn awoke my eyes,*
> *I saw you come back to me.*
> *But as each day nears its last hour,*
> *Stolen like the sun, my hope is gone.*
> *The children beg and beg for you;*
> *Three children to care for alone;*
> *They cry and call for your return.*
> *But just as the sun will rise,*
> *I will wait at the crossroads,*
> *Dreaming you will be home once more.*
> *I will still be here waiting.*
> *The dream that I dream will never be.*

Her voice was beautiful. The purity of her song carried across the field and the people who heard her toiled the land with tears in their eyes.

* * *

One morning, the Khmer Rouge announced that a special dance performance would be held at noon. The entire village was required to attend, and all fifteen hundred grown-ups and children convened in the open fields, raising questions as to why there was a dance play. Larger and smaller meetings were becoming more frequent, but to have one for a traditional folk dance was strange. Under the hot sun I squeezed into the crowd, squatting and waiting, when two soldiers stepped forward.

A hush fell on the crowd when the black-clad soldiers took the stage in the front, hauling a man with his hands tied behind his back. Nervous gasps broke out. He was Vietnamese, from the country on Cambodia's eastern border, the country the Khmer Rouge hated the most. Soon a cadre wearing a red headband wrapped once around his forehead yelled, "This person has betrayed our Angkar! He is a conspirator and a spy that tried to escape! What shall we do with this person?"

The crowd sat still.

"Should we give him what he deserves or should we keep him?"

There was no reply.

I sat silent like everyone else. The Khmer Rouge soldiers in the back glared down, giving us threatening looks.

"You are either *with* ANGKAR or *against* ANGKAR! Is your allegiance with the ENEMY?!" the leader shouted in rage. They were very near to picking someone from the masses to make us cooperate.

"Kill . . . him . . . kill him . . ." the crowd murmured, raising their hands weakly in the air. "Kill him . . . kill him . . . kill him." Our cheerless chants slowly reached unison. We could not look at the man standing.

And just like that, good and decent people who would never have condoned such a thing at any other point in their lives verbally signed on for the execution of someone they knew nothing about. Only a few days earlier, any one of us would have taken great offense if someone suggested we would willingly participate in such a thing.

The cadre took the solid base of a wooden bat and struck the man on the back of his neck with such a force it knocked him to the floor. The Khmer Rouge soldier then pulled out a sword and jabbed it below the man's chest and tore it down his body. He ripped open his belly and pulled out his entrails, holding them high above his head, still fluttering. The children and women shrieked.

"Let this be a lesson to you all!" the Khmer soldier bellowed. "Do not betray Angkar, who has sacrificed itself to liberate the Cambodian people." He never, however, said what Angkar supposedly sacrificed in order to do that. "Long live Angkar! Long live the Revolution! Long live Democratic Kampuchea!"

The corpse was displayed for three days to remind every villager of where their allegiances should lie.

*　*　*

A month after settling in Nikom Kandal, nanny Yeay Sek's son returned, driving into the village for his mother. She again refused to go and the two argued loudly.

"You have no choice!" he shouted. "There will be a raid upon all Chinese people! Don't put yourself in harm! They will all be killed!"

We all heard his words, and Sihong told Yeay Sek, "You should go with your family. It's not safe for you to be with us." Without a choice, Yeay Sek sadly climbed aboard the motorcycle, side-saddled.

"Don't leave us . . . don't go!" Tears formed in Yeay Sek's eyes while the children ran after the motorcycle and cried when it veered away.

* * *

Before the end of the second month, armed soldiers surrounded Juiqui's house. They entered and pointed their guns at him to surrender. He was tied up and loaded onto the jeep. The soldiers took all his property, including his home, his animals, his farming equipment, and his prized re-milling machine for their own use.

Resigned to never seeing Juiqui again, and thus without a place to live, Father and I moved to the neglected shelter originally assigned to us. It was a compound where other residents also lived. The huts were connected to each other and were very small. Except for Chiv, who settled in the complex, the rest of my family found homes closer to where they worked.

The old Base villagers grew resentful of us. They began to mock and jeer those who did not come from the village.

"Why do they have to work with us?" they complained among themselves. "These people do not know how to plant rice. They only grow grass."

The city people were all unaware of how to distinguish between the green rice shoots and the wild weeds and were mistakenly transporting the wrong plants from one paddy to another. They stood with their backs bent in the muddy fields, stabbing unusable blades of grass into the wet earth. This made the old villagers furious. We were the new people—the educated, the landowners, the merchants, the teachers, the students, the doctors, and the businesspeople. Anybody who represented modernity. We were considered useless and weak.

Those who had lived a simple life, tilling soil far away from the corruptions of the city, were promoted. Villagers, farmers, and the uneducated, these people were upheld as better suited for Angkar's future.

The Khmer Rouge commanded us to discard our cooking pots and utensils. Dishes and spoons were handed over to the soldiers. We were prohibited to cook our own food; rations would come from Angkar centrally at the community kitchens, where we must communally eat meals together. It was now forbidden to take food from the earth, even if we grew it with our own hands. And no matter how abundant it was, foraging in the countryside would be stealing in the face of Angkar. The new government appeared to be angry over everything and determined to pay out punishments whether they landed on the guilty or not. It was all a display of power, and no one was exempt.

No more speaking of Chinese or any other tongue was to be tolerated. Khmer was the official language of Angkar, a dictate intended to prevent us from secretly scheming behind their backs, since oppressors are always fearful that someone is trying to cast off their yoke. Items from the city such as perfume and jewelry became forbidden. Gradually, everyone began to wear gray and black pajamas with red krama scarves around their necks, just like the soldiers and peasants, so we would all be "equal" in appearance.

In more village-wide meetings, we were made to pledge all we had to Angkar. They promised Angkar would watch over us, and provide food and shelter. Without currency to buy and sell things in the markets, only Angkar distributed what was deemed necessary for us. Angkar was the sole provider and therefore the sole owner of all our property, deserving our upmost performance, thoughts, and desires.

Or else they would kill us.

Our very lives now belonged to this Supreme Organization.

Although we could not see Angkar, every achievement and victory, each happiness and delight, everyone's inspiration and wisdom would come directly from the all-powerful Angkar. The high, venerable Angkar was the face of all things, even if we could not see it. We were forced to swear our loyalty to the magnanimous, never failing, farsighted, and awesome Angkar.

Or else they would kill us.

Angkar was our true parent. Our own will was the true enemy, which meant when they killed us, it was for our own good.

* * *

In the October growing season, Angkar announced it was holding a mass wedding ceremony. The young were allowed to have an official marriage with a partner. Those who did not marry were sent on projects outside the village. Father went through much trouble to find a wife for me, bringing me to see a Laotian girl. She was pretty, with black pebble eyes and fair skin. But I never expressed any hopes to marry, since all the girls I had interest in were taken. They feared they would be forced to marry a Khmer Rouge, and so they quickly found husbands.

"I can't marry her," I told Father. "I am too young and don't know anything about love yet."

Overlooking patches of schoolyard fields, when the late afternoon held the heat of the day, Angkar commenced the public ceremony. All the attendees, the entire town, wore black. In the center of the field, positioned on a table, were two crossed AK-47s. A Khmer Rouge soldier stood next to the table and called forth the first bride and groom. The first couple, wearing drab black garb and red scarves, walked side-by-side from the back, hands never touching. They faced the rifles and did not look at each other once.

"The gun is my witness," they recited after the soldier. "If I have an affair or divorce, then the gun will be my witness. We commit ourselves to Angkar—to make great efforts, to create life for Angkar, and to rebuild the country."

Each of the forty couples, pair by pair, stood at the table, making their vows to the guns, pledging loyalty to Angkar: "I promise to obey whatever is demanded of me and will honorably work harder." Some of these arrangements had been fixed by the Khmer Rouge; a handful of them had not known each other until that morning.

For the feast following the ceremony, special rations were handed out: slightly better portions of rice, rather than porridge, and new cuts of beef, with pieces dropped in that were large enough to be seen. It was a rare occasion, as the Khmer Rouge would never slaughter a cow, except in instances when it was too sick or too old to stand. There was no music, dancing, or blessings bestowed from the elders. No gifts of generosity were given. No good wishes were offered. Missing were the cheers for happiness, luck, and good health to the newlyweds. We were expected to feel nothing at all.

After the wedding ceremonies, the single adolescent workers aged fourteen and above were mobilized for assignments outside of the town. I fell into this group and set out for the meeting point of my squad. We all stood shoulder to shoulder as the cadre leader Pal pronounced: "Comrades, you are the tall, strong Revolutionary youth. You will be the ones to restore the country to its former glory. . . . You are the strength of Kampuchea. The First Strength. The pride of the country."

Since we were the ones full of energy, we were bestowed the highest duties of Angkar: to struggle on the front line and perform the most intensive and laborious work. He pressed that before we could become masters of nature, before we could fashion the waters and forge the lands like iron, we must first harness our own natures. This meant to put the sole focus of our minds only on Angkar. We must eliminate any personal thoughts and complaints for ourselves.

"You must destroy this cancer at its roots before it spreads," Pal continued. "If you want to kill the grass, you must pull the root. Anyone found slacking in any of these will be dealt with."

After the speech, I went with the youth brigade to dig dike walls and water canals an hour's distance away. The ditches we dug would be used to irrigate the rice fields. Without buckets or shovels, we stood elbow to elbow and heaved bundles of mud from one person to the next until it reached the last person, who slapped it on the existing dam walls. In the midst of working, we playfully flung mud into each other's faces. For a moment, the little horseplay made me feel like we were back in school throwing rolled-up paper balls across the classroom.

For lunch, a trio of youths left for the communal kitchen and brought Angkar's food to the worksite. A small shard of rock salt was passed around, along with a thin soup of rice. I looked at the brownish gruel in my bowl. I gulped down a salty morsel and wiped the perspiration off my forehead. Caked in dirt and muck, we sat on the wet grounds and open peaceful fields, relishing every spoonful of the watery rice.

Over the course of a month, the mounds we built were getting larger and began flowing with waters to bring to distant fields.

* * *

Pal pointed me out one morning before we went off to the worksite. "You. Come here!" I walked slowly toward him, my stomach coiling in fear. "What did your family do before?" he asked.

"I helped my father sell ice in the streets." I lied to avoid disclosing incriminating information on my family.

He looked at me and said, "You're not. You're a bourgeois kid." I felt my chest tighten at his words.

"No, that's what I did for a living."

He tried very hard to get me to talk about my past life before he moved on. "Well. I have something for you to do. Prove to me you are not a bourgeois kid." I followed him and he pointed at an eighty-pound sack of wet sprouted rice. "That rice there is the seed. Carry it to the rice fields." The distance to carry the heavy load to the faraway fields was at least two and a half miles. Pal saw the twinge of worry on my face.

"One more thing. You have to carry it to the rice fields without ever stopping." He came in close and helped heft it on my shoulders. Heavy on my back, it felt like a bag of bricks. I strained to stay upright, quavering like a newborn calf trying to stand up. *I must not fall down.* I clenched my teeth tightly and summoned up all the strength I had.

He kept close behind, carrying nothing in his hands. I moved with imaginative strength and will. "You are not. You are a rich spoiled brat," he snarled. Droplets of water from the wet bag rolled down my forehead and mingled with my sweat. "You're Chinese. A rich Chinese brat. BORN OF AN IMPERIALIST PIG!"

I felt nothing, except my heart beating, thumping so hard my chest hurt.

"You used to have people carry for you. Now how does it feel to do it yourself? You vermin! Hurry!"

At last, when I had endured long past where my body should have given out, he directed me toward a grass tent, where a small fire was already burning inside. I dropped the sack to the ground. He gave me a long, hard stare, his eyes boring into me. I saw in his eyes that he was going to torture me from here on. I could not last around him.

Pal left without saying a word. I collapsed right there, my overwrought nerves sapped. As I gasped for air, tiny scratching sounds came from the rice sack I had dropped. A mouse had leapt from the grass and onto the leaning sack.

Without thinking, I took a thin stick and gave the mouse a glancing blow. Between my hard gasps, I picked up the tail of the stunned animal and threw it into the fire. The mouse was charred black and brittle. But I ate the mouse regardless. My hunger blocked any feelings of disgust.

Chapter 7

Water, Water, Everywhere

"You and you . . . and one or two others," said the cadre leader. "You there!" Pal finally pointed me out of the crowd. "Go there." I was told to move to another group of ten other youths who were assigned to do projects that required a long journey to the work site. He gave simple instructions: "It will be a while before you come back. Don't pack much. Angkar will supply all that you need."

I returned home to pack two sets of clothing and a hammock, and I said goodbye to everyone, not knowing how long I'd be gone. We journeyed alongside dirt roads and collected more young workers from other places, cutting through many bleak villages where no sound emerged. We arrived at a small, flat, clumpy island surrounded by hundreds of wide-leafed water lilies with bright pink flowers.

I inched toward the edge and saw that the water was dark and cold. My hopes of finding some small comfort—perhaps a little hut, a good fire, or a pond to fish—vanished. Men bathed themselves in grimy waters in areas close to where people had relieved themselves. Unabashedly, they dunked their heads in and out, while others used the same waters for cooking, scooped only moments earlier.

A haphazard assortment of stakes, wooden stubs, log posts, and bamboo shoots stuck up unevenly above the still waters. I hopped along the makeshift bridge to reach the island.

Sitting behind a table was the Khmer Rouge in charge of the project. He put me in a unit of a hundred unfamiliar faces. I was required to sleep in their section each night. Almost every bit of land was taken, with nowhere to tie my hammock. So I opened it on the ground and slept on top.

I arose to a haze of morning fog. As I hiked to the back side of the island, I saw only water that stretched far beyond my view. I became thirsty. My only choice was to dip my hand in and drink it.

"Everyone will live here until the project is complete," the Khmer Rouge said. They handed out blue plastic tarps to build tents for ourselves. Without any trees to hang them on, we retrieved skinny branches from around the island and used them as shoddy posts to tie the tarps to. Our tents hung pitifully like frayed rags; we had to stoop or crawl on hands and knees to get through the drooping openings.

The cadre leader of my group spoke: "You have been chosen by Angkar to be part of the front lines. Angkar has provided food and shelter for all of you. We must be proud of ourselves and show gratitude to Angkar with the combined work of our strength and labor. The purpose of the revolution is physical toil. We must commit ourselves one hundred percent; commit all we have to Angkar, toward rebuilding the country." He called on us to raise our hands for chanting: "If you obey Angkar. Anything is possible. Long live Angkar! Long live Angkar! Long live Angkar!"

Shovels were passed, and in a long line we followed our cadre leader into the night-chilled waters while he balanced a gun over his head. The water reached up to my chest. I quickened with panic, afraid they would let the deep floodwaters swallow me up. A brisk wind came with the smell of mud and rain. It swept over my head and ran over my skin, bringing lonely shivers inside me.

For three miles, we muscled far through mud and silt. Fatigue began to set in our arms from holding the shovels above our heads. Soon we reached an area prepped with many square sections of rope attached on sticks above the water.

"Dig into here." The Khmer Rouge soldier pointed to the square segments. "The entire way back to camp." I lifted a shovelful of deep mire from beneath, raised it above my head, water pouring on my hair, and dropped it into the square plots. The fragile wet mound crumbled, sliding apart. It took several strenuous heaves for the mound to take shape and become high enough to pack in. When I became too weak to pull up the heavy mud from the bottom, I dunked my head beneath the waters to lift the watery mass up.

Lunch buckets barely half-filled were delivered to the project site. We held our small, meager meals just above the water to eat.

The evening skies shone brightly, the moon white like a rice cake, glittering on the waters. Because there was light to see by, the soldiers worked us late into the night. Afterward, I staggered with half-closed eyes, hungry and exhausted, coated with crusts of mud, longing for the dirty but familiar shelter of my tent. I yearned for moonless nights, where we did not have to work past dusk.

The days became long and the nights short. The whistles split early at four-thirty, each day the dam rising, growing slowly back toward the camp.

* * *

Before the first month passed, I was making the last scoops of the day when a sickly, tingling feeling coursed through my body, as if I were slipping into a deathly spell. I became cold.

The next morning when the whistles blew, I awoke sick. My temples hammered and my body was in a feverish cold sweat. I staggered out and approached the waters, but the sunlight reflection brought an ache to my eyes.

I approached the cadre leader before the meeting started and said, "I am ill." He looked me in the eye to see if I was faking it. In fear, I let my back and shoulders sag and narrowed my eyes further to make sure it was enough to convince him. He allowed me to stay behind with the other sick boys. I splashed water on my face and went back to my tent.

Most of the tents were now empty. Then I saw about twenty other boys curled in pain in their tents. Their upper arms were covered in sores and rashes.

The air was stagnant. I fell asleep and awoke sweating. The hot sun burning the blue tarp baked me inside it. I heard a voice and then sounds of soft shuffling, venturing from tent to tent on the island. It was the Khmer Rouge nurses, three of them, much younger than myself, aged thirteen to fifteen. Each carried a black medicine bag like a purse. Inside was a Coca-Cola glass bottle filled with young coconut juice, capped by a bark cork. The boys in the other tents began screaming in pain during the nurse visits. They were administered IV shots of the coconut juice to bring down their fever. The syringes were reused on the next patient, the needles rusted and bent.

I was afraid as one of the nurses began approaching my tent. She came ducking beneath and asked, "What kind of sickness do you have?"

"Just diarrhea." I sat straight upright, my heart bumping strongly against my side. I did not want to tell her I had a fever.

She reached into her purse and pulled out a clump of about twenty homemade pills: honey rolled into tiny pearls. She placed it in my hand and I bit into it, chewing the pills contentedly. It tasted like a cookie. A slow-moving energy flowed in my body and the headache dulled away.

"Can I have some more?" I was happy when the kind girl gave me another batch of twenty and left.

I savored it bit by bit, like a cow chewing its cud. It felt so good to be spared from work and allowed a chance to rest. Since I was no longer in the water and was recovering in the tent with more breathable air, I felt as if I would be able to work again tomorrow.

* * *

But the fever did not break, and the next morning I felt no better. The whistles sounded. I dragged myself out to the soldier at the gathering point.

"I am still sick."

"Are you trying to get out of work?" He leaned in closely to examine me. "What kind of illness do you have?"

"I have a fever and diarrhea. I don't feel well enough to work." After I appealed to him that I was too sick to work, he dismissed me for the day. Feeling somewhat relieved, I doubled back to my tent to sleep.

Later that morning, the nurse came and asked, "You're not feeling any better? Are you sure you don't have a fever? I should give you a shot."

"No. No . . . no." I shook my head. "I have no fever. Just give me the pills."

"If I give you the shot, you will feel better right away." I refused vigorously and she gave me the same honey pills and extras when I asked again.

As I lay semiconscious, I stared at the blue fabric of the tent, watching the ball of the sun through it. I felt cramped, wearied, and starved. For a waking moment, I thought I was looking into the sky. The tarp was cooking, deteriorating while it gave off a stale, acrid odor. My heart grew numb and my joints ached. I pulled my knees to my chin, shaking uncontrollably.

I was alone, and no one knew how sick I was. Formless thoughts stirred in my mind. Painful pictures of Mother caring for me and maids bringing me hot water and soup to my bedside. I was troubled with little turbulent memories I had forgotten of my family. *Is my family alive still? Is Father still there?* I was driven to madness.

The whistle shrieked again. I was still stricken. I felt no better than the day before. Although I had a sick heart and a sore head, I went and forded the waters with the rest of the group for work. I did not want the soldiers to suspect me of trying to skip.

The air was thin and cold. As I worked, my teeth chattered and my body shivered with violent tremors. I fought every urge to take a break, believing my strength would fail me if I stopped. The Khmer Rouge soldiers watched as I tried to work, sick and wet.

When the day was over, at last, I stood sweating and trembling and heaving on the dirt summit. I could not lift my arms for a single stroke more. The ground was swaying and unsteady, and swept by a tremendous dizzy spell, I slipped from the dam walls, plunging into the waters. I started drawing water into my lungs before the other boys came to my rescue. Cambodians I never knew lifted me up, with their hands under my arms. They carried me heavily through the waters back to camp. Wet and covered in muck, I went straight for my tent while the others got dinner; I was very sick and no longer hungry. Without even the strength to walk to relieve myself, I slept all night.

My eyes could hardly pry open the next day. My throat was taut and it burned to speak. This time the Khmer Rouge did not question me. They saw I was sicker than ever. Once I returned to my tent, my mind harked back to thoughts of my family, more than on any of the previous days.

When ten o'clock came, the noisy movements of the nurses walking between the tents temporarily lifted me from my loneliness. Then I heard the surprise call of an older man, a high Srok leader, for all the ill to gather for a meeting. With these words, I rose stiffly to my feet and picked my way out to join the rest of them already sitting in front of the leader.

"Comrades. Now you are sick and cannot work. Would you like to go back to the village?"

Nobody answered. We all looked at each other.

"Do you want to go back to your village?" he asked again. "Because I will give you a permit to travel across the county lines to go back to your village." We sat silently, blank faced. *Would he let us go like that? Are they trying to frighten us?* I did not believe him. It was too good to be true. Something in my head said it was a trick.

"If any of you want to go home, raise your hand. If not, I will leave."

The voice inside me changed. There was deep longing to go home. *I'll take my chances*, I thought to myself.

My hand shot up. The only one of the thirty kids.

The kid beside me looked at me. He suffered a fever himself and without giving it another thought, he also raised his hand. Then, the hand behind him quickly went up. Then the fourth beside me followed . . . the fifth, sixth, seventh, another . . . until ten of us held our hands up.

"Is that it? Anybody else want to go? This is the last chance."

The other kids did not raise their hands but looked at us, open-mouthed, with eyes that said it all: "You're being deceived." Although I was filled with cheeriness to leave, I did not know what would happen next.

Filled with a mix of happiness and fear, I quickly retrieved my belongings and returned to the Srok leader. He did not give us a certificate, but instead handed over a single sealed pink envelope.

"Take this pink envelope to the Srok leader at the next county. Do not open it," he commanded.

We headed east, nervously wondering what was in the sealed envelope. "Are they going to trick us?" one of the boys asked.

"This letter must say we are the lazy ones that don't want to work," said another. "It must be telling the next Srok leader to get rid of the ten of us." We anxiously examined the pink envelope again. It had a red decorated sticker on the seal.

"Do we give it to him?" I asked.

"We must. Without question they will catch us. We have to do whatever they told us to do," one more kid said.

After two hours we arrived at a beaten brown bungalow with a red clay slated roof. The spacious yard was bright with blossoming mangos, banana trees, and tropical flowers. I was half-convinced I was entering my executioner's house. Just as we made it to the front, the Srok leader came out of the doorway. He was elderly with salt-and-pepper hair and dark nut skin.

We fearfully pushed each other to give the letter to the Srok leader. The letter switched from hand to hand before someone forced it into mine. In showing him the letter, I discovered how much my hands were shaking.

The old man gazed at our faces intently before he opened up the envelope from the sides and pulled out a small, folded square of paper. His brows furrowed as he mouthed silently the text on the page. The silence lengthened—my heartbeat slammed in my chest.

"All right. Who is first? Tell me which village you are from and I will make a travel permit for each of you."

We lifted a smile at each other.

From there on we romped. We were jumping and laughing. At a crossroad, we said our goodbyes and our paths divided. With a certificate in my hand, I walked on the highway for home.

* * *

I saw Nikom Kandal, and rice fields on both sides of the road leading into the village. The fine waves of golden stalks with their white tassels curled in a breeze, gently bending toward the warmth. Simple sounds reached my ears: riotous cries of sparrows, the raps of a hoe and spade, the rhythmic tossing from a sifter. The noises seemed to hang in the air.

The village was different than when I left. Standing before a radiant sea of harvest, I felt an old lift of the heart. There was a soaring sense of fullness at the sight of this seasonal abundance.

I came to my house and stood by the door. I caught Father's face first, as he tried to recognize me. The family gave a sudden gasp of surprise and stared at me in disbelief. The person they saw was a cadaverous body, someone they had no memory of.

The grown-ups said something to the children and they sprung up to get me a pounded rice dessert called *ambok*. On the brink of starvation, it was the sweetest and tastiest thing I had had since I left Poipet.

On this day, instead of waiting in line for watery rations, I finally had solid food that came from the care of my family.

Chapter 8

Catching Cattle

Months after the rice planting and harvesting season, summer was approaching. The dry season parched the land and the village needed to make sure to graze the cows on lush grasses until the rains returned. I was picked as one of four people to herd Nikom Kandal's cows to the mountains thirty miles away.

I was clearly the youngest in the crew. The eldest was in his fifties and was the only one who brought his wife, to cook for us. He looked like an old wild radical, thin and dark like a tribal native with short, frizzled white hair. The other two were in their twenties and thirties. We packed enough supplies for two months on the backs of the cows, once we had gathered all the cattle. We set off for the road, leading them five miles to National Highway 5.

Alongside the highway lay wide scrubby fields, bare from the heat. It felt good to see National Highway 5. It had been so long, since I was always kept on a project or in the village. We drove the cattle onto the quiet, open tarmac. Then, all of a sudden, a few broke from the pack and headed for an untamed tangle of rice stalks. I moved close to shoo them from the grass nips they were tearing off in mouthfuls. Once I got near, I saw tattered and sun-beaten Lon Nol uniforms sticking out between the stalks—the unmarked graves of executed soldiers. There was nothing that could be done for them.

* * *

The few straying cows returned to the rest on the highway, and soon the hum of machinery approached. The herd sauntered to one side, allowing a motorcycle carrying men in black shirts to squeeze by. Shortly after, a military caravan rumbled on the road with its dreadful *romp*, sending the frightened cows trampling wildly off the blacktop pavement. As the roofless truck bore down, I glanced inside and saw men, women, and children, whole families, weeping.

Five armed Khmer Rouge guarded them. I knew they were being taken to be slain.

Once they passed, the sounds of hooves and bells took over again, and with my cattle stick I shooed the cows back onto the highway. In the late afternoon, we broke off and herded the cattle through a stretch of dirt and grass plains until dusk, when we finally reached our destination: a sole cottage surrounded by a sparse ring of trees.

We let the cows ruminate, contently munching in the meadow, while we perched high on hillocks and trees to relax and take in our surroundings of golden peaks and deep, still meadows. The mountains had a way of nurturing peace in me, the gentle green hills undulating far out in the distance. Cries of birds and monkeys hidden in the mountains mixed in, resounding in rhythm-like music. It was an oasis. This is how I remembered Cambodia—beautiful and untroubled.

For about a month, our only duty was to gather and feed the cows, and explore other areas once a grazing area was chewed down. Upon returning one evening, we found two cows missing from the herd, a male and female. The next morning, the younger man and I went and searched for the pair on our own.

We found a pack of cows overseen by another villager who also brought herds to the mountains during the dry season. The overseer said he had not counted any extra cows in his pack. After trekking for a few hours we became lost, stumbling upon several unused cottages in the jungle, barely visible through the screen of trees. We both decided it was best to find our way back.

We came into a bare valley and I made out the hard outline of numerous blue tents pitched on the dusty foothills, their flaps snapping in the stiff winds. Loud revolutionary music played. The din of a woman's voice, harsh and shrill, sang on the recording: "Commit to hard work! To overcome the feelings of suffering! Make your mind strong!" The sound of dull metal thuds echoed in the dirt.

I stood, aghast. The earth had been gouged out, almost scorched. Workers in rough blackened jackets shoveled and leveled the cracked land into place. They snaked over the sides of earthen mounds like little black ants, raising whirlwinds of drifting sand. The Khmer Rouge on guard toted guns as the workers dredged dirt in a basket from one area and threw it on the broad earth elsewhere. The strikes of shovels were both loud and numbing—swing after swing, toss after toss, while baskets passed from one person to the next. It was like the drumbeat to some nameless event.

According to the man with me, this was Phnom Kamping Puoy. The Khmer Rouge were trying to build the largest handmade dam ever. It had become the place of the hardest work and the worst of losses. Thousands of struggling youths were down there, much younger than me. He said that little boys developed night blindness, malnourished from their golf-ball-sized rice rations. The blind boys begged the Khmer Rouge to let them rest at night because they were unable to see, but the soldiers pushed them down into the pits and forced them to hoist up dirt. I felt sorrowful when he told me that. I could have easily been drafted into this project, toiling at the bottom of this pitiful valley.

We retreated back toward camp, into the solace of the forests, and found the pair of cows running wild on the slopes. The male had tried to mate with the female and had chased her all this way. We took out some rope and tied it around their necks and led them back to camp.

On the last few days of feeding in May, before we had to head back to Nikom Kandal, it showered and thundered all night, signaling the approaching rain season. The morning air was warm and full of heavy smells and dampness, and the light noise of dripping branches. Pools of flowing water emerged where fields and the trodden paths had been.

Near the end of the day, we were herding the cows when several of them discovered a muddy pond and raced for it. Baked from the midday heat, much of the water had evaporated, leaving only a brown sludge. We shooed the cows out, and one by one they left.

As the herd dwindled around the pond, a baby calf was left drowning in the shallow waters of the middle. Coated in thick mud, she flailed her legs up frantically on her side to stay above the muck. The calf dropped her head in the mud several times, each time rising weaker than the last, and then she sank beneath for one last time and lay motionless. We stared for a few moments, before we were quite sure the calf was dead.

"What do we do now?" the thirty-year-old asked. "We are supposed to report it. The comrades counted how many cows we took with us. We're in trouble when they find out the baby cow drowned." None of us wanted to acknowledge that fact.

Before any serious discussions started, the old man said, "We will keep it for ourselves. If we report this to the Khmer Rouge, they will come to get the baby calf and will probably eat it themselves. We must swear to each other not to say anything."

Even for a baby calf, she was still heavy. It took four of us, feet slipping on the mud, to drag her out.

Back at our camp, we cleaned the calf and cut her apart, the smell of fresh blood filling the room. The old man smiled widely, joking about how much meat we had struck. His demeanor was always happy, as if he was enjoying himself at any given moment.

The cutlets of meat were divided among the four of us, and everything else the cow had to offer was placed in a large pot: a chopped mixture of heart, lungs, liver, innards, and bones. The old man grabbed a handful of marijuana leaves from the backyard—from bushes that grew as tall as us—and tossed it into the soup. The leaves sank like cotton bits and filled the cottage with such a great aroma. He stirred it up, hot steam rising, and once it was done, we all dug into the pot at the same time with our own spoons. The soup was wild, creamy, and delicious; the marijuana gave a bitter tangy taste that simmered well with the hearty beef. It was so delightful I had to force myself to slow down. We slurped and ate the last scoops in the pot. We looked at each other and cackled and chuckled.

The weather changed during the night. Winds outside wiggled through the cracks of our dismal hut. The noise was like the rustling of cardboard. We had a surge of nervousness about what we had done with the calf. Uneasy, we whispered to each other, paranoia passing between us.

The wind strengthened, loud and bitter. The posts of the cottage shook, scaring us to take to the corners and pull covers over our heads, quivering. The sounds amplified our fears and turned them into things

I couldn't recognize properly. The heavy rustling of branches. The ominous creak of the cottage's wooden boards. Trampling hoof steps right outside. Animal grunts in the wind. In my troubled imagination, it sounded like we were being surrounded by an army of black shirts out there in the sharp shadows.

"They know we took the cow. They're coming to get us!" one of the young men yelled.

But the old man went mad with laughter; instead, he sang and joked in high spirits. He flung the door against the wall and laughingly cursed into the wind, frightening the cows. He then lifted his head and howled like a wolf. We were sure he would be heard by the Khmer Rouge and they would send soldiers here.

The threatening sounds continued throughout the night, terrifying us until dawn.

Chapter 9

Phnom Kamping Pouy

Hunger and death had befallen the townspeople. People were being abducted every day. Nikom Kandal's numbers dwindled from disease, starvation, and murder. Those who remained were gaunt in appearance, their skin stretched over thin, bony cheeks, their hair sticking up like wires.

One day in the afternoon, a Khmer Rouge soldier came to my hut and told me, "We have an assignment you must do for us. Pack your clothes and be ready to leave tomorrow." I was given no more information, except one other person would be joining me. Father was especially worried.

"Why would they choose only two people in the entire town?" he asked. Every day, many continued to be taken from the village. And once they left, they never came back. The mood over the town darkened every day. While there was always a heavy sadness when I departed for one of these jobs, this time I feared for my life.

The other boy chosen was named Dangdi. Both of us were Chinese, adding to my fears that we were going to be eliminated. We were given a travel permit by Pal and told to go to Tuol Krasaing, a place located in the elevated lands where soybeans, vegetables, and tomatoes were grown instead of rice, since not enough water could be transported up there.

We were to travel several towns away, to be picked up along with other workers at the village of Thma Koul. National Highway 5 was deserted, without a single person traveling on it. We hiked on for some fifteen minutes before we turned onto a strange dirt road passing through empty abandoned villages. Soon we heard the sound of repeated leather slaps and a group suddenly approached out of the distance. Three Khmer Rouge soldiers dragged a man leashed like a donkey. They were beating the prisoner with a whip and the butts of their guns, and he looked half-dead. We dared not look more when we passed them by.

We reached the designated roadside pickup spot and waited with the other youths. While we stood there, Dangdi showed me the travel certificate Pal had given us, and he asked what I could make of it. "These are two people at Angkar's request to send out to do the project," I read. It was signed "Kadeb," the name of our village chief.

An olive-colored cargo truck puttered up the road. Dangdi presented our certificate to the driver and we climbed in the back. Dread settled in my stomach. This was the first ride I had taken since the Communists took over. I thought back to the families on the truck that were heading to be slain when I oversaw the cattle. Riding in a truck almost always meant you were to be removed. However, as I looked around, I took a bit of solace. The driver was a villager and there were no guards. About twenty middle-aged men were already in the truck. We sat on the floor facing them. They appeared to be as nervous as we were.

The truck picked up two more men. One of them was shaking and mumbling regrets about his wife and children. Later in the day we arrived at our destination, a tiny bush village at the edge of the woodlands.

The person in charge was an older Khmer Rouge in his mid-fifties. He and his wife smiled when Dangdi and I presented our permit.

"Well then," he replied. "I've got more Chinese kids coming."

I had no idea what he meant until I turned around and saw a throng of workers returning from work. Many of them were Chinese: yellow-cheeked, clean-looking, a healthy glow to their skin.

"Go clean up," he said. "We're going to have some dinner at six o'clock."

At the community kitchen, I was given larger than usual portions of rice, tomatoes, cucumbers, soybeans, fresh basil, lettuce, mint, and fish. I found other youths that I knew back from Poipet who had been there for two years and they looked healthy and appeared happy. They worked in the hill fields, pruning tomato and soybean orchards, cutting the rough stems off basil leaves.

My arrival at Tuol Krasaing seemed like a deliverance. The chief leader was not like the rest of the Khmer Rouge. He was a good man. The work duties were much less arduous than before, and the man would encourage us to eat more when we were not full.

"Ah. I never thought at my age I'd be blessed with so many Chinese children!" he often joked. Even in the midst of all this betrayal and misery, moments of decency—all too rare—could still be found.

In two weeks, I gained back some of the weight I had lost and my stomach ailments vanished while I performed tasks like gardening, watering plants, and hoeing. I even had time for breaks to chat with others. Women and men were allowed to work alongside each other. I began to ponder whether I could possibly live the rest of my life under the Communists in this manner, and settle with one of the women here. There would be no more projects, no more orders, no more meetings, no more hard work, and no more having to move around. I almost laughed with joy.

But my happy interlude in Tuol Krasaing only lasted three months.

The leaders changed. One day without warning, Khmer Rouge soldiers wearing blue checkered scarves instead of the typical red came into the commune and tied up the dear old leader. They spoke with an eastern Cambodian accent and looked very hardened. It seemed Khmer Rouge was now pitted against Khmer Rouge. They took him away as a prisoner without any explanation.

The chief was replaced by a more ruthless man, and things were not at all the same afterward. We had to work longer days and food was cut back to meager rations of watery rice porridge. After being in position for two short months, the new leader ordered all single men to leave for another project. Only married couples and girls were to stay in Tuol Krasaing. I felt cheated, having something good taken away from me, since even this shrunken life was better than my former days in slave camps.

Instructions were given to travel to the opposite mountainside to meet a truck that would be waiting to take us to the project site. If we had to be transported, I judged the assignment was far away. We set out on foot immediately. On the mountain trails, the paths rose dizzily into the hills, then plunged into the dense overgrowth of forest. Suddenly the forest gave way to wide open land. The red clay earth dipped into a valley.

I was arrested by the sight in front of us.

At my feet was a massive hand-built dam running through the center of the valley. It extended all the way from the end of the mountain where I stood to the next mountain, four miles in the distance. I remembered seeing it in its early stages back when I was caretaker of the cows. This was Phnom Kamping Puoy, and in the time since then, it had grown twice as wide as before, wide enough for a two-lane road. The workers walked the squat rammed earth walls, which stood at least six feet above the water.

It was now well known that this was Angkar's most ambitious project for crop production, to enable rice growing not just once in the summer, but three times a year. However, it came at the expense of thousands of people who had been forced to build it and died of malaria and starvation.

At the far end of the dam, two colossal wooden gates were partially open, feeding water into the rice fields. It was like a mountain stream, throwing up a shower of white spray and forming swells and bubbles.

Over a small ridge, we descended the incline beyond Phnom Kamping Puoy back toward the mangroves of the wilderness. We arrived at our location in the late afternoon. The truck, however, was not there as promised on the road that connected to the dam.

Rain clouds began to darken the sky and we covered ourselves with plastic sheets, feigning sleep beside the cold blue lagoon.

Early the following day, two trucks drove up. Soldiers issued a meager golf-ball-sized portion of rice to each person and all of us squeezed on to the two trucks. We were taken far away from the vicinity of Phnom Kamping Puoy.

The crowded trucks motored along the lonely highway for a long hour before turning on to an alternative track, winding over green low-slung hills and mountain ridges. The surrounding peaks jutted up high into the vast flat skies. As our truck staggered up an incline, a smudge of ropy smoke coiled in the hot air. I saw trails of it drifting over the trees like poison in the wind. The contours of the green mountains soon took on a bald look. The bare countryside was dotted with tree stumps and blackened spikes poking from the ground. Slashed wood burned in fiery stacks, huge piles of orange flames licking up.

The truck rode into massive columns of sweeping smoke spewing up and turning the sky ashen. Flames angrily climbed the trees that stood, glowing like torches and turning the trunks to a chalky white. I felt my eyes pricking, my lungs heavy from the burning soot.

I thought, *Angkar has torched the beautiful splendor of my country with blazing hot fire.* Only empty and blackened ground remained. Cambodia was always a land of tranquility and green calm. This was the greatest wealth she offered. The Revolution's Rural Transformation plan was to clear distant mountains and open up the land for more rice planting and large-scale farming. But there were not enough workers to plant this land. The Revolution had swept so many of them away—with Angkar reckless to accomplish its goal, even if it meant the collapse of the population they were supposedly doing it all for.

At the base of a huge mountain, ancient taproots and vines grew ruinously out of boulders. Ropy tree limbs draped from hanging mountain brush, darkened with mud. Crowds of young men and women close to my age were broken into various working groups. Dangdi was still in my group, since we were both from the same village.

I went to the sleeping quarters designated for my group—banished to a horseshoe-shaped cove at the foot of a mountain. It was crowded with many other youths who were already staking a spot. There were many young workers and not enough tents; the place reeked of human feces, but no one cared.

Chapter 10

Blazing Red

*W**here am I? I do not know.*

All I knew was the night air had been cold and the morning was quiet in the way that typically comes before the rains. Soon the stillness was broken by the Khmer Rouge, ordering us with speed. The Khmer Rouge sent every able worker deep into the mountainsides, where we were to retrieve wood chopped by other men and use it to construct our own huts. Our daily requirement was to carry two teak logs a day back to camp.

Dangdi and I climbed to the top of a hill, watching a line of already exhausted men carrying logs downward. When we reached a pile of felled timber, we found the fresh teak logs to be heavier than either of us. Dangdi and I tried to carry one log together, pushing it up on our shoulders, but the soldiers on duty commanded us each to carry one teak log by ourselves.

I grabbed a log, first pulling it straight, then hugging it under my arms, but it was too heavy for me. I maneuvered the thirteen-foot log along my aching back and dragged it by one end, the other end digging the earth as I moved along. One slow footstep after another, I lugged it around trees and up hilly slopes, crisscrossing the mountain. Thankfully, there was no river to cross. The teak was so heavy, it would have sunk in the water even if the log was dry. This should have been work for an elephant to pull, as was usually done. At one point I paused to relieve my aching arms and legs. I feared that if I dropped the teak log, I wouldn't have enough energy to pick it up again.

In a few moments there was a shout like the crack of a whip: "Hurry up! Keep it going!" A Khmer Rouge on guard pointed the barrel of his rifle at me. I felt the panicky beginnings of despair. The distance was five miles back to camp; going back and forth for a single log would be twice that. Twenty miles just to retrieve two logs. It felt as if I had been ordered to scale an endless vertical cliff.

Somehow my body accomplished what my spirit could not imagine, and one painful log trip followed another without leading us to our executions. Each effort of grunt-and-shove work shot a new bolt of pain through us.

When I went to dinner, a Khmer Rouge with a rotund belly stood by the building. His round, sun-darkened face was callous and uncaring. He had short-cropped iron-black hair and a bull neck that was square and piggish. He glared angrily in my direction and, unsure of what he was looking at, I turned my head to see if there was someone else behind me. With no one else there, I turned back and his coarse, brutal eyes met mine, unchanged. I pretended not to see the hatred in his eyes and went into the community kitchen.

The next day, the same burly soldier gave me another cold stare, but this time a slow smile spread across his face. "Hi, Chink. How do you

like your new life?" he chortled. I held my head down and passed him
to walk inside.

The others told me his name was Don and that he was soon to
be promoted. I saw him in the very same spot nearly every day, and
each time I feared he would single me out, the same way Pal back in
Nikom Kandal did.

* * *

On the morning of the two-week mark since Dangdi and I were sent
for the project, the whistles summoned us to roll call. As soon as we
all assembled, the cadre leader counted the line and found two youths
missing.

He gestured to a gunman and went in pursuit of them.

Later, the evening whistle blew, calling nearly one hundred of us for
a meeting. Once there, we saw the two soldiers had returned.

"We got them! They are done!" said one of them. "If any of you
think of disobeying Angkar, let this be a lesson. Angkar will destroy
you, like it destroyed the bourgeois and the capitalists. You must devote
yourself and your gratitude to Angkar. You must destroy all your personal attachments!"

Then the cadre leader pointed to one of the youths. "Comrade!
Stand up! What will you do for Angkar?"

The kid stood up. "I will devote my life and energy to the awesome
Angkar. Long live Angkar! Long live Angkar!" He chanted and pumped
his fist, and the other youths clapped with him.

"What about you, Comrade Mae?" He pointed at me. "Stand up.
What will you do? Tonight, we shall all share our testimonies."

A nauseating wave of dread flooded through me. I had just been
plunged into a position where I had no choice but to outrightly lie,

to save myself from torture and a bad death. My deep shame was only exceeded by terror. At the time I did not realize this is the perfect state of mind for a government victim.

I stood up, thinking I'd better get this over with. "I will obey Angkar. I will work with all my power for the purpose of Angkar." I threw my fist up and did my best to act with conviction. Deep inside my heart, there was nothing except seething anger that was turning into pure rage. The work we did was meaningless for us, the very workers these liars claimed to champion. We would never see the harvests and rewards of our efforts. It made me feel sick to work so hard to tell convincing lies. My rage distilled itself into a thing of greater power. I saw our captors for what they were, and I had nothing but hatred for all of them.

* * *

Over the course of a month, the sounds of the great forest deadened as the mechanical sounds of humankind increased. Swaths of workers crawled like invasive ants over the hillsides. Different groups were tasked with woodcutting, carrying timber to other piles, or loosening the soil with their hoes.

Then we were ordered to begin sowing the cleared land into a soybean plantation. In mere days, the lush forest land was razed to bald mounds and bare earth, exposing the darkened soil. The snakes, tarantulas, monkeys, lizards, and raccoons had been flushed out of their homes and eaten by whoever was quick enough to snag them.

* * *

In the middle of the fourth week, my group was returning to camp when we saw a new brigade of recruits arriving. As I searched their faces, I spotted an old friend from Nikom Kandal. His name was Gip.

"Gip! I am Mae!"

He turned around. "I don't recognize you," he said. Then his eyes went wide. "What happened? You are so skinny."

"They give us very little food here." I was impatient to know about the village. He did not have good news.

"Our village land has been ravaged by a terrible flood. The heavy summer rains were too strong and the river waters from the Tonle Sap rushed out, collapsing the dam walls that held it in. The rice fields are bursting and the harvested crops are wasted. People have drowned, but now many villagers are dying of starvation because there is no more food."

I stood stunned, fearing for my old father. The last time I saw him, he was afflicted with a bad cough and had a festering infection on his feet.

"Do you know anything about my father?"

"Sorry. I don't know. I was sent out right after the village was evacuated."

What was Father going to do? He had no one to take care of him or help him escape the rising waters. Who was going to bring him to higher ground? I missed him even more after I heard this news.

I returned to work but kept thinking about him as the day passed, sick at heart. Finally the thought struck me: *I've got to go see him.*

After work I went to the Khmer Rouge and asked, "Can I have permission to go back to town to see my father? I heard my hometown was flooded and I just got the news that my father is sick with a bad infection. He needs help. He is living alone now."

The soldier did not hesitate. "Seeing family is forbidden." He raised his voice to a threatening pitch. "You must devote to Angkar first! Personal feelings are not allowed. You must lose your every personal attachment, including your father! No one here is allowed to go back to their village to see their parents! No one!"

I left and went up the sole hill that had not seen deforesting and worked on one side, chopping alone. Thinking about Angkar now struck a nerve with me. I had worked so much and then they did not even let me see Father. We knew no other purpose than to be slaves to this mysterious Angkar.

Their idea of a perfect revolutionary soldier was someone uncorrupted by the past. A human being with no thought. No love, except for Angkar. No grief, unless for this Supreme Organization. They had dismantled everything: money, medicine, religion, schools, personal property, languages, music, dreams, and now they were destroying the very notion of kinship. I was forbidden to think about Father, or any of the others I knew and loved. We, the victims of this revolution, were expected to purge all feelings for our spouses and children, because there is no god but Angkar.

We were without souls of our own. Our only reliable companions were illness, work, and death. All hail the revolution.

I thrust the ax into the tree in a spasm of anger and frustration. I had to go see Father, with or without a permit. I had to find a way out.

* * *

At the start of work the following day, I hiked past the blackened hillsides, gradually making my way upward, hoping no one would take notice. It worked well enough for me to reach the top of the mountain. I tried to orient myself by peering through a window-like opening through the trees and foliage. Down in the right corner of my vision, the earth was a rich golden brown with a farm tucked many miles away. Behind it was a blanket of green woodland. Off to another side was a dried-up riverbed. I pointed to my right side and asked an older man up there, "Is that side east? If you walk in this direction, where does that bring you?"

"Yes, the east side. That direction, only more forests and wild animals."

"And the left side?"

"In that direction, you will find a small river."

I asked him again the following day, "If I kept onward past the forests, where would that bring me?" This time he had a little more information.

"Well, if you kept following the river, you might eventually reach some villages and Highway 5."

I was sure from his answer that east would bring me toward Nikom Kandal.

For three days, I studied the path of the sun as it rose and set. At night, from outside my hut, I charted the stars to establish the direction they would take me.

Once I had the chance, I whispered to Dangdi, "Have you heard what is going on in our hometown? It's been flooded."

He looked stricken by the news. His mother was also back home.

"I'm planning on escaping back to the village to see my father. They won't give me permission to go. Would you come with me? You can see your mother again." It did not take long for him to answer.

"Wherever I go," he replied, "whatever I do, I will follow you. You have my trust."

"I might be going tonight."

"How long will it take us to get back to the village?"

"I don't know," I said. "I am only following the direction of the sun. But we need supplies to walk through the jungle or else we'll starve or become dehydrated. Especially if we get lost."

"How can we get supplies? We have none here."

I already knew the answer. "We have to steal them," I declared.

When night arrived, I watched from a distance while the other workers entered the community kitchen. It was dark and quiet, with only a single lit candle on the table. Once everyone finally sat down and began to eat, I sidled to the back of the kitchen. Out there, half an acre was filled by rows of yucca trees planted on mounds. Their spiny leaves shook in a slight breeze.

I snuck to the innermost part of the grove with my nerves tingling and senses sharpened. Never had I stolen in my life. Lacking tools, I used a piece of wood to scrape the dirt from the roots of the tree. Once exposed, I twisted off two of the roots and hid them in some bushes. I was shaking; if I was caught, the punishment was death.

I quickly went to the community kitchen to get my food and sat in front of Dangdi. He quietly ate his meager dinner.

"I got two pieces of yucca root," I whispered. He glanced at my eyes for a moment and then went back to eating out of his bowl.

After we finished eating, we went and picked up the yucca roots and tucked them in our shirts. We returned back to our sleeping quarters and saw the flame from a campfire behind it, where some kids had tried to cook and feed themselves wild vegetation, an attempt to stave off starvation. They had left their fire unattended, without a pot. Grasping a stick, I separated some of the wood in the fire and threw our yucca roots under the hot coals.

We sat on guard with our backs turned away from the hut, watching the feeble firelight dance on burning twigs. I could see thousands of fireflies blinking through the high grass and jungle trees. Suddenly, we were alarmed by other voices. Dangdi stiffened and lowered his head as chattering boys came and asked what we were doing. We pretended to play with the fire, toasting our hands on the embers until the other boys shuffled into the sleeping hut.

After ten minutes of cooking, we took the yucca roots out. They were burning hot on our palms, so we let them cool on the ground. They smelled so good. I picked up the roots and blew away the ashes and burnt bits—my mouth salivating.

"We can't eat this," Dangdi said, looking at me. "Remember, it's our supply."

Before we went inside I peered at the sky. The wind was blowing and large clouds scuttled over the stars and the half moon, obstructing what I needed to see. The clouds were moving fast, though, and the gleaming rays of the moon shot forth and disappeared. I figured it would clear later on.

I wrapped my yucca root inside some linen clothes and used it as a pillow. Unable to sleep, I mentally replayed my strategy over and over. The plan was to escape at three in the morning. The earlier, the better. I looked outside the hut beyond the darkened plains, at the edge of the ridge where I worked. That was where dawn would first appear. Soon, I would be somewhere over that mountain. Then I had one of the most powerful feelings wash through me—guilt. It had been my idea to cross the mountain. Whatever happened to Dangdi was my responsibility. The guilt suddenly magnified. *If we get caught, Father will never know what happened to me.*

In that quiet and peaceful night, I wrestled with fate.

Dangdi slept in another row, four people away from me. I rose quietly. I was barefoot, and the bamboo boards faintly creaked beneath me. I stood silently at the edge of Dangdi's bed for a time before pulling his leg to wake him. He immediately got up, clutching a bag close to his chest.

Moving stealthily, we climbed down from the hut's waist-high platform. Once we were outside, pale moonlight shone down on us while we ran with the agility of tigers toward the mountains. Sharp winds lashed our faces and whooshed past our ears. By this time, the clouds had broken up and I could see every star. The field was flooded with a glowing lunar blur. I hit the homestretch, reaching the dark shadowy trees, and I watched Dangdi disappear into the woods first, then I lunged in after him. We darted through the trees, which formed thick walls on all sides. The faint inky world disappeared behind us. Running into the womb of night, our eagerness to escape into the forest was replaced by new fears.

The eyes of the moon were everywhere except here.

Chapter 11

Everything Is Dark

The darkness yawned all around us. Leaves on the haunted trees fluttered wildly as the boughs breathed and danced and moaned. The yell of the wind sounded like frightful human voices. Alert to every noise, I could feel my head and shoulders shaking hard. I felt suspicious of everything—there was nothing I could trust in the forests.

Shouldering past a thick tangle of dead growth, we fell upon a stony riverbed. Through the tatters of the rising trees, the sharp moonlight was fighting its way in, bleak rays darting on the dry bed, giving the slick, pale pebbles a slight glow.

Suddenly, a violent shaking sound came from a nearby bush, along with the cry of a strange, mysterious animal. We had no idea what it was. Cobra. Python. Wild elephant. Panther. Leopard. Bear. Tiger . . . My thoughts raced. Some creature of the forest was hiding there, thrashing about in great agitation. Then, with a low cry, it scurried free of the bushes and fled away. We ran in the other direction.

We trekked deeper into the darkness. Sharp objects poked up from the forest floor. One lightly pricked the ball of my foot. I moved on and ducked a low-hanging branch, but it snagged my hair and partially tore out a patch of my shirt. I was still squirming to break free when Dangdi stepped on a bamboo thorn and gave a loud yelp.

"I can't take this anymore!" he cried. "There is no way I can do this!" He hobbled on one foot, stammering in fits and tears. "There is no way we are going to find our way out of this jungle. I'm going back to the hut."

"Dangdi, it's too late to go back."

"There's a chance we won't make it anyway."

I yanked Dangdi close to my face. "We can't go back now. They already know we are gone. You and I are wanted now. They will kill you on the spot. I'd rather die trying. It's better than having them kill me."

At that point we were both bawling. I had not planned it like this. How did I get myself into this? I felt terrible for bringing Dangdi. Yet, I needed him to come with me. He remained tight-lipped, as I kept telling him I couldn't do this alone. After he nursed his foot, my persuasions seemed to sink in. With a low sigh, Dangdi gave in.

He painfully limped and tentatively poked the ground around him before he firmly planted his foot. I pushed him, faster. He cried, hopping on his toes.

"Hold the pain. We can't let them run faster than us. We have to make it before sunrise."

Blindly waving our arms in front of us, we knifed our way through darkness, groping from tree to tree, plant to plant. Bamboo thorns continued to litter the forest floor. Stepping on the pins and needles, the brittle stones—I felt no pain. I was free from it, unaware of the effort my legs made beneath me.

After sunrise, daybreak progressed slowly as dim gray light wavered into the woods. The quiet was interrupted by a stir of leaves and the trampling of fallen branches. In patches of dappled light, we spotted muddy black torsos advancing our way.

Terror shot through me. We frantically broke through a clump of bushes clustered at the base of the trees and hid among the brush. The crunching noises grew louder. I held my breath and froze.

Three soldiers approached. They wore blue checkered bandannas on their heads and carried guns propped above their shoulders. One of them held his rifle behind his neck with two hands. They rushed noisily past, apparently preoccupied with some other matter besides us, and disappeared into the shade. Inside the brush, we waited until we could no longer hear them, then we crawled out and sprinted in the opposite direction.

We passed trees, some sort of featureless vegetation, some familiar patches of yellowing fallen branches, and deeply piled needled plants that we swore we had stepped on before. We realized we had been circling around.

"We are getting nowhere," Dangdi said. I looked up to search for the sun, but the thick trees and bamboo leaves blocked everything out.

We found ourselves standing at the foot of a massive tree that towered above the canopy of leaves and trumped all the other trees in size. The base of its trunk was thick and branchless with a girth larger than my own arm span. I could not find a way to climb it, so I chose a smaller tree beside it, hoisting myself onto its slender arms. Branches crackled under my feet, but I managed to take hold of the limbs above and pulled myself upward. I paused to gather my courage and then leaped out of the smaller tree onto the first low, broad branch that spread over from the larger tree. I was never much of a climber, but the need to survive had me shunning fear. I climbed dangerously high, from limb to limb, more than seventy feet from the ground, and at last I saw a break in the foliage, bits of light.

I poked my head above the roof of leaves and saw green treetops scrolling away into the distance.

"I see the sun!" I yelled down and pointed to the direction of it. When I screamed at Dangdi, he looked up at me, appearing so small. "East is that way! Don't forget!"

We pressed onward. Every time I took a step, pain flashed through my feet. I trudged stiffly with my toes curled under, crimped in pain. All my attention was on my feet, gently placing one heel ahead of the other. After a few hours we made our way through a cluster of prickly bushes, stumbling to the fringe of the woodland. Here we found some shriveled bamboo trees, and before our grateful eyes we saw a sandy road. Just the sight of it tempted us with a sense of triumph.

I had been here before—it was a path I had used on my travels as caretaker of the cows. We picked out the thorns that stuck to our feet, rubbed our soles in the sand, and soaked them in a nearby pond. It helped, but it was not enough. Our feet were blistered, with red cuts and swollen gashes. We pressed on to return to Tuol Krasaing, which I knew was nearby. I hoped we might be able to stay there with the women long enough to let our feet heal.

* * *

The village of Tuol Krasaing was unoccupied. We combed the empty rows of thatched huts containing a strewn wreckage of broken beds and splintered pieces of tables.

We wandered to the tent I previously was housed in and now found it a tattered cluster of roofless walls. Standing in the dreary ruins, I saw a chalky sliver of smoke rising from the community kitchen.

Without the crowds of people, the community kitchen looked larger. An old lady sat cooking before a fire. She was the wife of the former chief leader, the one who had been arrested.

"Where is everybody?" I asked.

"Every single person has been sent off. Nobody works here anymore."

"Can we stay here one night?" We explained to her about our escape.

"They will come to every area you used to work at. You cannot stay here."

She hurriedly packed up rice and grilled fish in green banana leaves and slipped it to us. "You have to go," she said urgently.

It was the first good meal we had had in days, and we ate it on the road while we headed onward toward Nikom Kandal. I forced myself forward, my feet burning every time they touched the ground. My limbs were like rubber. I summoned the willpower to block the pain, putting as much strength in each stride as possible. Our slow pace made me think it was going to take more than a day to get to Nikom Kandal.

At the hour of darkness, partial moonlight illuminated most of our path. Then, far up the road, a bright bonfire blazed. Winking candles flickered like a multitude of fireflies, scattered beneath four thatched huts that were organized around the fire. We headed for the first doorless shack in the small commune. A dark figure slipped out from the hut and approached. The man was from Nikom Kandal and recognized me.

"Your brother Choa is over there." He spoke softly and pointed at the last hut in the group. When I heard Choa's name, I raced for the hut, past the bonfire, feeling the heat emanating to my face and body.

It was dark outside the hut. The lit candles sent eerie-looking shadows dancing over many faces. In a far dim corner, I spotted Choa

sitting upright on his bamboo mat. When I neared him, Choa startled and stared back at me. We had not seen each other for more than
six months.

We were overjoyed to see each other. I told my brother I needed a
place to stay for the night. He happily retrieved leftovers for me and
then went to ask the commune chief if I could remain here. When he
came back, he said I was not permitted to live here, as it was only for
the married. I pressed him to go back and ask if I could just stay
for the night. Upon his return, Choa said with great regret that I was
only allowed one night, but no more.

* * *

At sunrise, I felt nothing at first. But then my sore feet throbbed, swollen like melons; angry red cut marks crisscrossed at various angles.
The flesh was solid and hard when I pressed on it—threatening to be
infected. When I stood, a searing shudder went through me. There was
no way we would reach Nikom Kandal in our condition.

Dangdi and I did not want to be the only ones in the huts, so we
made an effort to limp to work with the rest of the residents. I had
a fleeting wish that the leader might let us stay here if we showed we
were capable of good work. This would buy us enough time for our
wounds to heal.

The workers carried their farm tools, baskets, and sacks to the fields
in silence. Dangdi and I retrieved a hoe and imitated what everyone else
did. We stood and struck the dirt, loosening the soil. All around me in
rows, left and right, were men hacking the ground at an easy rhythm,
which I found myself comfortably breaking into. Among the workers
and the racket of hoes, I kept on with the swinging and huffing. But
then the workers slowed their motions. They stole anxious glances at

me. Without a word, moving only his eyebrows, one worker gestured for me to turn around.

"Comrade Mae."

The air went dead behind me. My eyes saw long shadows to my right, and there stood a soldier with an AK-47 and my cadre leader. My heart sank.

* * *

"You think you can escape?" the gunman said calmly. "You don't like it there? I have a better place for you." I looked around and saw that Dangdi had already disappeared. "Drop your hoe and come with me."

They escorted me across the field, the gunman close at my back. Lying on the ground were two Chinese-made bicycles—one black and beaten and the other silver with a metal rack just above the back tires. I sat on that one with my cadre leader in front. He pushed onto the bumpy road, while the gunman on the black bike stayed close to my rear, making sure I did not jump off and run away. Either way, I knew what the punishment was. As I looked sadly to the woods in the distance, it summoned images of what they would do when they killed me out there.

With only one set of pedals, my cadre leader did all the work himself. The bicycles creaked slowly across the sandy farm road, wobbling while my cadre leader strode to keep the bike from listing too far to one side. On a moderate hill, he pedaled while standing, huffing and puffing to reach the crest. He told me to get off at certain times, and he would walk the bicycle long enough to regain his strength. Once we reached a steep decline in the path, he re-mounted and allowed gravity to take us down the hill to the highway.

We rode until late in the evening, finally turning in front of a row of barracks facing the highway, the cyclists dragging their rubber sandals on the asphalt to brake. When we stopped, I suppressed a cry. This was Chrouy Sdau. My house was less than two miles away! I felt an intense longing to see Father. We entered the barracks, where a Khmer Rouge soldier bunked on the wall in a hammock. The gunman raised his hand to a vacant corner and told me to sleep there. My throat burned and suddenly I felt the need to speak out.

"The reason I made an escape is because I wanted to see my father. I heard he was ill. My father is living in Nikom Kandal. It is very close. Please let me go."

Instead of answering, my cadre leader handed me a bowl of rice soup. By the light of the moon, his long shadow bounced across the teak floor. Then, after a brief pause, he said, "If you make another escape, I'll finish you." He turned and went to his own hammock.

It was late. The cold moon was beaming bright into the barracks, splashing through the open doorway onto the floor. I peered at the door, then at the soldiers sleeping soundly. All I had to do was tiptoe unnoticed to the doorway and run out.

Restlessly, I went through the different scenarios, filling my mind with all the possibilities. "If I escape, I will be alive. If I don't, I will be finished," I kept telling myself. "But what if they catch me right after I leave? I'm a goner here anyway. I must go to see Father. I might as well try. But if they find me missing, they might go after Father."

Many times, I very nearly ran out. Yet there were so many Khmer Rouge out there. I did not think I stood a chance to make it. They would kill me for not having a travel permit. Hopelessly, I decided not to go.

"Please let me go see my father," I continued in the morning. The soldier that lounged in the hammock stared at me angrily, as if I were a criminal, but I pressed on. "Please let me go see him. He lives only three kilometers away. Right there. Let me see him for the last time. Then you have me. You can do whatever you want with me afterwards."

I fell on my knees and begged them. I felt an extreme violent pain in my chest and a tremendous wrenching cry came from my throat. I uttered pleas and tears. To see him just once. For mercy just this once. My throat dried up, a sharp pain catching it, and my voice started to crack.

"Enough! STOP!" the cadre cried. "This will be your last wish. You can go see your father." He went outside and called two younger soldiers on duty to escort me. We left with neither the gunman nor my cadre leader following. Just the two young soldiers.

A single sandy path led from the highway to my dwelling. I would soon find out Father's fate. The dirt road was lined with huts for a time, but they were bare and abandoned. Then a villager appeared at the other end of the road. When I glanced his way, the man immediately put his head down and looked away. He was afraid to even associate himself with me, since the soldiers were following me.

* * *

The village had been washed away, left with pools of standing water and sad, flowing creeks. All around lay a thick wreckage of floating debris and soaked banana trees that looked like rags. Half the houses had been leveled, roofs splintered and walls broken. The trees had lost all their leaves as if they had been struck by a disease. They stood stark and naked under the hot sun.

I reached my hut and it looked smaller in the wreckage. The bottom half was covered with green and black muck. It was misshapen, with one wall crushed inward, collapsing the roof halfway and exposing some of the inside. The wall seemed to have sustained a few repairs.

Someone had been there after the damage was done.

"Ba! Ba!" I helplessly called for Father, before I crept in. An ache welled inside me. I thought the place was empty.

"Son? Is that you?" A weak voice reached my ears. A thin, pale face was propped upright on the bamboo bed. It could have been another man because at that moment, I saw little of the father I had left. He looked decades older and frail—the graying in his hair accelerated. The infection on his feet and legs was like a wild flame, caked with pus.

He leaned forward and attempted to get off his bed, but once he saw the Khmer Rouge soldier standing behind me outside, he stopped. He sat stock still.

"Son . . . What happened?" he asked in Chinese, despite the presence of the Khmer Rouge. His voice was unsteady and there was a sense of fright in it. The question rendered a hopelessness in me. I felt something deep inside me twist and then collapse.

I went close to him, crouched near his lap, and cried. *My father is alive*, I thought. His hands trembled while he brushed my hair.

"You're so skinny," he said. Soon he was captive to tears. I managed in half-choked breaths to tell him in Chinese that I had escaped and got caught. We cried too hard to speak to each other. We wept uncontrollably, trying to catch our breaths between sobs, before I was able to talk again.

"How did you manage to survive?" I asked. "I heard the town was flooded."

"I was unable to walk . . . but your sister rescued me. Sihong put me in a giant clay pot and pushed me to higher ground as I floated inside." I had never known my sister to be so brave.

"My boy . . . my boy . . ." He kept brushing my head. "How come you are so pale and skinny . . ." We both continued to weep in each other's embrace, saying no more words to each other.

"That's enough now!" one of the soldiers shouted. "You have seen your father. Time to go."

"You take care of yourself," I said.

"Don't worry about me . . . Don't worry about me . . . Wait." He reached for a lump of sweet potato sitting at the end of his bed and handed it to me. "Have you eaten yet? Take the potato and eat it before you leave."

I pushed it back with both of my hands. "No. Keep it for yourself. I'm fine. Really. I'm okay."

When my last words left my mouth, I headed for the door and turned back once more to see Father's eyes still on me. It was the toughest thing for me to do. The moment I broke away, tears overflowed my eyes and a wave of deep regret swept over me. I wished I had never come back.

Without saying a word, the soldiers walked again, and I quietly followed, thinking, *That was the last embrace I will have with Father. Why did I do this? Why did I bring this sadness to him?*

The Khmer Rouge brought me to the nearest community kitchen, number five out of six. They sat me at the long picnic table underneath the shaded tent and then one of them went over to the cook.

"Bring lunch to me," he said to the cook. The cook quietly set a pot of rice porridge right in front of me, going back to retrieve grilled fish and vegetables. No ordinary person got food this good, especially in one sitting.

No one else was seated. The few workers inside glanced at me strangely, having the same resigned thought: *The boy's last meal.* I meekly stared into the bowl; the porridge for once was not soupy or runny, but rich and warm with thick clumps. I swallowed my tears and gorged on my food, spooning it in as quickly as I could, despite the tension in my stomach. I was fearless. I did not let anything hold me back. As I ate, in a strange sense I found solace, even knowing that I was living on borrowed time.

I thought about the five minutes with Father. Though the time was brief, it felt long. It was frightening to see him so skinny and old. I was helpless to do anything for him. Yet, having seen Father, I was now at peace. I was able to say farewell properly. I was ready. Maybe this is how it should have been. How a son leaves the world before his father.

The soldier allowed me to eat until I was full. I polished off everything in my bowl. I savored the last hot sip and licked the spoon clean. He then walked me out. "Well," I said to myself as the food settled in my stomach. "That was the last meal. I know if I go, I won't be a hungry ghost."

The soldiers led me back to Chrouy Sdau, and the villagers who knew me covered their faces or put their heads down without saying a word. They shuffled by me as quickly as they could.

At the end of the sandy road, one of the soldiers had me sit alone in front of the highway before he entered the barracks. I sat with my legs crossed and looked sorrowfully at the morbid fields ahead of me, quiet and dead like everything else. I spotted a weary man, his back bent, wandering down the highway toward the dirt road to the village. He was gruesomely skeletal, just hair and skin. No muscles or meat except his large, bulging stomach. The man hunched forward with no energy at all on his ghastly thin legs. I could not take my eyes off him.

And then I heard him say, "Uncle Mae? . . . Uncle Mae?! Is that you?" The man waved his stick-like hands at me. I thought this sick, sixty-year-old man had confused me with someone else. But then I recognized his voice.

"Uncle! Uncle!" Sen called as he came toward me. "It is you. What are you doing here?" he asked. Sen was my sister Sihong's eldest son. His cheeks were so sunken that his lips peeled back, showing a large number of teeth.

"I've escaped and been caught." I did not say much else. I could not get past how terrible he looked.

"I was caught sneaking a break from work to look for food and they punished me," he said. "They just released me after locking me up for three months." Then Sen looked to the side. My ears registered a noise, a low hum in the air. A thud and sharp screeching followed a second later, growing louder—it was the sound of a truck approaching.

Sen made an instinctive step backward, cautious, as an old diesel-fueled military caravan lumbered to a halt right in front of me. My mind raced, darting from thought to thought. The engine panted and puffed out black smoke, expelling acrid rubber fumes into the warm air. From where I was sitting, the massive tires towered over me. The deep whir of the idling motor sent a shiver down my spine.

Two Khmer Rouge inside the bed of the truck vaulted out of the back and went into the barracks. Before half a minute passed, the gunman who had brought me in exited the barracks and gestured me off the ground and onto the truck. He hopped in behind me. The deck was threateningly large and empty. I stood and grabbed the hot metal railing to balance myself. It stung in my palms but I clenched it tight and my knuckles grew white, the veins standing out on the back of my thin, trembling hand. I saw my cadre leader outside the barracks, staring at me. I read in his eyes a terrible certainty: I was going to be executed. This gunman would finish me off alone.

Once the truck pulled off, lives suddenly flashed before me in a split second—the women, the children, the college students—all at once, they flooded my memory with such vividness, all the moments that I had seen others on trucks being sent away for termination. Now I was sharing the same fate.

I glanced over the shoulder-high railings of the truck and through my tears I saw only Sen's frail back now, as he walked on apprehensively down the dirt path, hunched forward. Sen gradually turned to look steadily back at me for the last time. It was as if a skull and bones stared at me, a walking skeleton sending me off.

Chapter 12

Concentration Camp

I closed my eyes to fix my thoughts on Father. *What would Father think if he saw me like this?* He would have to carry the burden of not knowing what happened to me, grieving about the final moments of my life. Feeling isolated, I crouched in the corner, my knees drawn to my chest, staring out at the distorted view. The scene was crippling, emitting an overwhelming sense of dread and sorrow. It was utter loneliness, driving by the fields as the sun was going down.

For two hours we drove, passing field after field. A single distant mountain hovered over the road ahead. Gradually, rusty tin roofs came into view, dotting the side of the road, contrasting with the lush green mountains. These gloomy gray structures were the barracks of the district.

There was a large, old mess hall with a long line of youths waiting to enter to get some food. The youths were all hollow-cheeked; their scrawny necks seemed to be wilting under the weight of their skulls. Their skin clung to their bones like paper and their navels shrank into their spines. I could count all the bones on their bodies. A large, beefy Khmer Rouge was standing in front of the mess hall.

The Khmer Rouge walked toward the truck, wobbling as he came. The minute I set eyes on the man I knew who it was—I never forgot that walk, the bumbling gait. It was Don, the Khmer Rouge soldier from the mountains. The same man who stared me off when I went into the community kitchen.

An instant later, it was confirmed. "Don!" the gunman called out. "I have a new guy for you." He jumped down from the back. "You take care of him."

Don lumbered toward the back of the truck and slowly peeked in. A round, grubby face with thick lips loomed at me. "Ahh! Big Brother!" he said in Chinese, intentionally mispronouncing it *Bean Brother*. "I've been waiting for you for a long time. A very long time." His face beamed. "Come out." He motioned with his hands. "Come out. Don't stay in there."

I hesitated to get up, terrified. He yelled louder, veins popping out of his neck. "*Bean Brother!* Did you hear what I said? Get out and stand in line behind those kids!"

The youths in line stared back at me with sorrow in their eyes. Don proceeded to the very front and had them count out their number. Each one screamed as loud as they could when Don walked by them. They counted up to me. There had been thirty-seven so far.

". . . Thirty-eight," I said, but my shrill voice cracked and the sound died in my throat. I went cold and numb all over. Don's face twisted.

The world tilted and my head dropped to the ground with a thud. Don had kicked me in the back of my leg. "You should shout like a soldier!!"

He gazed down at me then threw his head back and broke into laughter, his barrel-sized chest moving up and down. "Ha! Ha! Ha!" The laugh was booming loud and evil, the kind that bores into your skin. "Let's go again." He went back to the front and had the youths recount from the start.

"One! Two! Three!" they called out, until the count came up to me. Don turned to me. Saluting like a soldier for good measure, I shouted, "I'm thirty-eight!!!"

"That's how you should say it." He laughed again. There was no humor.

They gave us a cup of watery rice, more liquid than rice. We quickly gulped the soupy mixture, and no more than fifteen minutes had passed when Don said, "Everyone walk out by the numbers." As he led in front, two Khmer Rouge soldiers trailed us from behind.

It was dark out. We arrived at a wooden building where the doors were shut with a large padlock—as big as two feet put together. The soldier unlocked it with a key, unhinged the heavy-duty metal latch, and swung the old doors open. "All right now! Go inside there."

As we slowly crammed into the dark room, the soldiers shoved us further in. The wretched stink of unwashed bodies and stale urine assaulted my nose. In that pool of foul darkness came the dispiriting sound of the door shutting behind.

The padlock clanked closed.

The overcrowded room was suffocating, no larger than a one-car garage. Up high near the ceiling was a single window, fenced off with wooden bars. The boys quickly assembled into their sleeping positions on the hard cement floor—each crammed sideways with their stomach against the other person's spine, unable to lie flat on their backs in that confined space. It was a jumble of elbows and knees. I stayed near the doorway, hoping to vie for that spot.

But then Don said, "No. You go over there." His hand pointed to the only unoccupied corner in the room, right next to the urinal vats lining the walls. Flies buzzed. The rims overflowed onto the floor in a large puddled mess of dead insects and human droppings.

With a large pot of food taken from the community kitchen in his hand, Don opened the door to the adjoining room and I saw a single wooden bed with folded clothing on top and a solitary lamp that lit his room. He called two boys into his room and closed the ill-fitted door. Only a weak light came through the worn wooden slats, a view obscured by the sheet of cloth that Don hung on his side.

I lay with my back facing away from the cement vats, swatting away the flies near my cheeks. My only choice was to press my right shoulder and hips against the thin and filthy kid next to me. He had not bathed in weeks. I thought I could even smell the dirt beneath his fingernails.

Don laughed every so often in his room. Then the lights went off and it was black all around.

The space around me felt tighter. I lay awake in silence. Hunger and fear pulled me into a tide of grief. I drowned underneath it. The sorrow entangled me in a pitch-black sea.

I'm left to be forgotten.

* * *

Long after the boys fell asleep, I thought about Dangdi. Where was he now? Since he had disappeared so fast, I thought he might have made it to somewhere safe. Suddenly, I heard a scream and a cry, then indistinct shouting nearby.

"You tell me the truth! Who are you?!" A heavy thud followed with a brittle sound, like bones breaking. My heart thumped like a hammer.

I sidled up to the wall and looked outside through the narrow cracks. A dim light was coming from a nearby barn. Then the voice.

"I don't know what you want! It's not me!" a man pleaded. "You got the wrong guy!"

I heard groans and more panicky thrashing—once, twice, three times. Terror filled me.

"No! Stop!" Strangled screams resounded. I heard the cries as if they were my own.

"You are spies!" the Khmer Rouge shouted. "You are all spies!"

I stayed perfectly still, knowing they would do the same to any of us. We waited, fearing our turn.

* * *

In the weak morning sunrise, weary streaks of light crept in under the bottom gaps of the walls. My thighs were stiff, and my head and shoulders were sore from being hunched on the cement floor. I watched flies dart and buzz around, settling on the sweaty ears of the sleeping boys.

I sensed a soft tread, lazy footsteps from outside the doors. The key rattled loudly into place. The door swung outward and a soldier said, "Everyone out. Stand in line."

Don came out of his room and stood in front.

He pointed me out of the group. "Bean Brother and Toew! Go and carry those poo-pots!!"

I looked back and saw they were overflowing with refuse. I searched around, and within just a few steps were banana leaves. I went to get them.

"What are you looking for?" Don's face flexed, hounding us. "For something to protect your hands? I'm gonna make you lick it. Go in there, reach in, and carry it with your hands!" Don's lips curled in a half-smile.

The cement vats were so large and overflowing that Toew and I had to carry one together. We pulled the slippery, glistening rim of the pot, rousing a whirlwind of excited flies. Waste sloshed inside. The heavy tub tilted too far to one side, spilling the contents over our hands and feet. The stench was nauseating, turning my stomach. We found our balance and learned to evenly carry the vat to the corner of the jailhouse. We overturned it and brought the other vat out, quickly washing our hands in the gritty sands. But the reek could not be banished.

We collected our tools and caught up to the group. Don commanded us to get in line and put the shovels at our shoulders like guns. He started, "One!" and we followed with "Two!!"

In the slow march to death, we paraded like lunatic skeletons on the road, fists stabbing the air. "One! Two! . . . One! Two! . . . One! Two! . . ."

Just off-site of the military camp, we passed some fields to our right where boys from another commune were farming. They gave us sympathetic looks for being camp detainees.

We traveled far on the paved road until it turned into a large circular path with a grass field in the middle. Surrounding this were more rice fields and tall, slender sugar palms, shooting up in the back. They appeared like giant green dandelions crowning the forests, steady and unmoving. The soldiers commanded us to dig holes to plant coconuts. We spread over the field, all thirty-plus prisoners, while two armed soldiers stood guard at opposite corners.

Driving in from another connecting road, a small jeep with a tan plastic soft top made a half revolution around. When it approached my side, I got a glimpse of the passengers, a trio of mainland Chinese men dressed with white collared shirts. The sight of them lifted my heart. *What if they could stop and rescue us?*

But none of the men made an effort to look our way. They turned onto the other vein of the road and drove away. I seethed under the sun, angry and slighted. I wanted to break my shovel. How did they not see I was an enslaved Chinese person?! I felt rejected by my own kind. They did not care to help us.

"Dig deeper!" the soldiers screamed.

We resumed work, riddling the field with our holes. When we switched off to burying the coconuts, two youths decided to make a break for it. They dropped their shovels and ran. Don's face contorted in confusion and the soldiers were slow to react.

"Those kids!" Don finally shouted, shocked into rage. "Shoot! Shoot them!" The boys bolted faster, like rabbits, already deep into the fields.

Don went after them, shovel in hand, running with short, heavy steps. The two youths disappeared into the bushes and Don, now very far behind, lost sight of them. He smashed the shovel-head against the ground in frustration.

"Don!" a soldier said. "You go after those kids!" But Don did not move. He roiled with anger and the soldiers could see this.

"Don, we need to wrap it up and go back to the jailhouse before all these kids do the same." After there was no response, the soldiers turned to us and said, "Don wants you to go back."

"Wrap it up," Don then said.

"Wrap it up," the soldiers repeated. "Go back to jail."

Before we could count off as we returned to the jailhouse, the Khmer Rouge shouted, "Go in! Go in!" They quickly locked the doors. I immediately retreated to a peek-hole in the wall and saw Don and the two soldiers pedaling fast on separate bikes to search for the two youths.

Three hours elapsed before they returned. I knew they did not catch them—it was written all over Don's face—he was furious.

It was a tiny piece of satisfaction for us.

Don had Toew and I carry the vats out again in the morning. I had not even washed my hands from the prior day. When we dumped them in the corner, I saw the backs of two prisoners, hands tied, just taken out of the rusty building. I never saw either of their faces but I could see they were injured, beaten on the soles of their feet, unable to stand straight. Other soldiers led them forward. With their heads down, they limped for the thick bamboo grove of the forests.

Toew pointed to an abandoned well near our jailhouse. "They don't take them to work. That water well is for them. It is filled with people they finished."

For the fifth day in a row, we slept without showering. The confined room was putrid. The thirty-six boys sulked in sweat and the buckets beside me reeked of raw sewage. Maggots freshly hatched from flies laying their eggs slugged from the urns and crawled up my neck and face. I swatted them off. The boy I lay next to had oily, soggy hair that touched my nose and it smelled like the sour stench of hairy unwashed dogs.

As time passed, we would hear the accuser's voice yelling angrily again outside. More prisoners were interrogated. Their harsh cries rose and abruptly ceased. It shook me even more than the first time I had heard it. Each time, as the hours wore on, I heard less of the tortured screaming cries, the dying pleas. One by one they disappeared.

My heart was locked in so much pain. I wanted to put an end to it. How good it would be to have a rope to hang myself. But it was no use. The room was too overcrowded.

Now my greatest fear was not my death, but the heartbreak I would put Father through when he learned of my death. The distance from him pained me. The only consolation was that my hurt and pain were mine alone. He would not have to see me suffer.

* * *

Every so often, we found a spout of muddy water while digging. It seeped up, collecting in a shallow puddle. At one of these, I kneeled down on my hands and blew aside the dirt and insects on the surface and wet my cracked lips. The muddy warm water trickled down my throat, coating it with grit, and slow pain spread. It dried my mouth, feeling like sandpaper in my throat. I became thirstier than ever.

The Khmer Rouge had us toil for hours without rest. Overworked, four boys fainted during the week. They were dragged by their hands and feet, uttering wordless moans and ramblings amid the hollow racket of workers. We remained silently in our place, digging the earth at our feet.

"Don't worry," Don said. "They are going to the hospital. They will be fine." No one was fooled each time these statements were made.

Those who left never returned.

Before a week had passed, Don imposed more hardship on me, still angry over the loss of the two boys. A large boulder sat at the bottom of the pit where we dug; it had been avoided by everyone else, who chose to dig for small ones instead. Don commanded me to carry the boulder with another youth. The work was becoming more gruesome.

The boulder was too big to carry by hand, even between two people. We were given two bicycle tires to strap to both ends of the rock and then a long rusty pipe that was threaded underneath the tires. The other adolescent and I hoisted the boulder up on shaky, trembling legs. The pipe bent under the weight.

"Stand up!" Don screamed behind me.

When I raised the rock up, I gathered my last strength. My heart raced and my vision blurred with intense rings. I felt my legs go numb, my body twisting on itself, weighed down like a lead coffin. When my legs went limp completely, I lost my grip and the heavy rock slipped. The recoil sent me tumbling backward and the rock rolled down the pipe. The crushing weight stopped just before it reached my legs and body.

Don spat on me. "You bourgeois son of a bitch. How does it feel to actually do hard labor for once? Doing all the same things you had people do for yourself."

He kicked me in the stomach twice. I let out a gut-wrenching yell. The pain was excruciating. I couldn't breathe and the wind was gone, pried out of my chest. My world blackened as I faded in and out. I steadily became less aware of Don's muffled yelling. I wanted to stay here, waiting to die. One more breath and the world would seem no more. I lay clutching my stomach and gasping for air, anticipating another blow, but it did not come.

Don laughed. "Are you almost dying? If you are, I will finish you up. I can do it right here."

Fury inside me rebelled. I managed to get up, squatting low on my feet. As soon as I rose, the world spun. I fell once more.

Don looked on with a devilish smile. "You are not going to last."

When I heard those words, I willed myself to the rock—crawling with my body shaking as if everything inside of me was shriveling up. In forced motion, I lifted the metal pipe over my shoulder. My whole body ached; my bones, my muscles, and my nerves screamed in pain.

"Lift!" he shouted.

I was so weak, my knees buckled after a couple of steps before I tumbled over again. I couldn't pick up my feet anymore.

"Lift!! Can't you lift it?!!" When I inhaled, my lungs were on fire. My throat closed up. Before I could get slammed again, I made one last effort and staggered to my feet, all my bones crying. I clenched my eyes tight as if every ounce of pressing down would help me carry the weight.

The rock slowly moved from its place. I lifted the boulder up the incline, inching it along with strength I never knew I had, bringing it just far enough.

"You saved yourself today," Don remarked.

* * *

It was ten days since we had touched water and a glistening sweat coated over our pores, leaving a persistent itch from the permanently ingrained dirt on our skin. My limbs, my stomach, and my ankle joints swelled. The flesh ballooned, tense and firm. My legs were too heavy to stand, to move, like I was an elephant walking. Every heaving step was difficult. They would work us to death and had no concerns over it, since replacements were plentiful.

It was after work on the tenth day that Don ended our work with joyous words. "Today I will let you clean up."

He brought us to the pond and said, "You can jump into the water and wash up. But I will count to ten. If you don't get out after ten, I'll end you right here."

We plunged into the cool water and scrubbed our thin brown bodies as quickly as we could. The water felt wonderful to be submerged in, if only for a few seconds. Just by skin touching the wetness, I was invigoratingly refreshed, even if still sore and hungry.

Before Don's lips rounded to ten, everyone darted out and lined up. Since I stood last in line, I stole a glance at my reflection at the edge of the pond. A long, cadaverous figure with deeply sunken cheeks and popping eyes stared back at me. I was looking into the face of a corpse. In less than two weeks I could hardly recognize myself. My head was big with matted black hair sticking out in all directions. My stomach was bulging as though it was a big hump. But everything else was bones.

* * *

Upon returning to jail one evening, one of the Chinese adolescents went searching through his possessions and retrieved a silver watch. He rubbed his thumb across the glass face and rewound the watch, holding it against his ear. It ticked away, still working. This was a big mistake.

Don saw the boy toying with device.

"Gimme it." The boy sat still. He said nothing.

I saw that Don really wanted the watch, and so, desperate to get on his good side, I offered him the best I could. "Don. Take my clothes." I handed Don my only extra set of shirt and pants.

"I don't need your damn clothes!" Don threw them back in my face and looked right through me, right at the boy. "Give me that watch." His lips peeled back, baring his clenched teeth.

The boy remained silent, blankly staring at the floor and then slightly shook his head no. The room grew deathly still, fixed on Don. His grim eyes began to swell, popping from their sockets. He clenched his hands in a trembling fist, his breathing short and fast, and the veins at his throat stiffened red. Don's nostrils flared, and the muscles of his cheeks and jaws rolled in a furious grind like an enraged animal as he stared at the boy.

He then proceeded to his room and slammed the door behind him. The room stayed silent, no one daring to move at first, afraid for the boy.

I did not believe the boy had any chance of living long to enjoy his watch. He loved that watch more than his own life. I went up to the boy and whispered to him. "He wants your watch. Why don't you just give it to him? You either give it to him or he's gonna kill you to get it."

"No. I'm not going to give it to him. This watch was given to me by my father."

"You'd rather keep your watch, put yourself through torture, and lose your life?"

He sat perfectly still before he responded back. "This is the only thing I have of my father's memory."

I felt suddenly shamed when I heard that. It brought back memories of Father. I went to my corner to sleep. He had his watch to hold the memory of his father. I had nothing to hold on to. There was no point in telling him to give it up.

The next morning, dust danced in the early light. The room was very bright from the light through the open windows. The boy was no longer there. Somehow he had scaled the walls and broken through. I sat up and suddenly jerked my head toward Don's door. It cracked open and he peered out.

His wild eyes dropped from the window to look at us all.

We did not return to the jailhouse at the end of the workday. Instead we were moved to the death house. The inside was empty except for a few rows of benches and a shovel propped in the corner. The floor was strewn with different sets of iron claps—stained the color of rust and stale blood. There was nobody in here; all those former prisoners were gone.

The Khmer Rouge locked my foot with an ankle shackle. I felt the hard, cold press of iron painfully tight. We were commanded to all sit on the ground with our feet pressed against the side of the wooden bench. Then a long metal rod was slid between welded cuff rings in the bench and the shackles, the sound of iron scraping iron sickening. Don secured the end of the metal rod with a lock.

The worn and weathered barnyard doors were not closed. The mosquitos feasted on us. Through the night, there was constant jangling of manacles, clinking against the iron bar from the prisoners jerking their legs to avoid the insect bites. We lay on our sides, holding our knees close to our chests, moving in any position to cover ourselves. It was a den of grotesque shapes and blackened figures in the dark, each of us filthy from work. We were all half-dead, so skeletal and haunting.

Late at night, my stomach protested for food. It moaned and whined loudly; I could almost have mistaken the sounds for a person's voice. The constant sharp churns and painful jabs would not let me sleep. Hunger had eliminated everything in my body, gnawing down to my bones. I reached for my krama, the checkered scarf we always wore, and untied it from my neck. I wrapped it around my abdomen, pulling it tight to restrain the sounds.

I could not leave to relieve myself. I had no choice but to soil myself right there. In my own shit-caked pants I saw my emaciated body, the thigh bones jutting out at harsh angles without any flesh. It hurt to sit on a hard surface, as the ends of my bones rubbed together when I moved or lay still. I wanted to escape it, the empty tomb of my body. I wished to break away, my legs released and unbounded.

"Why are you so blind?!" I pleaded to the gods. I could feel tears welling up uncontrollably. "Why have you departed me here? Where is your mercy?" I tearfully begged the gods to release me, to cut short this suffering.

Of course there was never an answer.

I woke each morning with a new shrunken face—more gaunt than the day before. There was no flesh on me anymore; we were starving until our bones were picked clean. Forced to suffer in the cramped, stiff position for so long, we were almost incapable of picking ourselves upright. Once the manacles were removed at dawn, I massaged my calves nervously, nursing my threadbare knees with my lean hands. Freed, I rose with hunched shoulders and withering muscles, bumbling awkwardly out of the barn house. It did not matter how weak or hungry I was. Whenever they opened the jail doors, I always went.

At nights when we returned, I dragged my feet along the ground, pulling my heavy, skeletal body into the barn house. I took out a plate I had stolen from dinner and used it as a receptacle for my refuse. When I finished, I threw it across the room, aiming for outside.

* * *

One afternoon, in a rare instance, we were brought to a meeting just outside the barracks. When we entered the building, the other adolescents who worked in the neighboring fields were already seated. They stared at our gangly bodies while we crowded the back wall.

The Srok leader proceeded to the front and spoke. "We must work hard to grow black peppers and soybeans," he began, speaking in an eastern Cambodian accent. "We must commit ourselves to better efforts to grow these things. Our soil can grow anything. We can do anything as a people, anything for Angkar. And we are in demand. America cannot grow a thing. All they are able to do is build machinery. All they own are big mechanical plows, cars, and tractors. We, on the other hand, can grow black peppers and soybeans. And when we do, we will trade with America. Why? Because America is the 'Land of the Cold.' They are unable to farm a thing. Their materials are only steel, tin, and aluminum—only metal machines. They have no choice. They have to trade with us. If they don't, they will have to eat their own steel."

I weakly brought my arm across my mouth, trying to hold a swell of laughter inside. I let out a short chortle. It was such an outlandish thought. The Khmer Rouge in the back cast a long glance at me, so I feigned a cough behind my arm. It worked. They turned their heads back to the leader, who was deeply engaged in what he was saying.

"We can grow plentiful amounts of crops, especially black peppers. America can't grow any foods. All they have is steel. No black peppers. They want our crops and will have to trade with us: one thousand pounds of black peppers for one machine. We will give it to them for very cheap. America has no choice." He ended the speech with, "Are you willing to commit yourself? Will we commit ourselves? Against every enemy and obstacle! Are we prepared to sacrifice EVERYTHING?!!"

"YES!! We commit ourselves!" the whole room chanted. "We commit to work for Angkar!! To grow and trade with America! Long live Angkar! Long live Angkar!"

I did not take part in the chanting and instead tried to suppress my laughter. It was so outrageous. How could Americans not be capable of growing anything, yet they could go to the moon? Angkar could not even cross the river. They could not even build a bridge or a mere simple bicycle.

The work routine suddenly changed. We were made to harvest the rice fields planted by the other adolescents outside our camp. Yet the proper season for cutting and shredding the rice stalks had not arrived. The premature paddies still welled with water to our shins and the rice stalks were slick and rubbery with a tinge of unripe green to them. *Why were we harvesting the rice before the season had come?*

There was no one to explain it.

Hilly mountains crested over the far range of the rice fields. More Khmer Rouge patrolled the fields, armed to the teeth: extra bullets, stick grenades, and knives mounted on their belts. They stacked sandbags around themselves, standing silent, irritably fingering their rifles.

There were tens of thousands of green stems to harvest. To pick them, we groped the handful of rice stalks, and then thrust our other arm with the sickle-blade under the flooded waters to cut the armfuls of grass. We retrieved the first batch of cut rice-grass and stacked it neatly on top of the wooden wagons. No matter how fast we went, the soldiers on duty ordered us to hurry.

"It doesn't matter. Just toss them on top of each other. Hurry! Cut as much as possible!" They spoke with a lick of nervousness in their voices.

Somewhere in the distance near the mountains, intermittently, massive thuds exploded. The bombs sounded like demolition. I supposed the Khmer Rouge were conducting another project in the mountains; perhaps mining for minerals, gemstones, or precious metals.

"There is something going on here," I said to one of the workers beside me. But of course he knew no more than I did.

A week passed, and the Khmer Rouge pulled us into another meeting. This time the leader had a terrifying message.

"Other countries want to invade Cambodia," he announced. "They want to start wars with us. If these foreign nations are allowed to invade, the first thing they will do is arrest all the men and kill them. Then, they will have their own people from their lands come in to rape all the women, so they can interbreed. It will become their country after that. This is how they plan to conquer us. By mixing their blood and seizing our great race. These people are savages." He asked all of us to fight against this sworn enemy and protect the country.

This time, the room cheered softly. Everyone was bottled up with fear.

When we returned after supper, instead of placing us in shackles, the soldiers brought us to the old jailhouse again. The insides were boarded up; every vulnerable spot nailed with haphazard wood panels.

The window was sealed closed with crudely tacked-together planks. The two soldiers urgently pushed us all inside.

A final shove. The door banged shut. The sound of the lock bolted. After that, silence. It was pitch black. We were left to inhale the dust of the room. Don's light was not glowing in the other room. Then we realized Don was not with us, and we had not seen him since the meeting.

Dread thickened the darkness. The longer we waited, the deeper the quiet became.

Chapter 13

Waiting for the Bullet

A depthless silence hung around the campsite in the late afternoon. From far away something was soft and muddled, as if it was a rifle shot bottled up. I crept to the wall and strained to see through a peek hole in the wooden boards. There was no sign of anyone, not a single person—only barns, granaries, and a single scraggy tree. The Khmer Rouge had not come back in the morning. They had abandoned us here to waste away.

Hunger and thirst had set upon all of us. Through the knothole I noticed a grain sack leaning against an adjacent building, where soybean seeds had spilled on the ground. But it was not close enough to reach.

Two other prisoners sought a twig to grab the seeds and used their fingernails to peel off long, flimsy splinters from the side of the wall boards. After they managed to get some seeds for themselves, they gave me a stick to try it.

I knelt down, my cheek pressed against the wall, and threaded the stick under the rotten, warped ends of the wood panels. I shifted and flicked the sand, fishing for a single soybean, half an inch away. I stretched my shoulders as far beneath the rotten boards as I could reach. Touching the round unevenness of the surface stirred a chill in me. I poked the yellow bean with the tip of the stick and ever so gently wobbled it back.

Don had not taken his possessions: a lantern, a lighter, and an army field pot. We gathered some of the hay lying around, lit it with his lighter, and fed the fire with wooden splinters. Inside the army pot we roasted the soybean seeds; each of us had managed to retrieve one.

I placed my one seed in my mouth when it was hot and bit into it with my back teeth. The hot bean wedged into a cavity, sending a shocking jolt through my tooth. I yelped in pain.

Even then, I tossed it back and forth with my tongue to cool it down and chewed on it lightly, like I had nubs for teeth, rocks in my mouth. I painfully chewed it all, before it got too cold and hard. It was dry and tasteless, almost powdery. Though a phantom crumb, it filled the emptiness a bit. The difference made me a little more whole again.

Sounds of gunfire startled the room: *thut thut*—familiar sounds we knew all too well. The dull fire cracks picked up, fast and furious, and the fighting closed in nearby. It lasted about half an hour. Then, in a lull in the shooting, I heard several pairs of feet breaking into a run. I searched the side wall and looked through a yawning crack. Two black shirts dashed wildly from one of the buildings, crossing into another.

Rapid bursts of gunfire came from right outside, the claps amplified in our small space. Panic spread in the room. The inmates banged against the wooden door, trying to knock it down by brute force. They kicked and pounded, and threw their weight against it. The door did not move. We grasped the door's crossbar and pulled, yielding the same result. Outside, I saw more Khmer Rouge fleeing anxiously, lowering their heads amid the gunshots.

The prisoners grouped in twos and threes, pulled several steps back, holding their shoulders together. They charged, thumping the door with their small, frail frames, recoiling after each hollow thud, their faces grimacing on impact. The door would not budge. A larger group of four tried once again and collided with the door. A series of repeated attempts only rattled the door in its frame. Another group of four lunged, replacing the first worn-out group. The posts of the door shook, remaining solidly intact.

Several of the prisoners hunched side by side, leaning with all their weight against the door. The others came, standing from the back, close up to the wall. We all pushed hard from our shoulders, our backs, our thighs. The door warped, then bent under our collective weight. The heavy metal latch began to give. We gave a gigantic thrust. Another hard push and heave. The door gave partway with a slight crack. The wood holding the latch snagged. Two and three more shoves. At the last loud crack, the screws of the metal latch popped off and the prisoners at the front landed on the floor in a collapsed pile.

The prisoners stood, wincing from the sting of the fall, and began running at breakneck speed through the AK-47 rounds that were bursting from the trees, hacking the bushes around the jailhouse. My heart thumped in my chest.

War is coming, I realized. *There is no stopping it.*

My feet were nailed to the ground with fright before I saw a prisoner waving his hands at me. He screamed, "Come! Follow me into the trees! To my uncle's house. I will lead the way. I know how to get out of here."

Shots rang out around me, but I ran on, heedless of the danger, thinking only of not losing sight of the boy. Toew and another adolescent named Maaw also followed the boy east, for the forest.

Starving, I felt lightheaded and weightless, an empty frame floating. I ran, so emaciated that a single blade of grass brushed me and tripped me up at the ankles. I fell to the ground. So light, yet so heavy.

"Stop!!!" I screamed to them.

"C'mon. Get up. My uncle's house is not too far from here. His house is in a town called Dukcla." They pulled me back to my feet. Moving at the fastest speed I could and calling on all the strength I had, I plunged onward with them, between the trees.

The woods were full of smoke and fire. Orange and red flames blackened the trees. Soldiers moved through the smoke. The air was alive with gunshots—so many of them. From afar, combatants fired artillery, blasting in the upper woods. The surviving black shirts fled while the combatants chased them, firing more artillery rounds. Disoriented soldiers suddenly rose up everywhere. Bursts of firing. Grenades exploding. They sprinted for cover to get away from their pursuers. We ran. The soldiers ran. The cadres ran.

Bodies were sprawled in the woodland, innocent people killed by the Khmer Rouge. One body rested against a tree, head down. From the angle of the head, I was sure they had cut him in the throat. Another few sat impaled in their abdomens with sharpened spears that held them to the tree trunk. Their eyes were wide with the final shock and agony. I did not want to go further into the thick of danger. But I had to trust this guy.

Making turns right and left, the three of us followed the boy racing through the deep brush and overgrowth. We crouched low to the ground, away from the fire, while the hammering shots faded. The gunfire dissolved into a lingering echo in the distance.

The boy brought us to a little cottage nestled in the hushed recesses of the forest. The home was vacant, but we did not want to stay inside, where we could easily be seen or be struck by flying bullets. So we snuck underneath the raised bottom floor, behind the entrance staircase.

It was roughly five o'clock in the afternoon. The boy said, "We haven't had any food. You guys stay here. I am going to find some for you." He disappeared, but after about an hour he returned with a machete and a burlap sack stuffed with sticky rice, dried fish, *prahok* fish paste, palm tree sugar, and salt.

"Where did you get all this food?" we asked.

"There was nobody at the warehouse. I just broke in and got the food. But it looks like we have nothing to cook with." He went back out to check around the house and found an ugly, tiny pot sitting in the dirt. He also saw a steel combat helmet and picked it up. We cooked the food in the pot and boiled water in the inner shell of the army helmet. It was the first real meal we had had in a long time. Each bite spat life into me, the colors around seemed richer, the dimness turned sharp and clear.

With dusk approaching, there still had not been a single trooper around our hideout. For the moment, this area was under no one's control. Soft gunshots burst from far away. We thought it must be Khmer Rouge fighting against Khmer Rouge.

It was a relief to no longer be cramped inside with some thirty-odd people. I felt released from the heaviness of our prison, replaced with the lightness of learning to be free again.

But I felt so alone. My weak and starving body shivered with cold that came from inside me. I was highly alert, hearing all things moving. The wind blowing the leaves. Animal cries in the distance. It was the first time in a long time I heard a group of foxes crying.

Early the next morning, the boy asked if we wanted to eat sugarcane. We salivated thinking of its sweet taste, so he picked up his machete and went to cut some stalks.

Two hours passed and he had not returned. "How come he's taking so long?" Toew asked. "He only went to the bridge and river. That's nearby. I'm gonna go look for him."

After Toew left, it was just Maaw and me. We waited again for several hours, but neither of them came back. "Something's very wrong," we both said.

We waited until midafternoon and still they did not return. The gunfire was growing closer and louder. Concerned, I told Maaw we had to find a better place to hide.

"What do we do with their backpacks and belongings?"

"You have to carry one and I'll have to carry the other. If we see them again, they will have their clothes to wear." We got out of the house and headed for the highway. I thought staying near the road was the best idea to not get lost. We searched for a bunker but instead found a suitable dry pond just before reaching the highway. Several other women and children were already crowded in the pond. Maaw and I climbed in.

The ground rumbled. The air filled with unnatural clanking. Something enormous and heavy rolled toward us. The strange death rattling of metal became louder. The mechanical whir was powerful, dangerous, stunning me into silence. I stretched my neck cautiously above the pond and made out the large gun of a tank on the highway. Three greenish black tanks moved toward a nearby footbridge. Each tank successively fired a rocket, nozzles smoldering from the blast.

The Khmer Rouge fired back from the other side. And then dozens of troops, wearing stiff gaudy green, poured out and attacked along the roadsides, advancing on the Khmer Rouge.

At first glance, I thought the green infantrymen were Sihanouk's troops, and that the old king of Cambodia had returned, successfully rounding up his loyalists to reconquer the country. But after taking a closer look I realized they were not Cambodians. They had round, squinty eyes like Chinese troops. *Who were these mysterious soldiers?*

The firing ceased and a detachment of troops headed for my pond. I ducked down. The soldiers came to the rim of the pit, four of them, guns drawn high. They spoke very fast, very irritated.

"Why don't you speak to them in Chinese? Those are your people," a middle-aged woman in the pond said to me.

"They are not Chinese." I listened more closely to their heavily accented speech. "They are Vietnamese. And I don't speak Vietnamese."

The soldiers walked around the pond, pointing their guns at us and flashing many hand signals. A soldier stopped and pointed me out of the crowd, speaking in his language. I did not understand what he was saying. Then his fingers motioned backward, calling for me to come out. Maaw was also called to leave. We climbed out and they had us walk at gunpoint. They stopped us just short of a patch of bushes.

The soldier pulled at my knapsack and began shaking it, screaming into my ear to take it off. We dropped all the packs. One soldier tore through the packs. He tossed everything out. He threw out my shirt and pants. He went through Maaw's pack. Nothing different.

His hands then dug through our friend's pack—he pulled out a coil of copper. Their faces lit with rage. They turned and shouted at each other.

The soldier forced me by the chest to kneel down. They aimed their rifles straight at our faces. I stared down along a barrel and saw, behind it, an aggressive, piercing glare. I heard a click of steel. A sharp blade released several inches from my eyes. I sat in terrified shock. *Why are they about to kill us?*

They yelled in high agitation. Still glaring, the soldier reached in and stripped the krama from my neck. He gestured with his hand to me but I did not know what he wanted. He twisted my arm and shoved me to my feet. He took my krama and trussed me up, tight.

What am I going to do? I thought. *I can't do any sign language now.* He started profusely ranting at me. Of all of it, I only understood the two words I knew in Vietnamese: "go" and "motherfucker."

The man retracted his bayonet and pushed the cold muzzle of the gun against my back, prodding me to walk. He forced me to enter the forest and then into a dense banana grove. The scent of unripe banana leaves wafted to my nostrils. Passing through the grove, we plunged into damp, cool darkness. I thought he was going to shoot me right there, instead of in front of all those people. He continued to push me toward a clearing up ahead, where I could see tiny bright embers, the glow of fire. A silver pot shimmered. *Wow. Maybe he is bringing us to have dinner.*

The soldier's rifle stabbed Maaw and I toward the campfire, where I saw more Vietnamese soldiers. Armed men paced the camp, eyeing the wilderness. In the back there were about eighteen prisoners tied, rounded up beside a log, under the watchful guard of three soldiers. I had flashbacks of the Khmer Rouge's vivid words burning in my head again: *"Other countries want to invade Cambodia. . . . If they start wars with us, first thing they will do is arrest all the men and kill them . . . this is how they plan to conquer us."*

The soldier pushed my shoulders down to make me sit with the other prisoners. With my paper-thin skin, it was painful to squat on the dry earth, as though scraping on sharp, jagged boulders. I felt as if my tailbone would wear through my skin. On the opposite side of the fire sat a pair of soldiers who smoked and stared at me.

They had just finished cooking. The troops took out their bowls and tin cans and filled them with chunks of stewing food from the cooking pot. The fragrance of cooked rice floated to me. It was overwhelming. My stomach churned in anticipation. I had the faintest hope they would give us some food. But they rapidly devoured their meal without so much as a glance our way. They did not give a damn.

It was half dark; a full moon brightened the sky in purple twilight. The platoon leader came up to us. He had an angular face, a big red flag on his combat sleeve, and a large handgun on one side of his leggings. The commander was furious, barking orders. The Vietnamese soldiers stood us up very aggressively in a long line. They brought out a long, rugged coil of rope and threw one end down to the beginning of the line.

They looped the rope along the length of my arms. As they pulled tight, the rope bit into my skin, squeezed my elbows together, and pushed my chest outward like the wings tied on a chicken. The nerves along my arms were on fire. Faintness pressed on my head and lungs. They bound each person in the same way, one behind the other, until we were all connected by this single line of rope.

Suddenly, sharp words erupted between the soldiers and they pointed at each other, trading insults back and forth. The circle of soldiers tightened, pushing on us, and they broke into loud arguments. They then hurled foreign curse words at us, and back at each other again. There was a long standoff of infighting. And then something unexpected hit.

A prolonged screech shook the air, whistled past our heads, and exploded with a heavy roar a few hundred yards behind us. Swirls of smoke rose upward to the sky. A stream of curses poured from the soldiers' mouths as loud bursts from automatic weapons erupted on the far side of the field.

The soldiers threw their food bowls aside and raced to their weapons, then broke for cover behind a sparse wall of trees to return fire. The trees danced and shook with impacts from the enemy bullets. A couple of soldiers hurried into a nearby barn that was fortified with mounted AK-47s, and they fired shots into the trees.

I stood with the prisoners at the center of the crossfire, white with fear, while the night rang with volleys and we remained tied up. We were captive between the two sides.

I looked over Maaw's shoulder and caught black shapes and shadows at the bottom of the hill, climbing up a distant dam wall into the lower terrace of straw stubble. Three wagons came drawn by oxen, piled with goods of war. The carts peaked over into the field and the weapons were retrieved. It seemed the Khmer Rouge were using the oxen to deliver their ammo supplies over the bumpy fields and earthen walls, since the Vietnamese controlled the highways.

A crew of Khmer Rouge set up mortars on a dike and launched them—*PHROOM!!!*—*PheweeeeeeEEEEU*—I held my breath and waited. *PHOOM!*

A brilliant brightness consumed everyone for a split second. We hugged close to each other. The faces of the Vietnamese soldiers flickered orange, their mouths opened in enraged shouting. Kneeling and half-concealed behind trees, they shot faster, their guns kicking on their shoulders.

Then the Vietnamese soldiers came in with their own mortar tube—*PHREEWW!!!*—the missile screeched, striking the ground, rupturing in angry flames. The Khmer Rouge answered back. A large round flew in the air and overshot us. It crashed to the earth and sent up orange braids of fire on the grass near us. More rockets lobbed, the incoming sound gut-clenching.

The Vietnamese stopped their fire from the barn. The Khmer Rouge hurled two more shells: a quick whine running above. The bombs fell. White-hot pops and flashes, spewing up dust and black smoke.

The Khmer Rouge abandoned their positions and threw their arms into wagons, hauling away the cartloads of weapons to the side dam walls. Their oxen shuddered and slipped under the onslaught of bullets. Bright red flames burst close to them. The Khmer Rouge stood like anxious charioteers, hurriedly snapping their whips on the backs of the oxen, rushing them. The oxen fumbled more on the dam mounds, making the Khmer Rouge violently lash them harder.

The oxen plunged over. The shooting stopped.

A Vietnamese soldier screamed out in pain, wounded by shrapnel. Aides ran to his side, shouting, while angry faces circled around us. Many, many soldiers. The commander charged into the circle and shouted uncontrollably, the vein in his neck bulging. One prisoner began sobbing and shaking. It was clear he understood them. We turned around and asked him what was said.

"I k-k-know a little V-V-Vietnamese . . . but they s-said . . . they think we are Khmer Rouge . . . and n-now they are g-g-going to kill all of us."

We froze, our blood iced with terror.

They untied the young adolescent who spoke Vietnamese and separated him. For whatever reason, that action chilled me to the bone. The commander barked new orders. I thought he must have snapped and had gone mad.

Two soldiers grabbed my arms to pull me straight and they stood us all back in a line. Each one of us was flanked on either side by a soldier. Meter-long blades came out of their black leather scabbards. One of them rubbed his weapon on his scabbard like he was sharpening the edges. *This is it.* The blades shined. My heart pounded. *It is the end.* I closed my eyes. My lips went numb and my heart raced with panic. Maaw stammered in front of me. He violently shook and cried—I looked down and saw the ground becoming moist, a trickle running from his ankles. I clenched my eyes tight again, blood pounding louder in my ears.

I imagined the swords bearing in closer, the sharp, cold steel pointed at an angle to pierce my soft, bloated flesh. I muttered a hurried prayer to Mother and asked her to lessen the pain. In one last breath, I braced my stomach, and held it. The soldiers waited for the final words.

The commander snarled loudly and the soldiers put their blades back into their scabbards. Five other soldiers came forward, pointing their guns, and told us to walk down the hill, across the grass field to the woods. We marched in a single staggering line down the slope, through the freshly broken ground pockmarked with charred bomb craters. A single unexploded shell still lodged in the dirt. The rope weighed heavily on my frail swollen body.

When we exited the forest, we emerged at a set of railway tracks—its empty ties receded into the mystic darkness. The moon wavered bright in the sky, a hanging paper cutout.

A pair of soldiers moved to the front and led the march. Tied together, we lifted our feet up and stood on the tracks without any arms to balance ourselves. I was pulled along by the rest of the prisoners, forced to waddle from rung to rung in a clumsy lockstep. They swung back and forth, slipping off the wooden ties. The weight of their bodies tightened the end of the rope around my shoulders and arms. We lost all feeling and became numb. Afraid to stop, I lifted my foot and nearly hopped with my back foot to reach the next track tie. I lifted the other foot and lunged again when a person in the middle slipped and jerked the entire line back, pulling the rope even tauter. I struggled to stand upright, trying my best not to step on the others' heels.

Midnight came. After two hours of doggedly marching in strict step at an unbroken pace, we converged on an outpost of canvas tents alongside the tracks. Vietnamese soldiers slept or lounged outside, some cleaning their rifles. More soldiers walked around chatting. The first man to see us had been dozing in a folding chair with his arms crossed. When he opened one eye, he reacted furiously, leaping to his feet. The man barked at us in his fast tongue and spat at the ground near us. His report alarmed the camp. This led the men idling in front of their tents to angrily point and shout at us. Half-clad soldiers got out of their tents without getting dressed and joined in. This awoke more soldiers. Quickly, the whole camp was in an uproar, howling and pointing at us.

We numbly paraded through and reached a set of trees where soldiers were sleeping in hammocks with their shoes sticking out. They, too, woke up, swinging out of their hammocks and flailing one arm around, pointing and cursing at us, spitting at our feet. We passed onward, and their swearing and rough shouting lingered distantly behind us for a long time.

The hours passed slowly and wearily. A burning thirst consumed me. We walked the train tracks all night with empty stomachs, past the point of exhaustion. I had not had a drink since that afternoon. My parched tongue craved even a squeezed droplet of water from a wet rag. We all knew these people would let us die on our feet. Yet we all were determined to keep ourselves from falling. If one fell, we would all topple together.

I would not let myself think of fainting. I had to see my family again. When the soldiers had pulled their blades on me earlier, I was only able to think of my family. No one knew where I was. My burdened heart could scarcely take it in. I could not allow this mystery to descend upon them. I had to stay alive for Father. I wanted to be together, Father and son again: the only thing that mattered. I vowed that no matter the odds, I was going to see them again. I had to go on living to make right what never should have been.

The soldiers on patrol fixed their attention on us and one of the men detached from the group to come toward us. He spoke perfect Khmer:

"Only your fuckin' country would kill its own people. All you fuckin' Cambodians do is kill your people, then starve and torture the rest. Goddamn idiots! You stupid assholes, listen to me. In the morning, one at a time you will be interviewed by the officer. Tell him your identification. Don't you lie that you are not Khmer Rouge. Nobody will believe you. Get it? You stupid assholes!"

They kept us tied up all night lying on the sand before they released the first prisoner to be interviewed. When it was my turn, they loosened the rope and I felt bruises on my arms, black-and-blue marks etching tracks around them. They had me enter an olive-green tent, where a man sat wearing a sharp red necktie and a crisp short-sleeved uniform. Under the thin folding table, I saw a pistol on his belt. His interpreter, the same soldier from earlier, had me take the seat opposite the officer.

"What division did you control?" the interpreter asked sharply.

"How could you think I'm Khmer Rouge? You can look at me. My skin covers my bones like a rag. I'm nearly starving to death. How can you think that is me? I was in the concentration camp for almost forty days and they beat me. I broke out and got caught by your group, and now you think I'm Khmer Rouge?" My mouth ran faster than I could think. I said it so fast I did not know if they understood me.

The interpreter nodded and said, "Okay. You're not a Khmer Rouge. But you were in the concentration camp."

"Yes. I was in it. And many others were too."

"You are very lucky. I saw many concentration camps burn down with the prisoners still in them." He stopped and then started talking to the officer. The interpreter again nodded his head and then spoke to me. "We will let you go, but I can't do that right now. What concentration camp were you in?"

"My concentration camp was Jomka Ko," meaning Cotton Gardens Camp in English.

"You remember the people who tortured you?"

"Yes," I said. *How could I ever forget Don?*

"Well then, I want you to stay here in Sisophon. We need you to recognize who controlled the facilities at the time. Tell us who are the people who tortured you."

They had me stand outside where the vehicles came to park. Droves of trucks entered, loaded with people, wan and dull-eyed. They arrived moaning and crying, some unconscious, maimed and wounded—mutilated ears and faces, smashed heads, broken noses, some with blackened skin bleeding all over. Those towed in oxcarts were in the most wretched shape, nearly dead.

After hours of watching truck after truck at the Sisophon drop-off depot, a couple of soldiers asked Maaw and me to lend them a hand carrying some things. They brought us to a warehouse, dismantled the lock with a bolt cutter, and opened the doors. Inside was an unimaginable supply, stockpiles to last a small town for months: sacks upon sacks of rice and sugar on all the shelves. There were knives, hoes, axes, and pitchforks leaning against the wall.

I was furious. It was everything the Communists kept from us.

The next day I again watched hundreds of people getting hauled in but did not recognize a single person. Then one particular truck caught my attention. I spotted somebody familiar among the roughed-up passengers, and once I was sure it was him, I pointed him out to the soldier on duty.

It was Dara, the first guy that had left us to cut sugarcane, after our escape from the concentration camp. His angled face was bruised like the others. Then a few more trucks immediately arrived and I saw Toew, also in the same condition. I turned to the soldier. "How come your comrades caught all the good guys?"

"Huh. It's a good thing you are able to recognize them. We couldn't tell them apart from the Khmer Rouge."

When Toew stumbled off the truck, I asked what had happened to him.

"I went to find Dara and when I got near the sugarcane by the bridge, the Khmer Rouge appeared from behind and held me at gunpoint. They took me as hostage to the other side of the river. That's where they beat me up."

* * *

In the following days, I did not see Don or anybody else—just all kinds of misshapen people brought in trucks. The Vietnamese allowed us to leave for home to find our families. They gave us provisions of salt, rice, and canned food to take with us.

We all went our separate ways, except for Maaw, who had the same journey as I did. When I walked out from that place and was far from the campsite, euphoria hit me. An anchor had been lifted and everything was new. I did not once look back, banishing it behind me.

I was a free man. It was the first day I could walk without any permissions, certificates, or soldiers to hassle me wherever I ventured. I could go anywhere I chose. When we reached National Highway 5, the noise returned, a flowing river of people. Men and women, happy and smiling faces, carried possessions in their hands, trading goods.

We discovered a small bubbling brook just off the highway and went to wash up. We got in with all our clothes on. I had not bathed for too many days. The water was clear, sparkling like gold in the sunlight, shimmering off the bedrocks at the bottom. I lay midstream, a salty pain stinging my weeping wounds. The flow softened the angry knots in my stiff neck and washed my blood-raisin skin, showing its natural color. I let my head fall back and shut my eyes against the sun.

"Look!" There was a sudden shout from Maaw, pointing north at a flightless gray bird running across the field. Its head was flung back and it fluttered its wings in confusion, trying to go airborne, too young to fly. We soon captured it.

Leaving our clothes on the ground to dry in the sun, we prepared to cook the goose. This was an act we were now free to do without the Communists in control. Without bothering to pluck the bird, we burned its feathers into ashes. For lack of a pot to cook the rice we were given, we hollowed out a bamboo stick and punched holes in the top and stuffed the rice inside. We stuck it in the fire and turned it around periodically. By the time we finished the slow cooking, it was dark.

After we had eaten our fill, we continued along the highway until we were stopped by a Vietnamese tank blocking the road. We could not go any farther because there were still rough pockets of Khmer Rouge ahead. We had to wait until they cleared the area, so instead we lay down alongside the highway.

The dark velvet skies were strewn with an incredible number of stars. Random sounds of bombs bursting and of rifles shooting echoed from miles away. The Vietnamese were attacking the Khmer Rouge, their rockets spotting the horizon in dazzling flashes and thunderclaps. It reminded us of a fireworks display, and instead of terrifying us, it seemed like the cheery rumblings of independence. The joyful noise was everywhere.

Once the loud roars died away, a peaceful murmur took over. I could hear myself breathing calmly through my nostrils. Fireflies danced playfully around our heads and I traced their blinking for a long time.

"Comrade Mae—" Maaw's voice broke the quiet.

"Don't call me Comrade," I interrupted. "We are free now. Don't use that word. I hate it."

"What are you going to do now?"

"First, I am going to find my family. If I find them, we will go back to my hometown of Poipet. I plan on starting a business. Do like we used to."

"The same thing for me. I'm going to find my family, then a woman to marry, and pretty much be a farmer again. My family has been farming for generations. That is the only life I've known."

We became quiet. The differences were re-emerging between the lives we once had and the lives we could expect now. Even after years of having no notion of individuality, the Communist dream of everyone becoming the same equal class did not fool us. We still grew up knowing what our parents did and how our parents lived. I supposed we would always be products of how we were raised and where we grew up. The Khmer Rouge could not take that from us.

We talked more about the past, a relief after keeping it a secret for so long. Maaw and I found we were very similar to each other, a surprise, given the opposite worlds we came from. Both of us were simple people, who longed for nothing more than to live our lives in peace.

Then I asked Maaw, "What would you have done if you saw Don?"

"I wouldn't have hesitated," Maaw said. "For all that he's done to me, it would have been easy to just tell the Vietnamese. I would have done it myself if I had to." Then he looked at me. "But I didn't get it as bad as you. I could only imagine what you're thinking."

I never answered back. I did not have to. If I had gotten the chance, I would have made Don drink a tub of human waste.

Early in the morning, the Vietnamese took down their barricade fences and rolled their tanks to the wayside. Masses of people came from the opposite side, carrying their life possessions, holding babies, pushing wagons, the sick and wounded wearing cloth bandages around their injuries. The roads were filled with joy. When a truckload of Vietnamese soldiers drove by, people weakly thrust their hands upward, shouting, "Thank you for rescuing us! Thank you for liberating me! Thank you!" I gleefully shouted along, and like several others on the road I had hardly enough strength to raise my arms.

As hundreds of people hustled by, I kept an eye out for anyone from my village. I spotted one man up the road, arms wide to balance two baskets strung from his shoulder pole. Within one of the baskets he had sacks of rice and cookware, and in the other he carried his child.

"Brother Ga. Have you just come out of the village?"

"Yes. I am the first one out. There have been a lot of people killed."

"What about my family?" I asked him.

"Your family moved to Chrouy Sdau for safety. They haven't left yet for Poipet. You better hurry. They are waiting for you."

Maaw and I reached the point where we had to part ways. I felt reluctant to bid him farewell. He turned to me, his face shining bronze by the sun high in the sky.

"So . . . it's goodbye now. You're Chinese. Chinese people are smart. They always have successful businesses. When you're rich, don't forget about me." His eyes were welling up. "Make sure you . . . take care of yourself, Mae."

"So long, my friend, 'til we meet again."

I walked toward the beginning of the sandy footpath leading into the village. The desolate path had been a reminder that each time I left, I might never come back to see it again. This time, however, when I found the dirty trail meeting the highway, it struck me differently. I heard the soft laughter of children.

My little nieces and nephews were in the fields, chasing dragonflies. They spotted me and their faces lit with pure joy: "You're alive!" cried Siam. The seven-year-old broke into a run. "You're alive! You're alive!" Her words lightened my heart.

Siam skipped out in front of me. "He's alive! He's alive!" She curled her tiny hands on one of my fingers and pulled me along. My feet did not know where she was going. I just followed.

"He's alive! Uncle's alive! He's alive!" her little voice screamed. She let go of my hand and sprung ahead. "He's alive! Uncle's alive!"

Siam raced through the sprawling jumble of huts, screaming. I saw my family by a fire, roasting a pig for the first time in a long while. Father limped out of the hut with grateful warm tears in his eyes. They all stood up and I walked to them.

I felt the touch of my family surround me in their arms, bathing me in a luminous embrace. Tears of joy welled in my eyes.

JAMES TAING

From the start, I was considered an all-American in my family. I'm told that while I was still in my mother's womb, she had insatiable cravings for American dishes like cheesy pizzas, ice cream, burgers, KFC, mac and cheese, things she had never cared to touch before. But they all turned out to be things I loved as a kid.

Oddly, when she was pregnant with my younger sister, her cravings went back to her normal Asian palate of rice, noodles, and Chinese vegetables, dishes I didn't care for myself. But there was far more to it than food. While the Cambodian identity was familiar to me and a part of my upbringing, I had never swallowed it into my soul. Therefore, in my younger years, whenever my father predicted I would be like him when I grew up, I detested the idea. I had no background such as what he had experienced back in Cambodia. We didn't even agree on our diets.

All that ended once I began to learn his story, to truly *listen*. When I first committed myself to writing out his amazing story, I intended to merely take down his words and be a transmitter for them. But as we traveled back in time and moved from scene to scene, I was unable to keep from falling into the darkness of it. I was nearly the same age he had been when that all took place, and my empathy for his experiences caused me to take in their impact. I eventually came to feel as if I had partially lived through it all myself.

But feelings of empathy also delivered self-doubt. Would I ever have had what it took to live as he had done, as a prisoner and an escapee? His ordeal echoed within me. I often withdrew from the company of friends and went home to write up the most recent portion of interview material.

The story he told followed me at night into my dreams. In one particular nightmare, I found myself wandering the jungle groves with my father, deep in a mountain valley.

* * *

My father was off on his own, trying to find my family. Just as I see and call for him, a landmine explodes nearby, shaking the ground and knocking me flat. Shrapnel hits me. Thick, choking dust rains down, leaving me stunned and blind. Warm blood runs down my abdomen while my heart thunders in my chest. Alone on the ground, having no idea what may have happened to my family, I crawl toward the crest of the hill. Moving slowly, pulling with my hands, grabbing loose soil, I feel the cold earth and rocks scraping beneath me.

But now the earth yawns open under me. I fall into a deep black hole. It closes around me. Great avalanches of dirt press in, carrying the thick smell of blood and dust. I frantically try to flail my way out of the hole, but the dirt crumbles under my feet and I can't get a purchase to move forward.

Instead, the hole widens, its entire mouth caves in. I am hurled back into the bowels of the mountain.

* * *

That sick feeling of terror followed me back to my waking state. The impact was so powerful, I finally understood why my father feared this story would overwhelm me. It forced me to question whether I could finish documenting his journey. Was the nightmare some sort of a warning over my own mental state? What would happen if the nightmare returned? How many could I endure and still stay on the project?

And this story had already taken a life of its own, for me. After all, I was being allowed to take part in someone else's memories of suffering and vulnerability, with the definite goal of assuring that the long sojourn would never be lost to history. The nightmare resulted from my ownership of that goal. In a way, that awful vision gave me permission to carry my father's story with full respect for the gravity of it.

I had come to carry his spirit much the same as he once carried his own father.

It was as if I had descended into the valley of this story, and climbed back out with a new character. I was coming to resemble a side of him I had never known before, the side he kept concealed. I had internalized his story.

And so, nightmares or not, I realized that regardless of how this process might change me, I had already gone too far to fail to see it through.

For the rest of my life, I will be glad I did.

PART II

Red Shards

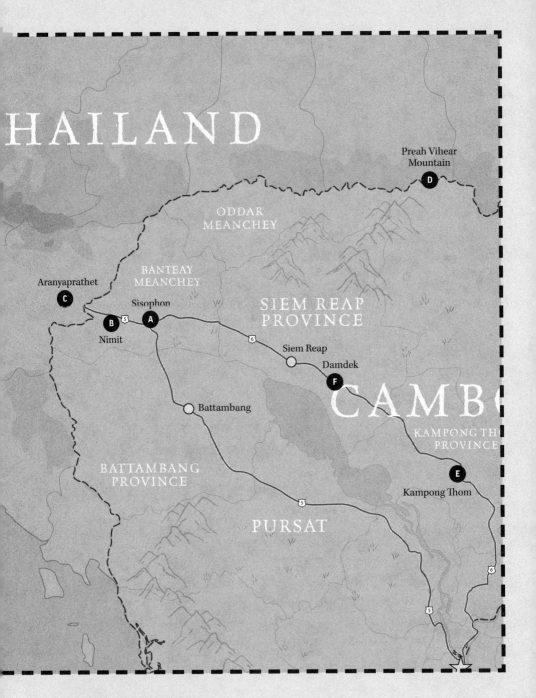

PART II – RED SHARDS

- **A** Sisophon
- **B** Nimit
- **C** Aranyaprathet
- **D** Preah Vihear Mountain
- **E** Kampong Thom
- **F** Damdek
- **5** National Highway 5
- **6** National Highway 6

Chapter 14

The Bone Fields

MAE TAING

Change was in the air. Thousands of people staggered along the highway. Pushing through the tumult, I was excited to find many old acquaintances from Poipet. They asked who still lived, instead of speaking of who had died. Most planned to get as close to the border as possible to make moves out of the country.

After two days of slow travel, our family arrived in the town of Sisophon on National Highway 5, the place where the Vietnamese released me. It was an important station for their military operations.

We reached the end of the station posts, where the Vietnamese had a military roadblock with two tanks. They explained we could not go on because the territories ahead had not yet been cleared of Khmer Rouge.

So we took shelter nearby, inside a large garage warehouse holding about twenty parked cars from America, France, and Germany— Plymouth convertibles, Peugeot 404s, Renault family cars, and Mercedes-Benz classics. The sight brought a sudden wave of nostalgia.

They came in many different colors: white, black, navy blue, teal, maroon, and tacky pink, all from the 1960s and early '70s. A few were long-nosed muscle cars and others were boxy convertibles with no roof left. The cars had been left there for years in fairly solid condition, except for the tires, which had been trimmed off to make Ho Chi Minh sandals. But the engines, the wires, rims, hubcaps, axles, and even the embossed leather seats, had been left intact.

The children ran about in play and injected the warehouse with laughter. They weaved between the vehicles, playing hide-and-seek, banging on the hoods and doors. A few sought to avoid being tagged by climbing onto the roofs, denting the tops. The smaller ones sat in the driver's seat, marveling at the steering wheel and pressing their cheeks against the windows, creating smudges and spots. I picked out a tan car as a place to sleep that night.

The sun sank into a belt of red clouds and disappeared. That evening we had a big feast of pork and chicken, cooked on spits over an open flame. As we ate, it was easy to remember the taste and smells of other roasted meats, grilled fish, boiled eggs, and soups we used to have in abundance.

When we finished, Father said, "Right now we are all safe and together. But danger remains if we stay in this country. We will not go back to our hometown. The new government will not recognize us as their citizens and will persecute us further." Father did not look in any of our eyes as he spoke. "I don't know the future of Cambodia. Nothing is for sure. I've already made one mistake by not going to Thailand. I cannot make that again. Cambodia is no longer a place we can safely live."

My brothers and sisters agreed, anticipating the dangers to come when the new Communists took full control. It was best to leave, for now.

This was not our country anymore.

* * *

We referred to Thailand as the "second country." Although we had no
idea what to expect there, we kept our minds on the second country.
The name Thailand itself had great significance. "Thai" means "free."
Thus "Thailand" is the "country of the free." This was what excited us
the most, and we patiently waited for the roadblocks to open. A new
country and future beckoned.

Even though the Vietnamese did not allow people to travel beyond
Sisophon, some families grew impatient and sneaked into the countryside. One morning, no more than a week later, a few young ones
returned crying. They had encountered Khmer Rouge, and these survivors hid in bushes watching in horror while the Khmer Rouge killed
their parents. They had not even made it back to Poipet.

* * *

After we spent two weeks living in the car warehouse in Sisophon, the
Vietnamese rolled their tanks off the road and allowed people to pass.
Many people traveled ahead, anxious to get back to their homes and
fearing that whoever arrived in the cities first, before them, would be
able to claim properties left by the former owners. Since we no longer
had the desire to return home, we decided to stay in the warehouse for
a few more days, hoping by then the Khmer Rouge would be eradicated
from the roads.

Several cars down from mine, my cousin Gao and his family stayed
in a white car whose roof had been bent by the children. Gao was
twenty-two, one year older than me, and we had found each other
again on the road coming here. I watched his family place bananas,
oranges, and Chinese pears on the concave roof, as offerings to the

gods. In front of this makeshift altar, his father lit improvised incense sticks trimmed from bamboo stalks.

They prayed to the gods, asking to know whether they should leave the country as the rest of us planned to do. They placed more incense and fruit on the roof, and prayed harder, trying to focus on receiving good fortunes. Unexpectedly, the car roof popped back up and snapped the fruits into the air. The oranges and pears rolled off and whomped onto the cement floor. That was it.

"I don't think we should be going," Gao's father said.

Sihun's husband, Wensun, had his precious Buddha statue set up in front of the car, and he had placed fifteen bamboo sticks in a condensed milk can right beside it. He lit the sticks and watched wreaths of smoke curl and slowly fade away while he sat there and looked for any signs from the divine. Once Wensun sorted out his fortunes, he called out to his daughter Bai to come and see.

"The smoke should go up. That is a good sign," he said, gesturing to the incense. "But these are curling at the point of ignition. It means I can't leave or I will face a big danger ahead."

Bored by their superstitions, I stepped out for a walk and stared down the sun-blistered street. The sky was bright and hot. Many travelers were making their way down the road, carrying homemade knapsacks and bending under the rippled air. Off in the woodlands, the cicadas hummed intensely. It was April, Cambodia's hottest month.

After walking for just a few minutes I recognized two old friends I had not seen in four years, Sudian and Ming, once my best friends from Poipet. I had known both since the age of twelve. We had often gone to movies, picnics, festivals, and nearby fishing ponds. Ming was a sociable yet obedient son of reserved parents, and he wouldn't dare do anything to upset them. Sudian was different, a brave-hearted woman, high tempered with a take-charge attitude.

As she approached me, Sudian carried her little sister in her arms. The girl was pale and sick, and although she was five years of age, her body was so emaciated, she appeared as a two-year-old. Ming and his three younger siblings carried the rest of their possessions.

"What is going on?" I asked them. "Why are you two together?"

They both smiled. "We are married, husband and wife."

Sudian started to tell the story. When the Communists evacuated the population out of Poipet, her mother was tragically separated from the family. All that remained were her father and her siblings. When they lived in Koub Touch, her eldest brother attempted an escape to Thailand alone. They had not heard from him since, and had no information if he was dead or alive.

Sometime later, Angkar sent Sudian to work in the youth brigade, and upon returning to town from a long project, she found that all of her family had died from disease and starvation—her father, two sisters, and two brothers—everyone except her baby sister.

The neighbors told her that friends of her parents tried to take in her little sister as their own, but the Khmer Rouge came one day and took her because she was exceptionally cute, with creamy white skin.

Sudian's face suddenly shifted into an expression of firm resolve. "They left me with no choices. I had to kidnap my own sister back from the Khmer Rouge."

Once Sudian learned that her sister was kept at the head chief's house, she disguised herself as an old woman, covering every bit of her face with a black shawl thrown over her head and wound around her neck. The chief lived in a small hut on stilts at the far edge of the village—crammed between tiny rice paddies. Sudian hiked back and forth throughout the morning, pretending to bail water from a nearby stream. She would overhear the conversations from the Khmer Rouge inside. For hours she did this, returning back, passing through for water. At midday, the Khmer Rouge departed for their daily meetings. Once they were clearly gone, Sudian darted in and grabbed her sister's hand and ran out.

For the crime of stealing her sister, Sudian could not stay in her town any longer. Upon entering the next town, she was abruptly stopped by a Khmer Rouge soldier. He asked for her travel certificate. Sudian gave him a piece of paper, a forgery she had made that read: "Please let this woman pass to her town," signed with an illegible scribble.

The illiterate Khmer Rouge held the piece of paper upside down, pretending to read it. He returned it, letting them pass.

Although she got through, Sudian needed a quick plan to find protection before the Khmer Rouge realized she had escaped with the little girl. She ran across different towns and villages, from one to another. Ming was in the field cutting and gathering rice stalks when he saw Sudian appear, pulling her sister through the stalks of rice grass.

"You have to help me," Sudian said with desperation in her voice. "I kidnapped my sister and now they are after me. You have to save us. You have to be my husband. I have no one else to turn to. All of my family have died."

Ming hesitated to answer. "I cannot be your husband. What would calling ourselves married do to keep the Khmer Rouge from killing you?"

"They don't have records of me here. You have to lie to the town leader. You must tell them that you found your wife and register me. If you want to save my life and my sister's, you have to say you are my husband. I'm your wife. And this is your child and you want to register us in your hometown." Ming relented. He registered Sudian and the little girl as his family, and brought them into his household.

* * *

The night after I encountered Sudian and Ming on the road, Sudian's little sister was losing weight and fluids to feverish diarrhea. Sudian watched her baby sister the whole night. The girl was burning hot, then racked with bone-rattling chills. The almost unseen rise and fall of her chest ceased altogether. A rattle sounded in her throat. Her pains eased, wrested away.

Ming came to me the morning after, visibly shaken.

We buried the little girl in a nearby mountain graveyard. Without a casket, Ming and I wrapped a straw bamboo mat tightly around her and carried her as on a stretcher. The body felt lighter than it looked when Ming and I lifted her. She was a limp, white, fleshless thing.

The area was scary and silent. All around me, for as far as I could see, lay a rough land strewn with rocks. Wooden stakes and stones were scattered over the dried hillsides, the grave markings placed by those who had buried their friends and families. A number of them were poorly covered dirt piles with bones sticking out of loose pieces of cloth—hair and feet and skulls.

Ming found a path of clear earth between the other mounds and, using a borrowed shovel, he broke up the chalky dirt. He dug up a hand that was so completely whitened it resembled a pale stub.

After Ming dug in several spots, only to unearth decaying bodies and bones each time, I took the shovel from him. I looked for an area full of rocks where there would be no bodies. It took two hours of searching and was the best we could find. Ming used his hands to help me cast the dusty gravel and pebbles to the side.

Sudian wept over the body in sad, drenching sobs. "The heavens are blind to everything," she cried. "Do the heavens have no mercy? She was so young. Why didn't they take me instead?"

I worked over the pit, digging fast until I hit something with a dull sickening thunk. It was the bedrock bottom, too shallow to provide enough dirt for burying the dead. The grave was barely big enough to hold her. Ming and I lowered her in. She was so fragile and light. A breeze could bend her. As Ming started to shovel rocks over the grave, Sudian was made hysterical by the sounds.

"God is not fair! Why did all my family die? One sister I was able to rescue and God took her away." The bitter sadness of her voice filled me with pity.

When Ming finished, we rolled a large stone over the foot of the grave. I took along a twig and stuck it in the ground. Sudian knelt beside the grave, tears wetting her cheeks.

"God has no mercy!" Her shaking, ragged sobbing was loud and unnaturally high-pitched in the mountainside. I was frightened. It was so quiet. There were so many nameless bodies here, the dead listening to us.

We tried to get her to go. Sudian leaned forward and placed a ball of rice on the gravestone. She sat, head bowed, her hair curtaining her face from us. Her husband pulled her arm to leave but she yanked it back.

"If you bought medicine for her, she would still be alive," Sudian bitterly yelled. "Why wouldn't you help me?!"

"If I had gold I would have helped you."

She turned and shot back, "You did have gold. But you wouldn't allow me to exchange it for medicine."

On the way back, Sudian and Ming chose to walk on opposite sides of me. They did not say a word or look at each other. When we reached the warehouse, Sudian muttered something under her breath, harsh utterances directed at Ming.

"Why are you claiming that I have any gold to save your sister?" Ming said. "I don't have any gold to exchange—"

"You *do* have gold." Sudian's whole body trembled with anger. "You have it. But you only care for yourself. You had no compassion for my sister!" Sudian screamed in his face and Ming shoved her off, then staggered away. He did not want to have any more of it. Sudian stood, tears falling down her face.

Before I walked away, I said to Sudian, "I hope you will find your oldest brother. Maybe he is still alive."

A couple of days later, after a silent meal of cold rice and salted pork, we struck out west for the next town on National Highway 5.

Among the hordes of people, I found many old faces from Poipet. I exchanged hesitant greetings, since I was unsure if it was really them. Their faces were thin and hard lined. We chatted and shared stories, and I learned most of them were also planning on escaping across the border, outside the next town of Nimit. It would be easiest to slip into Thailand from this place, given its proximity. They were all Chinese and shared our concerns over remaining in Cambodia.

My family spent the night on the side of the highway on uncultivated earth stomped flat by numerous travelers. Yet I slept well, overwhelmed by exhaustion from traveling and talking loudly with so many people.

Within two days of walking, we passed Nimit, a town of plywood shanties huddled along the highway. The town was now overpopulated with thousands of people camping in the fields. We wondered why, until we reached another roadblock set up by the Vietnamese army. This time they used soldiers and a barbed wire barricade. The Vietnamese told us they still encountered Khmer Rouge in skirmishes near Poipet. They did not have any estimate of how long it would take until the road opened up, or if it ever would. So we waited patiently, nervously, anticipating that the next trek would be just over the border into Thailand.

As night settled, I sat by a campfire cooking fish Choa and I retrieved from ponds in the woods. We were joined by my brother-in-law, Wensun, my cousin Gao, and Sihong's second youngest boy, Haileng. Cousin Gao was without his family, having come alone from Sisophon. Wensun asked why Gao left his people.

"None of them wanted to come with me," Gao said. "I wanted to flee out of this country. I argued and tried to persuade them, but they thought the danger was too much. It ended in a big argument and I left saying, 'I'll go with my cousins and actually get freedom.' That was the last thing I said to them. But either way, I figured my father and I can't be together. If I stay with him, one of us has to die. This is what a fortune teller told me when I was younger. Once I reached the critical age of twenty-one, she said we would have to separate. I can't be with him until I pass twenty-five years old, or one of us will have to pay."

Especially now without a radio or newspaper, superstition played a large role for us, and fortune tellers often found eager and willing audiences.

"You have a good future ahead of you," Wensun said to Gao. "But you also have danger. And this is serious danger."

"Who wouldn't have danger ahead of them?" I jumped in. "We are in war, lost, and trying to escape. There is danger every day we live, every place we walk, and every chance we take. Of course we have danger before us. There is no getting away from it."

"Judging by his face," Wensun said, "if Gao can pass this event, then you will live a pretty good life. If you can pass the danger."

"Well, you are a fortune teller," I said to Wensun. "What about you? What do you see?"

He took a moment before he spoke. "According to the day I was born, I can live well past seventy. If I can make it. I also face a big danger ahead of me." He stopped talking about himself and examined my face. "You're going to have quite a good and comfortable life."

It was a prosperous projection. I saw no reason to argue with him over it. "Okay, if we escape safely to Thailand, then we will all live a good life. Let's just hope we get there." That evening, we talked late into the night about our plans to escape, about what our lives in Thailand would be like, and what kinds of foods we were eager to eat.

* * *

The following day, a Chinese man came around shouting, "If we can collect enough gold, the soldiers will open up the roads and close their eyes to let us pass. I can speak Vietnamese to them. I also have smugglers waiting to take us across the border. The amount I need is a quarter ounce for each person."

He came around with a blue bucket. Inside were the dregs of gold that people possessed: their dull, grimy, and unpolished pieces of necklaces, earrings, and rings, as well as solid chips and blocks of gold ounce bars. We did not have enough for our whole family and gave him what we could.

Afterward, Choa proposed we strip the wood off the abandoned huts along the highway to build one of our own. We did not know how long it would take for the Chinese man to negotiate with the Vietnamese soldiers. It could be days, months, or even years; we wanted to build some shelter to live in.

Before I went with Choa to get wood from the huts, Wensun summoned me to help him husk a new batch of rice kernels that he had bought. He required another person to operate the small foot-powered polisher. Since I was needed there, Choa decided to take our cousin Gao and Sihong's two younger boys, Haileng and Kip, to assist him.

Wensun brought me to the mechanical press left behind by the Khmer Rouge. He put the rice in the bowl of the grinding device and

I stepped on the pedal to let the pestle drop and mash the rice kernels to separate the chaff. After we finished, I decided to go help Choa. I had just stepped on the highway when there was an explosion in the distance—a huge bang that hit the asphalt like a blown truck tire. *Mortar round, grenade, or rocket?* I feared the fighting was coming closer.

A man I knew named Ang cried out and ran to me, flapping his arms over his head. "Your brother and family have stepped on a land-mine!" he shouted.

"They stepped on a landmine?!—How could they have?!"

We sprinted to the clearing where a mango tree stood plump with fruits. Big overgrown bushes and yellow grasses lined the sides of the road. Haileng came staggering out from the bushes. His pale face trembled, bloodied with scratches. He burst into tears when he spoke. "Gao and Kip got hurt. I don't know what happened to them." Haileng quickly ran to inform the rest of the family.

We saw two people lying face down beneath the mango tree. I started to go in to save them, but Ang screamed, "Don't do it! There are too many landmines."

I could see Choa making his way out of the bushes. He explained what happened. "I was on the roof of the barn trying to tear it apart. The boys saw the fruit in the tree and went to go grab it, and the explosion happened. The Khmer Rouge must have planted landmines surrounding the tree. That is why there are so many mangos. No one can get to it."

A crowd of spectators formed, and two Vietnamese soldiers arrived carrying a metal detector and a stretcher. They went into the bushes, slowly sweeping the ground. I attempted to follow behind them but they put both their palms up for me to stay.

Underneath the mango tree, the soldiers dropped the stretcher and lifted a body onto it. Red blooming blood covered its face, torso, and arms, as if it had been splashed with bright paint. The only way I knew it was Kip was because of the shirt he was wearing.

Haileng hurried back with the family. One bystander translated from the soldier to the family. "There is a medical clinic in Sisophon. Your son will need to be brought there soon by one of the family." Sihong's eyes darted about, searching for transportation back to Sisophon. She saw a Cambodian man driving a wagon of straw with one ambling ox.

She rushed to the oxcart and begged the man to take her son to the Vietnamese army aid station in Sisophon, anxiously ruffling out one ounce of gold as payment. She put Kip on the cart and left the driver with a note for Gao's family in Sisophon, informing them their son was hurt in the accident.

Sihong herself did not go to Sisophon, torn on what to do. The window of opportunity to cross into Thailand was so small. There could be only one chance for her family, and if her four other children departed for Thailand in that time, they would be without their mother.

The Vietnamese soldiers then emerged again out of the bushes with the second body and I saw the damage to Gao's head. Small fragments pierced through his skull—two small holes leaked a yellow milky substance. Using a borrowed pushcart, we lifted Gao onto the cart and pushed him to camp.

* * *

Just one day. If Gao had only survived one more day, he would have made it.

The long wait we feared having to endure to leave the country turned out to be short. Before the morning sunrise, the gold collector said, "Now the opportunity has come. Time to leave."

Hundreds of people mobilized out of the fields, refugees of every variety. People carried their loved ones. No one wanted to stay behind. The human craving for freedom was universal. Almost everyone was willing to risk the escape.

Our family carried packs of food, clothes, pots and pans, whatever we could handle on our backs. Father was still in no shape to walk; the infection in his feet still swelled. Sen—Sihong's oldest son—and I put him in a hammock to carry him through the jungle.

We set off northward, each person trailing the shadowy clothed figure in front.

Chapter 15

Freeland

Cicadas chirped away as the throngs of escapees followed two dark-skinned, lean guides from neighboring villages. The trees were old, with thicker trunks and leafier tops, providing cool shade and bringing moisture to the rich black soil. This was the forest primeval.

But hidden in the dangerous jungle land were dozens of deadly booby traps, trip wires, tiger snares, and landmines. Our guides showed us a vague dark spot on a path and knelt down to the vegetation to brush away the leaves and reveal a freshly dug punji trap in the middle of the woods. At the bottom, sharpened bamboo stakes protruded from the water-filled pit.

Traps lay everywhere. Cradled in the bushy foot trails, white spikes pointed from the leaves, placed there by the Khmer Rouge to wound the feet of foreign invaders going into the country and refugees trying to escape. The guides claimed they knew this area like the back of their hands. With the knowledge they had, I felt safe in their company.

We threaded through the forest labyrinth for hours, never quite sure we were still headed in a straight direction. Each of the hundreds of people in the line aimlessly followed the person in front of them, losing sight of who was leading the pack.

In spite of whatever knowledge the guides actually possessed, word soon passed from the front of the crowd that the guides had taken off, leaving everyone halfway inside the jungle. They had had no intention of helping the refugees.

Unable to orient ourselves, we came to a bald, flat, open space recessed in the heart of the forest. Large pools of light shone down; the sky peered boldly through the gap.

A sharp cry resounded from the circle. "Soldiers!!!"

Many of the crowd raced away like scattered goats, just as a pair of helmeted Vietnamese soldiers emerged from the far end of the clearing. But one brave man walked up to them and spoke Vietnamese. After a moment he turned to us and waved his arms in huge arcs. "It's okay!" he shouted. "Don't be scared of these soldiers. They know how to get to the Thai border and will bring us there. They want to escape also, but they can't because they look like soldiers. So they want to blend in among us—we need to give them our clothing."

A monstrous tree loomed at the edge of the field, rising above the foliage. The soldiers held their guns by the muzzle and rammed them straight against the huge-trunked tree. Everyone was speechless; the reverberations of each impact echoed. The weapons bent out of shape, shedding broken parts. Then the disarmed soldiers stripped off their military cloaks, down to their combat T-shirts and underpants, and someone passed some clothes to them. The soldiers soon looked like us, dressed in tattered pants and rumpled shirts.

The soldiers told us the border was close by, and showed us a shallow trail. We trudged on for another couple of hours, picking our way through the uneven forest ground, when a pack of prowling Thai robbers jumped out of the bushes. The soldiers were taken by surprise and took a step back.

There were at least twelve thieves, with two of them hanging in the trees and surveying the threadbare crowds. A few wore sleeveless camo shirts, and a few were shirtless. But each thief had a necklace with ivory Buddha pendants hanging off it. Others had charms ringing the entirety of their necklace. On their chests were Buddha tattoos, with Buddha kneeling and holding one palm outward.

From this and the other religious symbols tattooed on their bodies, I knew they were of a particular sect. *These guys are not Buddhist lovers*, I thought to myself. They had us organize in a line and searched every individual. People mournfully dropped their last bits of gold, diamond rings, jade pendants, and silver wrist bracelets into the thieves' buckets. A few daringly swallowed their last bit of gold or stuffed it up their body parts.

Before they reached my section of the line, Father quickly turned around to me. "Mae. Put this in your mouth," he whispered, holding below his waist a ring. I grabbed it and stuck it under my tongue. A thief with long hair tied in a ponytail came up to me and searched my body.

"If you have any gold, give it to us," he said in Thai. I did not reply, keeping my eyes from revealing anger. "Open your mouth," he commanded.

I opened it. "Ahhh," I said, wiggling my tongue around. Fortunately, he examined my mouth for only a split second, missed the ring, and went to the next person. They continued searching the rest of the refugees and then finally disappeared.

We moved on and I took the ring out of my mouth. I held it in my palm, twisting it between my fingers. It was Mother's favorite diamond ring. Suddenly, it had more heft to it. I went to give it back to Father, but he told me to keep it a little longer.

We could feel that we were almost there. The sun was setting, a glint of pink between the clouds. Delightful strains of a gong rang far off and the crowd seemed to rustle softly to attention. The sound was so tiny, as if it reached me from a distant time and place. I started to remember things. Little things from before the war. I reawakened. Enchanting melodies with hypnotic chants swelled from a temple. My heart skipped. Those in front quickened their steps. We thought the sounds must have been coming from just beyond the border. We were so close to Thailand. The terror we had lived in was almost at an end.

Yet misfortune was not through with us yet. Another set of thieves fell on us.

We met men with faces just as cold and grins just as merciless as the others. These waited for travelers near the border. However, this second group of thieves was more forceful. There were at least fifteen of them and they were armed—each had two knives in his belt and carried a shotgun.

They told everyone to kneel. I quickly crouched down and poked a small hole in the earth with my finger and buried the ring. Then I got down and covered it with my right knee. When the thief reached me, he had me get up. They patted me down and examined my mouth more closely than the first thief had. They finished collecting jewelry in their buckets and fled into the woods. I got down and uncovered the ring, holding it firmly in my fist, and rose stiffly to my feet.

* * *

A strand of grayish light peeked through the vague dark forest. We went straight in the direction where we had first seen it. Winking farther through the woods were the scattered lights of a city. I felt numb with excitement. The sources of the light were revealed when we walked out of the forest into a large sandlot.

Although an inky lavender dusk had spread over the city, the slick black highway had light poles all along the roadside. A number of cars and vans cruised along it.

The sandlot was soon peopled with refugees, blackened souls clamoring—the sheer excitement, the ecstasy of seeing electricity for the first time since the Communists. We all broke into rapture and cheered mightily. Men were bent on their elbows and knees, kissing the ground and then holding their hands up in a *sampeah* to the open skies. Women knelt in prayer and cried.

The mood was like a festive Thai carnival. Families filled the night sky with hoots and cheers when they saw vendors selling steamed bananas. More sellers appeared with apple carts, each one having their own lamp and squeaky air horns. They sold an assortment of goods I had not seen in years: drinks, snacks, chips, peanuts, popcorn, shaved ice cream, rice desserts, and many colorful fruits.

As it turned out, I was not the only one keeping secret assets. Despite repeated robberies, it was clear many of us had the same ideas about hiding our valuables. I saw men cash out and drink soda pop like drunkards. Children ate pink cotton candy—dancing jubilantly. Some vendors carried yoked baskets on their shoulders, selling tidbits of dried squid and pork rinds. I was on sensory overload with all the sights and smells. The place was alive, thrilling, and even restless; the atmosphere was charged with freedom.

There was a woman selling soda, named Jie-Ah, with whom we had done some trading back in Cambodia. She was so happy to see us and offered free soda in a plastic bag with ice inside. As soon as I took my first sip, the sweet liquid burst on my tongue and made me shiver. I guzzled down a second bag. We all went and purchased whatever she had with our hidden money until we could no longer carry it in our bellies or hands.

Soon a steady stream of people moved to the other shoulder of the highway, where a few white-painted military trucks were parked. Thai policemen directed the escapees toward the vehicles, telling them they were going to the refugee camp. A truck already packed with sordid refugees drove away, sending them forth with a gleeful, rattling hum.

Another truck started to fill up as soon as we arrived, while the vendors kept up their raucous cries. It was a blessing to finally take my heavy pack off and fling it into the flatbed of the truck. We boarded, sitting on our untidy heaps of baggage. The truck started with a moan and soon we were moving. The murmur of voices in cheerful conversation and light laughter hung in the air.

The truck drove off toward the city, Aranyaprathet. I fawned over the streetlights and sign postings. Large and small advertising signs for different movies and hygiene products hung outside of shops and homes. Alongside the roads were Thai-styled teak homes, shacks built on stilts with rusty tin roofs, and other rich dwellings: cement stucco houses and painted villas with red slated roofs. The cityscape sights, the hiss of the truck brakes, the smell of exhaust, the horns honking, and the wind lapping in my hair; everything stilled me now.

The truck drove beyond a boulevard of two-story apartments and traveled down one small street after another before we were caught in an upsweep of traffic into the downtown area. The streets were alive with people, bicycles, cars, and motorcycles. Illuminating the storefronts we saw Chinese characters mounted below Thai script names. The whole area was bursting with lights. Pandemonium erupted.

The refugees in the flatbed jumped up and down and pumped their fists in a frenzy. "Freedom! Freedom!" we chanted, rising in one unfettered scream, thrusting our fists in the air in a frenzy. I wanted to shout it to the world. My heart was swinging. "We actually made it! Freedom!" Our rapture woke the neighborhood. People came out of their houses to see what all the ruckus was about.

The Thai people were crisply dressed in bright colors—red, pink, yellow, brown, blue, gray tones, and cheerful whites. The pedestrians, shopping bags at their sides, looked in our direction as we went through. The shopkeepers, street chefs, and side cart owners waved back at us. Being of Chinese descent, they knew of our pain and persecutions.

Traditionally in Southeast Asia, nighttime was the most bustling time of the day, when everyone was milling in the markets. Music blared from a street vendor's cart. The aroma of beef broth from a noodle stand salted the air with a smell of prosperity. We saw stores selling leather purses, wallets, red dresses, metal spoons and kitchenware, men's suits, shoes, belts, umbrellas, baked buns, buckets of beans, cubes of tofu curd, fish flopping on the sidewalks, wooden crates packed with fresh produce, fruits, and meats. It was the market, a sight vacant from our lives for years. The more of the street and commerce we saw, the louder our voices sang out. "WE MADE IT! WE MADE IT! WE MADE IT!" we cried out, until our voices became hoarse.

Gradually the revelry went silent. The truck took a meandering route, veering to the outskirts where the streets darkened and there were no more shops. When the truck finally stopped, it was nearly pitch black, but we could see barbed wires surrounding a shanty complex. People pressed against the fence gates holding candles and lanterns. Among us, they were searching for their loved ones and relatives. "Does that look like him?" they asked each other. "No, I don't think so." The truck slowly backed into the entryway and we shuffled inside the front gates.

The guardsman closed the big, creaking tin gates behind us, and we went afoot into the camp to look for our own spot. When we abruptly walked into one modest rust-roofed hut, other families who already lived there eagerly rose, hoping to spot any lost family or friends.

We unrolled our mats on the dirt floor of the hut. The smell of smoldering wood from cooking drifted inside. We could hardly sleep that night, stoked by the euphoria of being in a new place.

Freedom was still a novelty. It was far too early to understand what it meant.

Passport photo of Father (1968)

Mae in Poipet (1973)

The last family photo taken in Poipet (circa 1974)

Back row, left to right: Wenqing, Sihun, Sihong, Tai, Choa, Chiv, Luor, Mae; *front*: Mother and Father

Gathering at Father's ranch in April 5, 1975, for the Qingming festival. This is the very last photo taken before the Khmer Rouge took over Cambodia.

Left to right: Siam; Yeay Sek; family friend standing behind Min; Choa's wife, Meiyu, holding their daughter, Qing; Choa; Chiv's wife, Su, with son, deceased; and Chiv

Choa and his family after they were rescued from Preah Vihear mountain (July 15, 1979)

Left to right: wife, Meiyu; Choa; youngest daughter, Qing; and eldest daughter, Min

Sihong and her family in the refugee camp after they were rescued from Preah Vihear mountain (July 15, 1979)

Left to right: eldest son, Sen; husband, Yong; Sihong; third son, Haileng; youngest daughter, Siam; eldest daughter, Hua

Earliest photo from Buriram Refugee Camp (October 12, 1979)

Buriram Refugee Camp (October 12, 1979)

Tai and his family in the Biriram Refugee Camp (October 20, 1979)

Left to right: eldest son, Wusen; Tai; wife, Ying; youngest son, Qi; and daughter, Meizhi

Tai's family, Heng, and Mae in the refugee camp (December 1979)

Back row, left to right: Tai; wife, Ying; Mae; *front row*: Heng, Qi, Meizhi, and Wusen

Photograph of Mae in Buriram Refugee Camp taken by a Thai citizen (1980)

Last photo taken in Buriram Refugee Camp (February 1980)

Sihun and her family in the refugee camp (circa 1980)

Left to right: Sihun; youngest son, Guihui; third daughter, Ang; second daughter, Ou; eldest daughter, Bai

Sihun (circa 1980)

JOINT VOLUNTARY AGENCY OFFICE

American Embassy   95 Wireless Road
U.S. Refugee Program   Bangkok, Thailand

TO WHOM IT MAY CONCERN:

Re: *TAING BUN SENG AKA MEI*
T# 350056

The United States Immigration Service has accepted these
persons for resettlement in the United States and has asked
the Ministry of Interior to transfer them to Bangkok on

21 APR 1980

Linda Howey

Linda Howey
Khmer Section Caseworker

Immigration papers from the U.S. Joint Voluntary Agency approving Mae and Heng's
resettlement to America (April 21, 1980)

Mae and his family, taken in Seaside Park Bridgeport, Connecticut (summer 1983)

Left to right: Choa, Mae, Chiv, Luor, Tai, Yeay Sek, Sihong, Sihun

"Refugees reach new heights." Mae (Bunseng) Taing featured in local newspaper *New Haven Register* while at work painting United Church (September 14, 1988)

Mae with Robert P. DeVecchi, head of Indochinese Refugee Resettlement Program for the International Rescue Committee (IRC) (December 2011)

Mae with former U.S. Ambassador to Thailand Morton Abramowitz, 1978–1981, and his wife, Sheppie (March 2016)

Mae and Lionel Rosenblatt, U.S. State Department Lead Refugee Officer, 1976–1981 (March 2016)

Almost four decades later, Chiv and Mae have a chance to visit Preah Vihear and sort through what was left behind by the refugees (February 3, 2017).

Mae at the mountain site where he and thousands of refugees were perilously dropped
(February 3, 2017)

Plates, spoons, and rubber sandals still remain in the jungles (February 3, 2017).

The refugees had only taken with them a few possessions of cookware,
the clothes on their back, and their sandals.

Mae looking at a pair of rubber sandals that had belonged to a refugee. After all these years,
many possessions like these still remain buried beneath the jungles of Preah Vihear.

Chapter 16

Wat Ko Refugee Camp

I woke, aching to explore my new life in the camp. The children wildly chased each other. Their play was blissful and carefree. About four-fifths of the refugees in the camp were Chinese, and many of them were from Poipet. Like us, they also did not feel safe going back to the town and had fled for the protection of the refugee camps. Among them were many people I had not seen in four years.

The remaining refugees were Cambodians. Among them was a small group of Islamic Cham people. Back in Cambodia, the Cham people were a minority living in their tiny, isolated communities, rarely mixing with other races. The Cham women were exceptionally beautiful, tall with slender shoulders, big brown eyes, and fair skin. They appeared healthy, unlike other refugees, without signs of trauma or starvation. I was not sure how that could be; I knew of their afflictions. The Khmer Rouge targeted their people first and had killed many. But now, the Cham appeared to have recovered and were again following their own traditions freely. They sang and danced and prayed in their own Cham ways.

To my surprise, I stumbled across Ming and Sudian as I strolled to the camp center.

"My brother is alive!" Sudian exclaimed to me. "The one that escaped! He came and visited me in the camp yesterday."

I could only shake my head. "It's incredible that he actually made it," I said. "So he is alive and well. I'm very happy for you." Without thinking, I added, "I'm sorry your sister didn't make it to find out he is alive." Sudian began to cry. I said nothing more and we parted.

We shaved our heads, as did half the camp in fulfillment of their promises to the gods for their survival. Befitting of the barbed wires that surrounded us, we were skeletal, pale, and bald. On the other side of the barbed fences, vendors clamored for our attention. We drew looks from strangers who gawked at their new neighbors. Some of the passing pedestrians also stopped to look for their relatives. At the camp gates, a policeman stood guard to prevent people from coming in.

One day, Jie-Ah appeared at the fence and greeted me. She brought with her another lady named Jie-Ya, whom I had also traded with back in my days in Poipet. They had both searched for my family through different refugee camps in Aranyaprathet. We talked on opposite sides of the barbed fence, sharing stories of our hardships and crying happy tears. "I'm glad your family is safe," they told us.

Since we were now allowed to own possessions for the first time in a long while, we pooled our money and told the vendors by the fence we wanted a radio. They returned from the marketplace with a small lunchbox-sized Sanyo radio and a compact cassette player. Everyone listened to whatever music they liked. The old people listened to old Chinese opera. The young people listened to Mandarin pop singers. Some listened to Cambodian rock 'n' roll, which the elderly had hated before the Communists, but now, having a change of heart, they admitted to enjoying it themselves. Often, the children danced and sang to the "pocket music" playing from their hands. Even fenced in, with nowhere to go, healing strength emanated from everywhere, filling the camp with new song and laughter.

A small river ran inside the refugee camp and gave us a place to cleanse ourselves. The river had a footbridge leading to a Buddhist temple within the camp. A few monks lived inside. The refugees were permitted to cross the bridge to pray. We watched the day disappear behind the temple and we spent many nights lying beside the river with our chins on our crossed arms. This place became our sanctuary. It also became a site for reacquainted lovers and new romances.

Some of the other refugees surprised us all when they received letters with pictures from their families in other nations. One woman rattled on cheerfully about her relatives in France, what jobs they had, and how their children could go to school; they had even bought a used car. She read the letters out loud for everyone to hear.

She showed us pictures of her family, impeccably dressed in formal Western attire: a well-tailored black suit with a red single-toned tie dropping from the man's collar. The wife and little children were in bright dresses. Their hair was meticulously groomed. The photos had been snapped outside, amid neatly trimmed backyard gardens. They seemed to have been taken in places I had only seen in movies.

They had made it. They were there. They were free.

Excitement grew in me. I wanted so badly to be there also, one of these days.

* * *

One day, Jie-Ah received a letter from Chiv and delivered it to Father. Chiv's wife had been pregnant and was due for birth, so he had waited another week after we left before he escaped out of Cambodia.

"We made it safely to Nong Chan Refugee Camp. There are so many people in the camp and there is hardly any place to sleep. I have met some people who we used to do business with and they have brought food and clothing for us. They are taking good care of us. I am now helping the Thai vendors sell noodle soup within the camp. The family is well fed. Don't worry about us. We are free. We are all safe."—Chiv

Father was uplifted and relieved by the news. Every one of his children made it to Thailand and was now living in a camp.

The next day, Father came with emigration papers in his hand. He was unable to contain his excitement. "I've got some good news. We can go to any Western country. We can apply to any one of them. We have a future! What country do you want to go to?"

Without even a second thought, I replied, "I want to go to America," remembering my dreams at age eleven of the Apollo moon landing.

"Then we will go to America!" A smile crossed his face. He paced around the camp nervously, unable to curb his jubilation, and returned to share the news with other friends. I'd never seen him so excited. Each day he was getting stronger, able to walk on his own. His sunken and dark face became smooth and full. He forgot all about his concerns and losses, spending his days happily milling about, making friends and conversations in the camp.

Any photograph taken of the camp at this time would show a haunting and sorrowful scene of gaunt-faced children and skeletal limbs. But it would not be a true picture; we were living in happiness. Little by little, we were putting our fractured lives back together, preparing to put down roots in the new soil to come. Images of dwelling in other places were taking shape inside—the unlived years ahead. The youthfulness in all of us was returning. We had childlike dreams of going somewhere wonderful or finding something new and valuable.

We began to believe in such things once more. Our imaginations had been set free.

The two Vietnamese soldiers who had disguised themselves to travel with us now lived with a widowed Cambodian lady. She had three children and spoke fluent Vietnamese. As the only Vietnamese people in the camp, the two soldiers were nervous they would get spotted. Every day they hid inside the huts and worked hard learning Khmer from the widow. They never spoke a word to each other in Vietnamese, only Khmer. But there was nothing they could do to cover their thick Vietnamese accents, and they did not have the years it would take to become fluent.

One day, Thai soldiers came into the camp asking for the two men. The soldiers told the men they were going to be transferred to a Vietnamese camp. The widow cried and pleaded not to take them. No amount of imploring was enough to allow them to stay. The men were handcuffed and placed in steel chains, then taken to a jeep to be driven away.

I noticed the hatred in the eyes of the Thai soldiers who took them.

* * *

Two weeks after our arrival in Wat Ko Refugee Camp, the Chinese community in Thailand sent us a truck filled with donations from the local Thai-Chinese. The truck backed in and the guards unloaded the items on the ground. Five roasted adult pigs were brought out first, then packages of dried noodles, hulled white rice, canned foods, sardines, and used clothing and shoes. I was heartened by the outpouring of generosity from people we did not know, but who warmly cared for us.

I helped pass the packages to the other refugees. Hungry kids ran in the camp, waving cans of food, tins of meat and rice, even candy. Little boys who had never seen ice cubes before in their life held them in the palms of their hands and were blowing on them like hot cakes. The refugees gorged themselves until their bulging bellies hurt.

After we unloaded the truck, I sifted through the clothing and found a pair of blue bell-bottom jeans. These so-called street sweepers were out of style. I removed my scruffy gray pajamas and slipped into the pants. The fit was a little loose; however, I was sure I would gain the weight to fit them, in time. Putting them on, I immediately felt love and pride to be Chinese.

A Cambodian man beside me was mystified by all the packages waiting for us. "You Chinese people are very united," he said to me. "Helping each other out in hardship. You guys are a different kind of people. Cambodian people don't help each other out. All they do is kill each other."

But I thought what the man said was not true. Anyone could have ignored their own people. It was about the character inside of them, not their race or nationality.

Toward the end of May, a Chinese journalist and a photographer appeared and stood just behind the barbed wire fence. The journalist had a notepad and pen poised in his hands, standing with his head just above the chin-high fence. He called out in Mandarin, "Do any of you want to talk to me? What is the Khmer Rouge? How did they treat you Chinese people in Cambodia?"

A man in the crowd shouted, "You know full well how they were treating us! Your Chinese representatives were in Cambodia at that time. You were aware how they tortured us. Now you come and ask us! Why didn't you interview us in Cambodia?" More people came to listen.

The journalist did not answer the angry question, and merely replied, "If you tell me your story now, I can write it and let everyone in China know."

"Your government was there!" shouted the man. "You knew what was happening to the Chinese in Cambodia!"

"Our government doesn't want to interfere with Cambodian rule of law," protested the journalist.

Meanwhile the crowd continued to get bigger.

"You people are not Chinese citizens," explained the journalist. "You are Chinese-Cambodians."

The photographer lifted his camera, but the reporter covered his own face with his arms. We threw rocks, sticks, rotten banana peels, dirt balls, watermelon rinds, eaten corn cobs, dark brown mango seeds—whatever junk we got our hands on, anything small enough, we hurled in their direction.

A couple of spiky durian husks were thrown. Soon the wet fruit peels and rotten oranges from some forty-odd people smeared the reporter's beige slacks and white shirt.

"You want a quote?" screamed another man as he threw a rusty can. "Say that I would rather be an American dog than be a Chinese citizen! They treat their pets better than the Chinese treat their own kind!"

"You want to hear how they treated Chinese people?" a third man shouted from the throng. "Look at my throat. They left me there to die." He stepped forward and showed his throat with a long, fleshy scar driven across it.

A woman hollered, "They killed my son and my husband! I lost my whole family! Why are you asking us *now*? You were in Cambodia and had knowledge of it all. You didn't try to protect us!"

The reporter said, "I just want to make a report and inform the Chinese people."

"Yes! Do that! Tell them who we are and show them what we look like, if they want to know!"

"Now you can put all that in your report!" someone else in the crowd shouted. "Tell how you Chinese people treat your own!"

"Don't come and interview us. Get lost! We don't need you here." We pelted more trash and cursed at them in Mandarin.

"Get out! Get out!" the crowd yelled, spitting at the pair. The reporter and photographer retreated, back-stepping away.

A man in the crowd demanded, "Why are they saying we are not their people? What are we? The Cambodians don't recognize us as their own because we are Chinese. The Chinese don't recognize us because we are born in Cambodia. What are we, then?"

*　*　*

The third week in Wat Ko Refugee Camp, a two-toned tan deluxe coach bus made a smooth arc on the road before coming to a stop near the gates. It was long like a train car, with flat windshields that appeared like big black visors on someone's eyes. The large tinted windows gleamed, making it impossible to view what was inside. It was not a regular bus used to ride into the city. No, this was a bus with air-conditioning, reserved for special people.

The bi-folding doors mechanically opened, and several heavyset, olive-shaped men strode out. They were darker than most Cambodian people and wore long purple tunics, golden scarves, loose-fitting white trousers, and black skull caps ringed with white pearl beads. A few women also exited, veiled in bright-colored hijabs that covered the neck and head, with slits for their eyes.

The Islamic Cham stood by the camp gates, waiting to greet the visitors, who entered and hugged their people, speaking their language. The Cham cried tears of joy. They hugged each other like long-lost relatives.

But then the visitors returned to the bus and departed the way they came.

When they left, I went up to the closest Cham lady and asked, "Who are those people?"

"Those are my people. They are from Malaysia. They told us they are coming back in two or three days to take all of us Cham refugees back to their country." She was ecstatic, eager for their return.

*   *   *

Three days passed, and two buses indeed arrived at the camp. The buses were not fancy; they were normal transportation buses. A Thai soldier got on the megaphone and called out: "Any Islamic observers in the camp. Come out and register in the front. We are going to transfer you to another camp to transport you to your new host country. Your government has come to take you to their country, so get on the bus."

As soon as the Cham people heard this, a collective cheer-and-cry rang through the compound. They all went to their quarters to pack. Though they took their clothes, they generously offered their pots and pans to others in the camp. Ming and I watched them form a line at the registration table, an assembly of standing orphans with bags for suitcases waiting to be delivered from their shipwreck. All around me, Cham refugees talked excitedly to their friends and family. It was the happiest day of their lives.

I saw the same Cham lady before she got in line. She was smiling, standing there with her family. "Wow. You're very lucky," I said to her. "You really are going to a new country and starting a new life."

"I've never flown on a plane before. I'm excited to fly. That and to live in a new country." She talked about her people being minorities, how many of them were lost, singled out by the Communists. "I can't believe my people came to save us," she said. "I can't wait to move to a new country and live among my own people. I'm so proud to be Islamic Cham."

We said our goodbyes and every last one of them crammed on the buses. The Cham shouted their farewells, hanging outside their windows, hands waving. Ming and I waved back. The children were smiling, laughing, and jumping in their seats as if it was their first bus ride, their flattened palms and noses pressed on the glass panes.

I watched as the buses steadily departed, the children's waving hands becoming smaller and smaller. In the thick quiet, I felt a bit of loneliness, jealousy, and excitement. We wished to someday share in the same prospect. Why could not mainland China help the Chinese people in the same way? Who knew if someone would ever come? All we could do was wait.

There was something deeply unsettling about that.

* * *

We turned on the radio and twisted the dial until a Khmer voice crackled from the speakers. For thirty minutes each night after dinner, we crammed together to listen to the Chinese news station, spoken in Cambodian. It started with its introductory musical chimes and then the male radio anchor spoke: "This is a broadcast in Khmer from Beijing."

Usually it began with news about Cambodia, reporting the portions of the country the Khmer Rouge still controlled, various other fronts they were losing to the Vietnamese, or the recorded casualty rate. The Vietnamese, recently, were approaching the northernmost part of Cambodia, sending large divisions toward the strongholds of the Khmer Rouge. But today the news started differently.

"Thailand has been accused of deporting Cambodian refugees seeking asylum in Thai refugee camps. In the past week, it has been reported that the Thai government has expelled several large groups of refugees back to Cambodia. It is unclear how many refugees were taken in the process or why."

No other information was given. It was chilling. The air had somehow gone cold. We had just witnessed the payoff for the blind trust the Cham people had optimistically placed in the Thai government.

The broadcaster launched into reporting the other news of the day related to Cambodia. His calm, composed tone belied what he was saying. I stopped listening, distracted by thoughts for the Cham people. It made my heart sink. They were baited and tricked by the Thai government to leave.

From then on, we listened attentively to the radio, hanging on to the broadcaster's every word. Each day, the news did not change. Many did not believe it; it was too cruel. The Thai were resolute in sending the refugees back because their country could not sustain the populations.

Then, within a few days, on June 7, it was announced overnight that all people in the camps within the border of Thailand were to be sent back to Cambodia. The Thais were going to send a message to the neighboring countries that refugees were not welcomed in Thailand.

It was June 8 when it all got underway and the Thais began to clear the camps. Events started happening too fast for me to keep up. We listened in wait, wishfully believing the Thais would stop if they received supplies from the United Nations, or if the world pressured them to end it all. But instead the news announcement was repeated, together with the names of camp after camp closing down. Chiv's camp was named: Nong Chan. Father was devastated by the news.

We continued to hold out with expectation that the Thais would not come to our camp. One man said, "Maybe our camp will be fine because we are at the center of Aranyaprathet city. The armies, media, or governments of the world will protect the last two camps in Wat Ko. They won't tolerate it."

That was the sentiment. He was expressing the fortune we all thought we should receive. We would be spared from the first purge and there would not be a second one. We were meant to be safe. We had heard wrong; they don't want to frighten the people too much. This was the expectation I built for myself.

But inside of me, there was a feeling that everything was sliding, slipping out of my grasp, out of my control. My world was coming undone.

Chapter 17

Life in Exile

Sudian's brother, Gengdi, made a surprise visit to the camp in the afternoon. When we walked close to the barbed wire fence, Gengdi gestured to Ming and Sudian to step aside and speak privately with him.

He whispered, "I will come back tonight to get you guys out. The Thai government is already starting to send refugees back to Cambodia. Get your things ready."

"What about my brothers and sisters?" Ming asked. "Can my family come?"

"I can't take them," he responded. "Just you two for now." He handed them a bag. "I picked out clothes for you to wear tonight. Don't take anything else with you. I want you to blend in with the citizens at night. I will see you at eleven. Be ready. Don't be late."

Ming was distraught and confused. He and Sudian rejoined me, and as we returned to our flats they told me what Gengdi planned. Realizing it might be my last few hours with Ming and Sudian, I stayed with them at the threshold of their flat. The rest of his family was inside. Ming only had younger siblings—a little nine-year-old brother and two sisters, one fifteen and one twelve. He went inside, shuffled through his possessions to pull out an addressed envelope, and put money in it. He gave it to the eldest sister.

"I have to leave tonight."

"What about us? Can we go with you?" his sister asked.

"No. Sudian's brother can't take all of us."

"You're going to leave us?"

"Let me get out first," he said in a soft voice. "I'll come back for you guys."

"But rumors say the Thai government is preparing to send us back to Cambodia. We won't survive without you." Then all three of them began crying. They were only kids. "You promised our parents you were going to take care and protect us!" she screamed. "Now you are abandoning us!" He looked at his three siblings crying, begging him not to leave. Tears ran down his face.

"I'm sorry. Please take the envelope."

At half past ten, as Ming changed into the new clothes, his siblings bitterly cried louder. Over and over again, they pleaded for him to stay, but at length Ming said nothing, turning away from them, crushed under the burden from this forced betrayal of his loved ones.

The time came. Gengdi came on a motorcycle and parked across the street and waited in a dark corner. A conical light stabbed out of the darkness for several short flicks. It was the signal. Ming and Sudian sneaked toward the corner of the refugee compound. Ming lifted the bottom strand of barbed wire for his wife to crawl underneath. When his wife reached the other side, she held it for Ming.

But Ming did not move. He looked toward his flat. I imagine he could hear the cries of his family echo in his head.

He broke down. "I can't do it! I can't leave them. I made a promise to my parents that no matter what happens I would take care of them. That was my parents' dying wish. No matter what happens, I'm responsible. If I leave them I might not see them again. They need me. I'm the oldest brother, the only one they have."

"If you stay we might not see each other again," Sudian said, trying to hold in her fear and anger. "I need you too. You are my husband. You have to decide now. I am your wife, but you have to make the choice."

"I'm sorry, Sudian. I must keep my promise. If god is willing, we will see each other again." He turned around and began walking back.

Sudian bitterly shouted, "I'm not going to come back for you. You and I are finished!" She dropped the wire and the yawn of the motorcycle ruled the quiet air as it took off.

This was on the night of June 11.

* * *

It was June 12 when the consciousness of pain woke me up. A sharp stabbing began in my stomach, then faded into a duller ache. When the pain radiated a few more times, I hurried out of the flat and took to one of the latrine stalls, a set of wooden planks elevated above deep concrete trenches, sheltered by an unconvincing bamboo fence around the outside. I squatted over the opening, my head jutting out above the thatched-grass fence enclosure.

It was oddly still outside. Most mornings were filled with the sounds of muffled cars or motorcycles squawking by and vendors eagerly setting up shop. But now, through the barbed wires I saw Thai soldiers setting up blockades at the end of the road.

A single raindrop splashed on my scalp. There was an icy feeling at the back of my neck, all down my spine. I had to go to my family and alert them.

"They are going to send us back to Cambodia! They are well prepared already!" I screamed from outside the door of our quarters.

A light drizzle of rain came down while a row of buses trundled along the side of the refugee camp. Every one of us was petrified. We said to each other, "Don't get on the bus, no matter what. Refuse at all costs." The rain spilled, thousands of thread-thin needles.

A loud burst of mechanical static went through the camp when a megaphone switched on. I felt my chest tighten with anxiety. Face after face turned toward the noise while the showers intensified, cloaking the grounds.

"Listen carefully," a Khmer voice blared through the bullhorn. The echoes whipped across the expanse of the camp, bouncing off the walls of the temple. "If you hear your name called, please gather your family and belongings and hurry up to get on the bus." As he spoke, the refugees gathered slowly toward the center of the camp, wanting to see who it was but afraid to get any closer to the buses. Beyond the gates, I could see an Asian translator holding the megaphone.

"En . . . Dian Guan . . . Family of five."

No one moved, choosing to stay still in the falling rain. The silence that settled was oppressive, full of deep sadness. The man called the name once more: "En Dian Guan . . . Family of five."

Not a single person went up. Everyone was afraid to take the first seat, fearing the bus would bring them back to Cambodia. He moved to the next name.

"Li . . . Zheng Qiang . . . Family of six." There was silence again. The rain fell with relentless persistence. The speaker now had to scream out his words: "If your name has been called, please come forward and get on the bus! We will transfer you to another camp for paperwork and get you to the next country!"

Upon hearing this, the refugees all hurried to the front gate to take a look. Outside the entrance gate were several Western people in green military ponchos, holding clipboards and packets of papers in their hands. We realized they had come to rescue us. At that moment, I frantically ran to find someone to help me fill out an English application. Many of the other refugees were doing the same. People rushed, scattering throughout the rainy camp, shouting at one another. The place became a human whirlwind.

The man urgently read the names off one by one. Before their relatives went on the bus, families cried and held each other in a farewell embrace amid the sounds of sobbing, while people grasped for their friends, cousins, aunts, uncles, and grandparents.

Before long, the refugees had filled the bus. It left with water swishing from the wheels. Immediately the next bus rolled up, shaking to a stop.

They called many names, but not ours. I became distressed that none of my family members were being called. Then I felt the pain again, deep below my ribs. A stab of terrible pain spiking in my lower abdomen. I ran back into the toilet trenches, as the rain fell harder, the water rising, overflowing out of the concrete pits below the platform. But I still squatted in, ignoring the foulness passing between my feet. As the rain battered my head, I heard the next name called.

"Ear Wensun. Seven people." When he said my brother-in-law's name, my entire body tensed up, filled with excitement for them. I tried to leave because I wanted to say goodbye before they got on the bus, but the churning inside wouldn't stop. I clamped my eyes and ground my teeth, waiting for it to pass. I heard their name called once more. And again. At last I was able to get up, and went searching for

Sihun in the crowd. I saw her family already packed and ready, among the rest of my brothers and sisters.

"Your name's been called many times," I said to Sihun. I had to shout because the rain was so heavy.

"Yes!" she shouted back. "But I don't want to be separated from you guys. I will wait a little longer and see if the rest of the family gets called." She was nervous and confused. Wensun appeared very scared. He murmured between his teeth, "If I escape on this bus I will have a darkness ahead of me."

"Just go on. There is nothing to worry about," I said. "We will be fine." Her name was called again, and many more times. The speaker moved on to the next names.

"You go on," Father said to her.

She refused. "I don't want to leave you guys. We can't be separated."

The speaker now shouted the different names with a rapid urgency that made me cold. Suddenly he stopped. There was a void without his voice, except for the sound of the hard rainfall. I ran to the gate to see what was going on.

The Westerners were pushed back and two Thai soldiers came and closed the big tin gates, shrieking across the dirt ground. The translator persisted in calling out names, trying to hold off the soldiers. Then the soldiers told them to leave, gesturing them out. The Westerners stood there with looks of grief, seeming to feel guilty for not doing more. For once they tried to save a camp, but the Thais would not allow it, even for this little camp. The soldiers again commanded them to leave, wrapped metal chains around the gates, and locked the padlock.

The Westerners got into their white minibus and drove away from the camp. Abandoned behind, the sorrow stung like many daggers striking through me. Then two army trucks filled with roughly twenty soldiers each came down the street, causing the camp to descend into chaos. The refugees ran about, shouting with fear: "The Thai soldiers are coming! The Thai soldiers are coming!"

The soldiers leapt out and lined up along the perimeter fence. Then we heard the sounds of massive engines roaring like thunder down the street. A fleet of buses drove in with terrifying speed and parked one after another alongside the refugee camp. They were a burning crush of orange, a pack of metal coffins.

One man shouted, "We have to stick together for our own survival. Don't get on the bus!" That was the rally cry.

Frantic mayhem broke out. I was panting hard from searching for Father in the rain, running blindly against a current of bodies, a crazed throng. Terrified people ran wildly in my path, slamming into my shoulders, shoving for their children, shouting for their relatives. It was as if a bomb had been dropped.

The soldiers unlocked the gates and entered with black batons. They held a megaphone and said in Thai, "We are going to transfer you to another camp. This camp will get flooded soon because it is the rain season." He droned on, repeating the same words. Assembled by the gate, he and the soldiers slowly marched in.

The anguished people grabbed hold of their relatives and moved toward the back of the camp: back-stepping, racing, jumping, tripping over others who had fallen, until the wave of humans ended in one corner of the camp and stopped. More soldiers already surrounded the fences to secure the camp perimeter, and they began to close in. Bodies came together. We pushed and shoved, a shapeless mass jostling closely together so that only our heads were visible to each other above the crush. Once I found Father, the two of us were hemmed in by fifteen hundred refugees. The soldiers continued their march on us.

Each refugee fell to their knees, begging the Thai: "Please don't send us back to Cambodia. Just please don't send us back. Please have mercy." Others tried different words: "If we go back, the Khmer Rouge will kill us." Amid the panic, I could feel someone's short breaths on my neck. People sobbed and trembled, lifting their hands and pleading.

The soldiers watched us without moving further. At least they still possessed some humanity. They appeared remorseful and conflicted about what to do. Then one chief behind the line of soldiers picked up a handheld field microphone off the pack of one of his men. He said a flurry of inaudible things, drowned out by the sobbing crowd. When he finished, with a vague wave of his hand, he signaled for his soldiers to back off. They retreated and we looked at each other with nervous smiles and slight sighs of relief.

The sun broke through the cloudy skies. The whole camp was drenched, muddy, and trampled. We were starting to disperse when a second group of soldiers made their entrance through the gates. They marched in, their stomping black boots splashing heavily in the mud. These were muscled soldiers, with big shoulders and wide chests.

"GET ON THE BUS NOW!" they shouted in Thai. "OR WE WILL FORCE YOU ON!"

We scrambled wildly to the corner again. We knew these men would have no mercy on us. Pulled together by human tears, each person linked arms with those next to them, joining together as a collective. The swollen human chain stretched all the way around the back of the camp.

A soldier approached a mother cradling a baby in her arms. He made a move to snatch the infant. The mother wailed pitifully, holding on to the baby as she was pulled out of her sitting position. The father quickly tried to pry the man's hands loose. Both parents begged the soldier to stop. Another soldier kicked the father in the ribs so hard that he fell down. The soldier lifted up the couple's five-year-old daughter high above the crowd and threw her to the next soldier.

The little girl gave a high, shrieking cry as she was dragged by her arms across the ground. She screamed for her mother. Suddenly the soldier ripped the baby from the mother's arms and walked to the bus. The mother chased after them, crying bitterly with her hands on her head. The little girl was thrown on the bus, and she let out a terrible scream that fell like a blanketing shadow on the camp. It was only then the parents stopped resisting and boarded the bus themselves.

Father spoke with a friend beside him. They both agreed to stay in the camp together. Once I heard this, I turned to him and said, "Ba, we are going to get our things and get on the bus. Or we'll be beaten."

"I'm not going back. I've decided with my friend to stay here in the camp. We'd rather die here. Better here in Thailand than Cambodia. There is nothing for me in Cambodia. At least in Thailand they will give me offerings long after I die."

It was ancestral veneration. He feared the decision to leave Thailand would haunt him into the afterlife, as none of his children would be able to fulfill the filial obligations back in Cambodia to see that his grave would be kept clean and fed. Father believed his spirit would reside in the place where he died, whatever that might be. And if he died in Thailand, his afterlife would have some sliver of promise.

I grabbed Father by the crook of the elbow. He tugged out of my grasp and my hands went cold. He dropped his head.

A lump rose in my throat.

"No, Ba!" I cried. "I won't leave you here alone. We're going to leave togeth—"

"No! You go ahead!" He cut me off. "Leave me here. Go with your brothers and sisters."

"Don't say that, Ba! I won't do that. We've been through so much together. We've suffered too much already living through the

Communists. Take my hand, Ba, please!" I tried to grab his arm again, but he still refused to move.

"You go on with your brothers and sisters. Leave me here." He raised his head and his eyes met mine, then he glanced away. At that moment, I saw the pain buried behind his eyes, the heavy guilt for having led his children to danger twice. I knew how he felt, having been wrong both times. I was about to tell him it was not his fault when a Thai soldier broke through the crowd and headed straight for us.

"Is there any problem?"

"No, sir. No problem," I replied.

"Good. Hurry up. Get on the bus before I kill someone!"

"Yes sir. Yes sir." I nodded, too shaky to speak another word to him.

Still, I could not go. The guilt of leaving my father would never go away. I begged him.

"Ba. Please." Tears I thought had long dried up came back to my eyes. "Please don't do this. I won't watch you here from the bus window getting beaten on the ground by them. I can't leave you here, living with that for the rest of my life."

I grabbed his arm for the third time. He finally got up.

Before we got on the bus, we passed our flat, and I had him walk ahead to enter the last bus, where the rest of my family already was. I quickly ran inside, gathering Father's white tank top and his two pairs of shorts and stuffed them into a nylon sack. I ran out, abandoning all my possessions, taking only the clothes that I wore, and got on the bus.

As I stumbled to the back, I saw that Ming and his siblings were also on the bus, sitting in the forward left seats. He looked lost and confused, unsure if he should be here at all. The packed, airless bus was musty, and with our damp clothing, the windows steamed up. Mud caked the floors and stained the thinly upholstered seats. I approached Father, who was sitting still in the farthest right-hand aisle seat. He stared numbly at the floor in hard grief, burning with regret and despair. I passed into the window seat beside him and leaned my head against the corner.

Two children who had been taken from their mother cried, calling, "Mummy! Mummy!" But mommy was not there. The father held his children closely, weeping.

"It's all right. Your mother is on a different bus. We will see your mommy again when we arrive at the next camp."

The bus drove down a block, catching up with the rest of the buses that were slowing through the street. The feverish racket from the buses ahead was horrifying. When we saw the empty camp disappearing in the rear, we were stricken with terror.

The streets were at a standstill—the market activities had temporarily ceased as everyone stopped what they were doing. All the vendor carts and motorcycles were pulled to the curbsides. Men in parked cars gawked in bewilderment from their open doors. Shopkeepers watched the fleet of orange buses slowly drive through, rendered speechless by the horror of our cries.

I looked out the left window and saw the Western people again. They were all crying. There was nothing they could do to help us. A little later, I saw Jie-Ah and Jie-Ya, tears running down their faces, mournfully waving goodbye. Several motorcycles parked on a corner, where a clump of young men yelled. Their eyes stabbed mine, while they made a throat-slashing motion with their hands. I turned away from the windows. It was too difficult to see people who wanted to help us, but were hopeless; and then others, with callousness and malice in their eyes, who wished nothing but ill will upon us.

Chapter 18

The Shades of Mercy

Seven o'clock. The sky was darkening as twilight approached. We had been sitting in our seats for over an hour, and the bus had fallen gravely silent. I watched the silhouettes of heads and shoulders bobbing slightly, hearing the hum changing in the engine when the driver shifted speed in crowded traffic. Some of the passengers buried their faces in their arms. A pregnant woman wept and moaned loudly, choking on her fears for her unborn baby.

I just sat, numb, with my head back. Abruptly, headlight beams flicked on, shimmering on the ceiling. The light bounced around, filling the corners, growing more intense. The sounds of droning motorcycles came from behind us. I knew we were the very last bus, so I turned to take a look. However, when I pivoted around, it set off a tingling sensation running down my frame. I could feel my innards slowly twisting, then a sharp, gripping pain. It was like the squeeze of a fist.

My body went rigid and I fell back in my seat, hunched over, cradling my stomach. *Not here*, I said to myself. *Not now.*

Serpentine convulsions ran from my gut to my loins. A tremor went through my bowels. I gritted my teeth. I could not hold it any . . . longer . . .

Then my body lost control. I felt degraded. I could smell how gross I was. All I could do was feel shame. I sat rooted to the spot, my face expressionless. My clothes were drenched and soiled. I surveyed the bus. The recessed lights turned on, suddenly magnifying my humiliation that much more. My eyes darted from one face to another, waiting for their reactions, anticipating stiff, mean, disgusted looks. But no one looked at me. They sat with their eyes fixed on the floor or someplace else. The reek was everywhere, but it did not matter at all. Their faces were red, eyes swollen—morbidly subdued with dread and exhaustion.

After a few minutes, my sister Sihun turned to me with her sorrowful eyes. Her wan face was slightly puffy. "What's that smell?" she asked. "What happened?"

The humiliation burned in me. I blurted, "I don't know what to do. I have nothing to change into. I didn't pack anything with me on the way here."

"Do you have boxers under your pants? You will just have to slip them out and wear your jeans."

"How? There is nowhere to change."

"Go in the tiny space behind you and change. I will stand facing away for you."

I got up and looked out the windows and saw the headlights from two motorcycles trailing far behind. In the semi-darkness I could only make out a black helmet on one of the drivers. I slipped out of my pants and boxer shorts, and jammed the damp shorts into the corner.

With dull throbs still aching inside my body, I leaned my pounding head on the wall of the bus and closed my eyes. The world seemed faded. The noises of the old rattling bus vibrated in my ears—the shaking chassis, the sputtering motor rising and dying, the squeak of the wheel axles. I could hear every crumpled cough in the road. I spent a long time listening. The sounds lifted me temporarily. Everything was hazy and half-forgotten. Then new sounds, a stuttering engine. The sound of a motorcycle, one or more of them. A thrumming rhythm grew louder—droning right near me. I straightened up and peered behind to find the motorcycles directly behind our bus. One motorcycle broke away and drove to the side of the bus.

Unbelievable! It was Gengdi! He was on that motorbike and staring up at the bus while he held up a cardboard sign:

MING. I COME TO GET YOU.

The motorcycle veered up to Ming's window. His shocked gaze locked with Gengdi's, but in the next instant he realized what he was seeing. His eyes darted back and forth between his siblings and the motorcycle, struck by confusion.

The motorcycle fell back again, far behind the bus, its striking headlights beaming in the dark. I wondered if Gengdi had given up.

After about half an hour, the bus pulled into a brightly lit gas station at the side of the highway. The other buses flew up the road, driving farther ahead. We never saw them again. The bus driver turned off the engine and the lights went out, throwing half the bus into darkness. The workers in the service station immediately went to refuel the tanks.

The driver opened the door and got out of the bus. He began speaking with some of his friends out there. I caught the sound of indistinct voices and laughter. But though the driver had left us for the moment, the soldier remained in the aisle.

Gengdi boldly walked right up to the side of the parked bus and Ming leaned out the window opening. "I told you," he said, "I cannot leave my brother and sisters. Why aren't you listening?"

"You can't help them if you are trapped with them. You have to help yourself first. Then you find a way for your siblings."

"I can't leave. They are not old enough. This is the only way I can do anything for them. Why can't you take them?"

"I'm sorry. I cannot hide them at this time. I just can't. It's too dangerous to take all of them. The government won't allow it. We will all get caught."

"I'm staying then."

Gengdi could see Ming was determined, but he felt he had to try again. "This is your last chance. My sister has been crying all night thinking of you. She won't sleep or eat. Only cries. Sudian doesn't want to let you go. She misses you. She loves you. She says she can't live without you. That's why I came back to get you. Sudian can't think to let you go."

Ming searched for words for the horror of this dilemma, but they lay beyond his grasp. He looked back at the soldier guarding the aisle and realized there was nowhere to get off. Ming sat back into his seat, his head sinking into his chest with shame.

"Ming," Gengdi said. "This is your last chance."

The bus driver climbed back inside, closed the door, and drove off again. But it was not over yet. Gengdi got on his motorcycle and followed closely.

* * *

It was pitch dark outside. We were traveling at forty-five miles per hour. From the other lane of the highway, every so often, bright headlights popped up in the darkness. The vehicles blew their horns, but I was unsure whether they were greeting us or cheering for our departure.

Ming whispered to his siblings, "Let me get out first and I will come back and get you guys out." His sisters and brother softened their sobs.

Mist droplets struck the bus windows. It began to rain again—a soft pattering of raindrops. We closed our windows and stared out at the darkened highway, where a little distance away, a streetlamp shone through the murky rain. When the bus entered the edge of a city, more streetlights appeared, spotting the streets in their dim glow.

Maybe it would turn out to be just as they said, and this would be the other camp, a place where we could be safe for the time being. I wonder how many of us nurtured a last ray of hope without daring to put it into words. The bus now slid through a neighborhood of black, leaden streets that seemed quiet and felt deserted. We passed blocks of shuttered shop-houses and market-fronts, and I saw that beneath the Thai letters on the signs, the translations were written in Chinese. One sign took me back: Chen Groceries, written in Chinese characters. The family shared the same last name as mine.

It struck me like a gong. My memories of life before the Khmer Rouge rose to the surface. Back then, all my brothers and sisters had their own stores and shops—we too had our Chinese names proudly hanging in front of our buildings. But now I feared we would stay forgotten people, strangers who would remain nameless. All I wanted was a home.

The bus continued down the empty street until the driver slowed at a crossroad, where a lady dressed in dark and modest clothing stood on the street corner carrying an umbrella. Her eyes followed our bus as it slid past her to turn the corner and halt in front of a squat gray building. Both the soldier and the driver exited the bus while the engine was still running. The woman grabbed hold of her folding metal cart and dragged it, rattling toward the bus. We knew she must have been Chinese because of the area she lived in.

Wensun jumped up and opened his window in front of me. The smell of rain flowed into the bus. He asked in Chinese, "Do you know where they are sending us to?"

"I don't know," she answered solemnly, her face darkening.

"Are they sending us to die?" my brother-in-law asked.

There was an agonizing silence. Rain tapped on the roof and windows like tin tacks. Looking up with troubled eyes she said, "I have rice, water, and medicine. Please take it. You will need it."

While one hand still held her umbrella, she reached into the cart and took up plastic packages of rice. I dropped my eyes and shrank back into my seat. The sadness of what she said filled me with bitterness and I felt her pity go through me. I could not bring myself to take the bags. It was not dignity. As refugees we were never ashamed to accept anything. But here, now, taking charity was impossible for me. It meant allowing ourselves to accept the truth—to admit the lethal danger was real. Her pity showed it clearly enough. She saw how degraded, how hopeless we were at that moment.

Wensun abruptly turned to his wife. "We are all going to die," he declared in a low, defeated voice.

"Please. You must take the things," the kind woman said.

"How will this help us?!" Wensun snapped back, hoarse. "Where are they taking us to?!!"

Her face dropped. She was quiet again.

We saw tears well up in her eyes. She held a bleak gaze and in an infinitely sad voice said, "吃是有福气，死是天意." In other words, "If the fortune of eating is within your control, then death should be left to God's will."

The message cut through me. Instantly I understood it was true. A sickening quiet engulfed the entire bus.

The lady finally broke the silence. "I have a good home, a spare room to sleep, warm food. And I can take care of your children . . ."

There was no answer.

It seemed like an eternity before the woman repeated, "If I can't help you guys, I can still save a child."

"I have a four-year-old boy," Wensun said. "Would you take him?"

"Yes. I will give you my address. If you survive you can come back and get your child . . ." She reached in her purse and extended her arm, a business card in hand. "Or I can raise him like my own child . . ."

Wensun quickly took the card, and without even looking at it, buried the card in his shirt pocket. He reached over the facing seat and lifted his little boy, then shoved his head out the window.

"Nooo! Whaaat are you doing?!" A scream escaped from Sihun's throat, throwing herself off her seat to snatch hold of Guihui's leg. "Have you lost your mind!!" Her cry seized hold of the bus. She clung on to him and pulled back before his neck was fully out the window. "Why? Tell me why?!"

The little boy wailed.

"We had our chance to be saved at the camp!" Wensun shouted. "But we didn't take it! It was our mistake to begin with. And now they are going to send us to die. Let's not let all of our children die because of our mistakes!" Wensun tried forcefully to pry her hands off and push the boy out again.

"It's too late now!" Sihun cried bitterly, still holding on to Guihui. "Even if we made a mistake and lost our chance at the refugee camp, I will not give my child away."

From the middle of the bus, someone uttered a low, broken moan. The pregnant woman three seats in front of me was sweating profusely, short labored breaths escaping in and out. I was not sure if she was giving birth soon or not. Then she began crying hysterically. She passed out against the window. Her husband tried to hold her shoulders. He kept shaking her. "It's going to be all right, Darling. I'm by your side. We will be spared."

Wensun ignored them both. "It does them no good. As parents we should care for them. As least one of our children can still be saved. For the last time! Let go!"

"I will never give my child away. If we should die, then we all will die together," Sihun cried. "It is all we have. This little time together. Because then our parting will be forev—"

Then with a sudden wrench, Wensun pulled the boy out of his mother's grip and stuck him out the window. Sihun tried to reach for the boy's arm. Wensun positioned his body between her and the window. She thrashed madly against his back, slapping him as hard as she could. "You are out of your mind! You have lost it!" she screamed sharply at him. The other passengers dissolved into sobs. "You're giving our baby away!!" she uttered in a broken voice.

I looked at Father and saw a single tear run from his right cheek straight down into the collar of his shirt. I knew what he was thinking: *I caused this. I made my family separate.*

"He should be given a chance to live!!" Wensun shouted.

Tears rimmed the woman's eyes and she turned her face away from us. "Fine. Fine. Fine." She wiped the tears from her eyes. "You can keep your child. But . . . Please take the supplies. Please take the water . . . And I will pray that God will watch over you."

Sihun pulled her boy in, clasped him tightly to her heart, and rocked back and forth with stifled sobs. The child continued crying. "Baby. Baby. My darling. We are going to be fine. Everything is going to be okay."

The lady tossed the supplies in our windows and we reluctantly accepted. The water she gave us was wrapped in a plastic bag. As she walked along the side of the bus, passing the rest of what she had to everyone else, the husband of the pregnant woman spoke out the window. "Can you help us? My wife is pregnant. She is already passed out and barely conscious."

"I'm sorry. I can't."

"My wife is going to be due in a couple of weeks. Can you just help? She needs your help."

"I can't." The Thai-Chinese lady was on the verge of tears again, but bit them back. "I can't. If we get caught, they are going to put me in jail. . . . I can't help you. But I will pray for you." She dabbed her wet eyes with her fingers.

From the backseat, I watched the whole bus. Ducked into their seats, the refugees dissolved into hard, wracking weeping. I do not know if anybody was strong enough not to cry.

Once again, without warning, the pit of my stomach was seized with painful cramps, first in one spot, then all over. Knifing and twisting. My muscles tightened, my stomach soured. I held on like mad. I needed to go somewhere. *Anywhere.* But not in my one pair of jeans. I looked around for some kind of refuge. In the front, I saw that the soldier and the driver were still missing.

I dashed outside in the muted rain, feeling slight vibrations of the air on my skin, and raced behind the gray building. My gut emptied itself. It kept coming. My innards were turning inside out.

The metal paneled roof of the building pinged softly from the pattering rain. I heard two men whom I guessed were the soldier and Gengdi, talking in low tones on the other side. I only caught snatches of their conversation. Gengdi was bribing him. But before I got the chance to hear more they finished and returned to the bus.

I stayed rooted to the spot for a very long time. In the blur of the drizzle, I saw groups of two or three soldiers standing unmoving in the gloomy distance. There was no chance of escape. I hurried back to the bus.

The soldier and the driver were still not there. When I entered the aisle someone called to Ming from outside, "This is your last chance! Leave now!"

"You can't abandon us!!" Ming's sister and brother cried. They grabbed each of Ming's arms, trying to keep him from leaving. Alone in the seat across from them, the youngest sister lapsed into a quiet whimper: "You can't leave me. I can't be alone."

"I will be back to get you. I . . . I have to go," Ming sobbed. He yanked his arm out of their grasp and when they tried to grab him again, he shoved them back and hurried for the door. I slid into one of the seats to get out of his way. Ming concealed his face with his arm as he passed me, fighting back his tears. The youngest sister ran to the back of the bus, crying out the window, "Brother!! Don't leave us!"

The motorcycle rattled, sounding a haunting chant as it left, the brake lights and engine fading. Ming's eldest sister did not even watch him. Her head hung between her arms, and though she made no sound, her shoulders trembled.

After I got back into my seat, the driver and soldier returned. And still the kind woman threw supplies into the windows, this time white waxed candles, lighters, foil-sealed packets of Ya Tun Zhai Thai medicine, and Tiger Balm—all items we would need for the trip. The refugees barely had time to thank her before the door closed and the gears engaged.

She waved farewell while she watched the bus continue on. This lady, a complete stranger, was a saint to us. I would never get a chance to tell her that.

A terrible silence settled over the bus. I stayed still, my gaze set far away out the windows. For a moment, the jungles opened into fields, and on the expanse of the meadows were dull lamps shining within little farm huts. But of course I was not a part of any of that. I was somehow on the outside looking into the world.

"Nobody knows this, of our whereabouts," I said to myself. "Only death knows." And death was out there, hidden, prowling, waiting.

Chapter 19

Preah Vihear

A full night passed. The bleak dawn shone through.

The road hummed beneath the bus wheels. Light broke on the dirty, fogged windows, casting a dreary gloom. We sat tearfully silent. Some on the bus had awakened hours before. Few slept at all that night. I wiped the fog off the window glass with my palms and peered out. It was still the same endless procession of trees on both sides of the road, with no houses to be seen.

The bus cut off the highway and turned onto a shabby track. Gravel shot up, scraping the metal underneath the bus. Then the bus hit a steeper incline, lunging forward through a dark, chilling tunnel of trees. The rocking force momentarily knocked us out of our seats. Passengers were bolted awake when their heads struck the windows. The bus climbed upward with the suspension dancing up and down. Overhanging branches slapped hard against the windows and roof;

and the engine of the bus pounded and roared. The emergency lights tripped on again. I knew it was near—our destination.

Thai soldiers squatted alongside the dirt road. They rose to their feet on our arrival. The bus approached the squad of soldiers until they surrounded us in front and at the sides of the vehicle. Each one had an M-16 rifle in their hand or slung over their shoulder.

"We are here," the soldier inside the bus announced to us. "Get out of the bus." I instantly felt paralyzed. This was the place they were going to kill us. Nobody wanted to leave.

Bang! Bang! Bang!! A soldier outside violently pounded against the metal frame with his fist and forearm. "Everybody get out! Get out now!"

The folding doors swung back and two soldiers entered the bus with hate in their eyes, yelling, "STEP OUT! STEP OUT NOW!!"

Through the windows I watched the refugees disgorging, rifles pointing them into the forests. Ming's siblings and the rest of my family—Tai, Choa, Sihong and Sihun's families—descended the steps with the crowd and stepped into the unknown surroundings. I lost sight of them.

Father and I were among the last few aboard. I held his arm firmly and carried our belongings with my other hand while we stepped off the bus. After we got out, the soldier searched the bus thoroughly, looking underneath the seats for anyone who may have been hiding.

Then the bus took off, the wheels stirring up water and mud. I scanned the horizon, trying to grasp what I was seeing.

The sun sat high in the sky, shining on sweeping emerald-green forests that stretched forever. The treetops seemed so low, marching on endlessly to the horizon. Far beyond, fog swirled cloud-like, floating motionless in the trees. My gaze lost itself in the remoteness of the mountains. I had expected some sign of civilization or a city, but we appeared to be on the crown of a mountain overlooking a valley.

The Thai soldiers pointed us toward the downward incline. We headed in that direction, until more Thai soldiers stopped us and one of them said, "If you have any gold, currency, or valuable possessions, drop it in the buckets for us. You won't be needing it down there."

His words were too ominous to accept at face value. I surveyed the area and saw an older Thai soldier holding a box of cigarettes. He seemed to have a more merciful and gentler appearance than the others, so I walked toward him and spoke in Thai: "Excuse me, sir."

"Oh, you speak Thai."

"Yes, a little bit. Where am I?"

"You are on top of Preah Vihear Mountain."

"So if I get down off the mountain is Cambodia on the other side?"

He would not answer my question directly, but said, "Take as much water and rice as you can carry because there is nothing down there."

"Thank you, sir."

Before I turned and took Father by the arm again, the old soldier asked, "Do you have any money to buy cigarettes?"

"I'm sorry, I don't have any money." Then I asked, "How am I going to get down?"

"You just follow the other people taking the path down." He appeared frustrated that I did not have any money.

"Where are the other refugees who were sent here before?"

"Don't worry. They are long gone."

The words echoed in my brain: "Don't worry. They are long gone."

Then a man in his twenties came struggling up the slope in filthy, ragged clothing. He scavenged while he walked, picking up whatever he saw and putting it into his plastic bag. When he found some moldy rice tied inside a clear bag, he tore open the plastic and scooped his fingers in. He ate it quickly, then climbed up closer to our position.

He approached us trembling, with a look of horror in his eyes. "Are you a newcomer?" he asked with a shaky voice.

"Yes."

"Are there any more refugees coming?"

"I don't know. What is it like down there?" I asked.

"The dead are everywhere. People lost their lives from stepping on landmines. There is no water or food. The conditions are grave. There is no way out. I've been looking, but there is none. Is there food up there?"

"Yes. Lots of people left it behind." He looked up and saw the Thai soldiers.

The second my eyes strayed away I heard a gunshot. I threw a sideways glance and saw his body tumbling down the hill. There was blood on his shirt. He plunged forty feet, rolling, and collided with a tree stump. His crime was searching for food.

Four Thai soldiers stomped over to us and fired three shots into the air. One of them shouted, "Hurry up and get down!! Or I will shoot you all down. All of you guys!"

"Move faster!" I told Father. "Move faster! They will kill us!"

We needed to keep moving, even though I didn't see the rest of my family. I pulled his hand and escaped downhill between the thick wall of trees on both sides. My other arm flailed about, blocking the tree branches and thick bushes grabbing at my face. Staying up there was suicidal, but the same was true for going down. I was afraid we would fall into a minefield. One false step and we could end up dead. Although he had trouble keeping up, Father knew the danger and forced himself to match my stride.

On the flight down the mountain, we came to a stop on a cliff face. I looked over the edge of the bluff, where crumbs of loose earth broke away and rolled down the eight-foot drop.

"Find another way to get down," Father said. "I can't climb this."

"No, Ba. We have to. Otherwise they are going to gun us down here." I tossed my belongings of rice and his clothes sack over the precipice. I grabbed a fistful of vines streaming down the cliff and painstakingly rappelled off the sharp side.

When I landed on my feet, I held on to the vines and sprung onto a large rock that gave me height to reach halfway back up. "Lower yourself and put your feet on my shoulders," I said. Father gently eased his old body down, sliding into a sitting position. He grasped his legs and stretched them over the edge.

"Take your time," I told him. While I kept hold of the vines for support, he tentatively slid off and stepped onto my shoulders. I got off the rock and bent my knees so he would be level with the rock to stand on it.

Soon after Father gained his footing, gunshots from somewhere close by burst forth again. "Ba. Keep moving from the murder!"

"I'm very tired. I can't go on."

"We have to keep moving. Once we get to the next landing, then we can rest."

The next plateau was not as high. Like a rock climber, I held the little rocks sticking out and felt my way down, stepping on anything my feet could reach. Then I touched something foreign with my foot. It was soft, cold, and spiny, kind of sharp. I did not know what it was. I firmly stepped on it, and heard something crack and break. It was not ground. I could not see where I stepped because there was too much vegetation.

But once I reached the base of the little plateau, I saw it: a body slumped over, dead. It was a man in his fifties in a long-sleeved buttoned-up shirt and gray pants. I had stepped on his rib cage.

I immediately pressed my hands together and bowed forward. "Forgive me. I didn't mean to step on you. I didn't know. Please forgive me."

I was afraid I might have angered the spirit because I had invaded its resting spot and its peace in the afterlife. My people believe spirits wander around the body for a period of time after death and should be left undisturbed.

I helped Father get down, directing him away from the corpse, and breathed with relief when he was finally on solid ground. He untied the rubber band around the rice packets from the kind Chinese woman and offered some to me. He regarded me for a moment, then stretched out his hand and brushed my head. "You're so young," he said in a terribly sad tone. "Why have you endured so much misery? I thought we had made it after we escaped from Cambodia. But it's happening all over again. The Thai made it clear why they dumped us here. No one else would do this to other humans. We're here to be slaughtered. They want us to clear the landmines."

I had no response for that. It was so horrible I didn't dare speak of it.

* * *

Midnight. Suddenly a cry rose from the mountain. A mother pleaded, "Somebody help my baby! I beg you! Help me!" It was so loud. "Help my baby. Please. She has stopped breathing!" The cry continued and then stopped. Through the reverberating echo, I heard the thin, trembling line of the mother's sobs. After already living through so much during the Communist years, we thought nothing could frighten us anymore.

The sounds were joined by the voice of a man calling out for his family. So far down the mountain, I could hear the echo, sounding lost and forsaken. "Wh-ee-rr-eee-aaa-rr-eee you!" he called to his children. "Where are you guys! Ba got the water!!! I got the—!!"

A landmine detonated with a furious roar. So loud. The entire mountain felt like it was shaking. The earth was heaving hell. Unsteady silence reclaimed the air—his severed words made us tremble. His voice was no longer there. Then thousands of cries raised at once. Everyone on the mountain was mourning for someone we did not know.

Crying for him and for us.

Father's limbs trembled with dread. He wept bitterly, choking cries that made me sad to my bones. "Without hope of getting out of this mountain alive, our Chen family comes to an end. My children. All of them. Will not make it. This generation will be the last . . . The family will no longer exist . . . This is all because of me."

"Ba, it was *not* your fault! There wasn't anything you could have done. Or anything I could have done. Nothing would have changed. We gave it our all. We tried everything."

But my words seemed so empty in the situation; so powerless to overcome the grief and the horror. I set my hands on my lap and bowed down. For the rest of the night I lost my voice to speak. I did not sleep. I just wanted to keep my eyes shut because I was frightened of what I might see when I opened them. I was afraid things would be worse the next time I opened my eyes. The next time I woke from a dream.

* * *

Dawn brought in a new reality. There was no sun shining. The ground was moist and green, gasping with heat. The air hummed with flies. Foul, omnipresent reek of human feces and urine rose from the earth. Fearful to explore anywhere else, the refugees relieved themselves on the slope, certain these trails were clear of landmines.

Abruptly we heard a sound above, distant but low. We twisted our necks up, only to see the roof of leaves. The noise became something complex, a more lucid croaking. The sound of an airplane engine approaching.

The refugees became alarmed. The humming grew louder. We stood trembling for what seemed an eternity. A strangled cry rose and echoed out: "Please help us!" The plane closed in on our location.

"Please help us!" The refugees screamed as one, and picked up anything that helped to make sounds. Men frantically climbed up trees to get closer to the plane and yelled, hoping the pilot would hear them.

The plane circled above us. The whirl of engine propellers, a deep undulating bass, washed over our heads. Every human on the mountain, including every child, cried louder for help. Thousands of voices; a huge bottle of emotions.

Then the plane's direction altered. The metallic sound gradually faded away. Everyone fell silent.

The sound of the plane returned, back again from the distance. For an instant, there was a flash of joy in my heart. Someone called out, "Hurry and make a fire! The smoke will allow them to detect us through the trees."

I sprinted to help. One of the men responded, "Look at us. How many are we? Everyone has a cooking fire. There is already enough smoke for them to spot us. If we are to have any chance of getting rescued or have them drop supplies for us, we need to have something else to let them know our position."

I broke in and said, "A white flag should be the rescue sign."

* * *

We cut a long bamboo stem and tied a white shirt to the end of it. One man climbed a tree and I stretched up to hand the flag to him. The man was in such a hurry, he nearly fell out of the tree when he reached for it. The sound of the plane drew close above, increasingly drowning us out.

He took the bamboo staff and climbed up nearly three stories high, then raised the shaking bamboo stick the full length above his head.

"Higher!" we howled. "Higher!! Higher!!!"

The man climbed higher, to the very top of the tree, and stretched his arm as far as he could. The white flag poked out of the forest roof. He flung it from side to side. The plane swung low again. The whole forest was roaring: desperate screams rose from thousands of throats. Men perched in the trees shouted and slapped on the bark, shaking the branches wildly. The refugees below clanged loudly on metal pots and pans, and some of them banged them on tree trunks, hitting anything as loudly as possible.

A young girl knelt down on the ground, her body shaking, and put her hands in the air. She screamed and cried, "Help me!! I don't want to go back to Cambodia to be killed. My brother and I are the only survivors. Please have mercy!"

Despite our collective noises, the plane steadily continued away. We all watched the man at the top of the tree as if he had the power to do something more to change the outcome. He took a few vines and tied the flag staff to the tree. Thousands stood and watched, their faces fallen. That moment drained away all our hope. But we still held out, and our ragged sobbing went on. We screamed as loud as we could.

Suddenly, from somewhere near the top of the mountain came the loud, heavy reports of machine gun fire. The people fell into the silence of shock. For three minutes the gunfire went on. We never heard anything more of the plane.

A woman cried, "The whole world has abandoned us."

I was reminded of an ancient Cambodian saying: "In the water, crocodiles; on land, tigers." Tigers stalk, poised for a sudden dash to their kill. Crocodiles lie dormant, quietly under the water's edge, waiting for their prey to come to them. We faced two choices. If we went down to the river, we would face the landmines. And if we went to the top of the mountain, we would face the Thai soldiers. There was no way out. Nowhere to hide. No one could save us now.

We were caught between the crocodile and the tiger.

* * *

Night crept in and the mountainside path faded into shadows. Every now and then, explosions rent the air. The fear was inseparable from us, our own shadow.

On the ground around us, hundreds of little flags poked up near the trail. Refugees had used sticks with tied-on bits of cloth or plastic to mark areas where they found landmines. As we walked down the trail, my ears filled with insistent cries and moans of the wounded amid awful shouts for help. I brushed past outstretched hands that begged for compassion. I barely glanced at a whimpering girl abandoned alone at the bottom of a tree. I choked back tears, wiping them off my face.

Most of the path in safe territory was already overcrowded. We found a boulder-strewn area, a place that might be free of landmines and human waste. Every deliberate step I took on unstable rocks and stones, I got nervous jitters. My instincts told me I could still trigger a bomb even with refugees around me. I pulled out some grass and stones to make a bed. It was too dark to look closely for exposed landmine heads.

I carefully walked Father over and seated him down. I lay next to him and braced my arms across my chest, afraid of triggering anything around me. I remained perfectly still, embracing the loneliness. The constant shaking of the ground told me I was sleeping on unstable terrain, and if I rolled over in my sleep I might plunge into the void.

An unmistakable boom cut the darkness. This time, dozens must have been hurt. I heard the strained cry of a woman.

Then, nearer—*BWOOOM!!*

Cries of pain rose up from the injured, screaming to the skies. There were so many voices I could not tell them apart.

Soon, however, their screams ceased. There appeared to have been no survivors.

* * *

On the third day in the afternoon, two Thai soldiers smoking cigarettes tromped by on unsteady legs, reeking of alcohol. They carried a gallon of water in a clear plastic bag and a box of dried noodles. At first it seemed they had softened and were going to give relief to the hungry children. But they quickly demonstrated there was no compassion within them to do such a thing.

They approached a single mother with three children. Her youngest girl was sitting on her lap, crying for food. One of the Thai soldiers pointed to the box. "Do you want food for your children?" he asked in Thai. She nodded her head and kneeled before them, her palms pressed high together in a gesture of the utmost respect. She believed they were offering it to her children. The children stared at the box of noodles.

"Give me an ounce of gold for the noodles," the soldier said. But the mother did not understand Thai. Instead, she raised her empty palms out to receive the food.

"Give me gold for the food!" the soldier yelled.

I knew she did not understand them. I said to her, "They want to sell the food to you. Not to give it to you."

"I don't have any money or gold," she said. "Help me. I need food for my children." I translated back to the Thai soldiers.

"Fuck you," they said. "You think we're going to give food for free?" They began cursing loudly and walked away.

Her little boy cried, "Mama. They are not going to give us the food?"

"No, son. They are not going to give us the food. They want gold. Mother doesn't have any gold." The mother hugged the children and cried with them.

The soldier then asked another man, "You want this food? Give me gold." The man reached in his pocket and pulled out two hundred Thai baht. He got on his knees and held it cupped in his palms. One soldier grabbed the money and cackled, "I want gold. Not just two hundred baht. Give me gold."

The man could speak Thai, and said, "Please sir. Be merciful. I don't have any more money. That's all I—"

A hard boot struck the man in the stomach, knocking him to the ground. Lying on his back, stunned by the blow, he gasped the smallest breaths. His wife and children cried out and rushed to help him get up. The Thai soldier swiped their bags and shook out their clothes. When he found no gold or money, he burst into anger: "You think I'm going to take two hundred baht for my food? You are out of your mind! Give me all your money! You won't need money where you all are going. No one is getting out of here alive. Not this time; not ever."

We were convinced the soldiers would slaughter us right there, so everyone gave up money and gold to them. They appeared placated and stopped their threats, but never gave the food to anyone. Instead, the soldiers retreated up the hill.

One of them threw the water on the ground and smashed it with his boot. "God damn refugees!" he screamed. When they were out of sight, Father said he had never seen such heartless people on earth.

Chapter 20

One

By the fifth morning on Preah Vihear, we were depleted of our water supplies, so we headed down to the bottom of the mountain. Father and I took a route not many people traveled, cautiously funneling between massive sandstone cliffs and boulders. The terrain was rough with thick vegetation above and roots growing off the rock walls. We treaded lightly, avoiding the white cloth flags marking the paths. Hundreds of them stuck upward from the forest floor.

The path went vertical. Father grabbed slippery vines and tugged my sleeves to keep himself from falling. Together we clambered down from a shelf of rock and peered over the edge to confront the face of a feeble old Chinese man. The man was pinned between the rock walls, staring blank and motionless; flies creeping near his mouth and nose.

Father grabbed my wrist.

"Help me . . ." A voice spilled out from the ragged figure. He had a narrow face, a long snowy beard, and wore a silver Chinese traditional long shirt embroidered with folk patterns all over it. His elegant suit was worn over layers of other clothing. Not a scrap of skin showed from the rest of his body. A pot of rice and some food sat next to him, but it had not been touched. It was becoming rancid, flies feasting on top.

I knew his family had dressed the old man up and abandoned him there out of utter desperation. I thought I could never do that to Father. I was thankful Father was still able to walk, but I could not condemn the family who left the old man behind. If we had not had the month in the refugee camp to recover strength in Father's legs, I do not know what I would have done.

When we passed by the old man, he called out again in Chinese. "My children left me here. Can you help me?"

I looked at Father's face becoming overwhelmed with sorrow. "How long have you been here like this?" Father asked.

"Three days," he replied.

The man's weak windpipe wailed for us to come back, but we could do nothing for him. The words brought tears to Father, who turned his head to suppress his cries. I know he saw his own future in that man's plight. How much farther until his own children had no choice but to leave him behind also? Father might have felt he deserved it, blaming himself for not getting out of harm's way when he could.

I pressed his hands tight. "Ba. I promise I'll never leave you. You hear me? I promise."

Farther down the hill, we stopped before hundreds of other people propped against the rock walls, wearing ghastly faces. Their breathing was shallow, fading, as if past the agony of death.

My mouth clamored for water. The back of my throat was so dry it ached, swollen and cracking. We drank our last few gulps of water from the bag and continued moving down to the base of the mountain. The air was thick, humid, and baking hot. The combination of darkness and the lack of water was so severe that Father was losing his sense of balance and sight.

* * *

We stayed in a tightly packed encampment of dilapidated tents. On that night I heard pattering, thousands of tiny sounds on the leaves above me. I jerked my head back and my heart began to dance.

The raindrops swallowed the campfires, blinking them out one by one. The falling drops rapped and pinged on the crowded plastic tents.

The sweet burst of monsoon showers washed my scalp, face, neck, and chest, soothing my lips and tongue. For a moment, I was bonded to all: me and Father, the refugees, the forest, and the monsoon. It was all part of me. Eyes clenched shut, I shouted out in joy and tipped my head, sliding the water down my throat, until enough filled it like a basin. I moved it around to keep my tonsils and tongue as wet as possible. It felt wonderful. I guzzled mouthful after mouthful by cupping my hands to catch it.

The downpour continued, so I ducked under my plastic sheet, my clothes wringing wet, and went to sleep.

After we had rested for the night, we followed along a gully for a distance and heard the sound of prayers in the air. We came upon a clump of refugees gathered in a circle. I saw Tai, Sihong, and Choa huddled in the group, and felt immediate joy they had all made it down to the bottom safely.

However, we did not see Chiv or Sihun's family.

An old white-haired soothsayer stood in the center of the group, preparing a piece of paper and a wooden chopstick on the ground. The refugees surrounding her were asking for signs from the skies, forest spirits, ancestors, their lost loved ones, Buddha, their own gods. Whoever would listen.

The old woman held the chopstick canted at a point on the paper. After a moment, her hands twitched, led by the chopstick skittering over the paper, possessing a life of its own. The refugees clamored in excitement. It had been a week since we had arrived at Preah Vihear, and we were desperate to humanize our lives. Anything to provide escape for our minds. Anything to give us some hope where there was none.

"Show us the way," she murmured. "Show us the sign." The chopstick briefly stopped. The whirlwind of prayers and cries went louder; mumbling chants and prayers pushed their way deep inside me. The refugees wept and shouted, invoking the spirits of the forests, rivers, mountains, skies, and fields.

The old woman circled for many steps and paused. She spoke with total conviction. "Tomorrow . . . tomorrow someone will come to save us. We will be getting out of here soon . . ."

Tomorrow did come. Someone did not appear. But the illusion of rescue continued to inspire. On the eighth day on the mountain we tried again with the old soothsayer, who repeated, "Someone will surely come to save us tomorrow. That is what I have been shown. It will be tomorrow."

Yet again the next day, there was no evidence of help to be seen, no sign whatsoever. For a third time, we tried again and it was the same result. But desperation owned us. Even if it was all a lie, we had to believe in something, some force of good to intervene for us. We accepted the lie. It gave life. It was the only chance we had.

I spent my days looking out into the wilderness. My gaze often trained on the forest roof and for a second in my imagination I would jump up into the air to escape. My obsession with escape to freedom ran wild.

I thought of all the ways I could escape. My life compressed into this one basic instinct to get free. Perhaps I would simply fly away and be reborn—as a foreigner, a farmer, a city worker, an owner's dog. I would take that risk to be any place other than in Cambodia. I realized when we gave up our freedom, there was nothing left of us. There is no life. I peered at other men and women and wondered if they too had the same feelings.

It would not be long before I got my answer. On the twelfth day the fortune teller's words, her myths, became truth. In the late afternoon, word reached us from a refugee. A breakthrough. The Vietnamese had attempted to clear the minefield for many days. Their soldiers on the Cambodian border had successfully made a passage for the refugees. But it also left the Vietnamese vulnerable to invasion, so today was the only day the soldiers would leave it open for people to travel through. The man passed the news to everyone. "You better hurry or they will close it by tonight," he urged.

Sihong began to boil a modest handful of rice that she got from a Thai woman. She said, "We don't know how much longer we have before we can eat again. It is best for Ba to eat first."

"You can bring Ba after he finishes eating," Tai replied. "I can't stay here any longer." He took his family and followed the other refugees, afraid the window of time was closing.

Sihong had Father and I eat first, since Father needed to be taken to the passage before everyone else. Choa and Sihong's family would come after. Eating was a brief affair and once we finished, with one last word of goodbye, I took Father's hand and we ventured out, moving at a slow trot.

On the descent, our bodies now seemed stiff, almost frozen. I saw old men hauling their meager possessions down the rock hillsides. Though they were unsure of the chances of getting out, after hearing a mere rumor, they pressed on. They could tell themselves refuge was just around the corner. That's what we all pretended. Soon we would have a place, a bed, and a home to put our possessions in.

A moan of pain came from a woman in the vicinity. We passed a tight circle of women holding up gray U.N. blankets to conceal her. She screamed for short intervals, stopping with faint intermittent gasping. The feverish and rapid gasping intensified and the more I heard, the more I understood why. The cries of a baby suddenly piped up. The other women quickly dispersed and I saw the woman stand and lift the baby from the jungle floor, cradling it under her arm without a moment to rest.

* * *

When we reached the brow of the last steep descent, I scanned down the mountain flank. It was swollen with a dense sea of refugees. Only the tops of black heads and shoulders could be seen. A throbbing human tide stretched all the way back to where we stood.

People spread across the edge of a distant hill, standing clear behind treacherous tracts of landmines. Hundreds of dead bodies lay strewn in the fields. When I saw these bodies, I knew it was Cambodian land again. A long line of refugees had already spilled deep into the jungles, finding a narrow footpath by walking over the bodies.

Father and I made it to the lower base of the mountain, arriving at the end of the broken line. We waited for Sihong and Choa. Ahead of me, a tall man stood, leaning weakly on his wife's thin shoulder blades. He mumbled nearly incoherently, "What's . . . happening? Where . . . where . . . are we going?" His wife supported him under his armpits, while her right hand held both their bundles. She also had a frail, aging mother standing by her side. The line moved, and the man wobbled and staggered crazily like a drunkard. I feared he was going to detonate a mine.

The refugees funneled into the single narrow line, and the woman walking with her frail husband stood tense and distraught. There was not enough room for both her husband and mother on the narrow safety path. She could not hold them both, and one of them would surely set off the landmines.

She had to leave one of them behind. The wife stopped and asked her husband to rest. "You need to sit down and regain your energy before we cross ahead. I can see you are tired."

He grabbed her tightly and said, "Don't leave me. You cannot leave me."

"I'm not leaving you. Just sit down and rest." But he would not let her go. She dropped her bundles and pushed his hands off her. He clung to her shirt, but he was too weak.

"Don't do this!" muttered the quivering man. "Don't do this."

She did. The wife laid both her hands on the sick husband's shoulders, and quickly, but with all her strength, pushed him down into a sitting position. The man was already unsteady on his feet, and he fell over backward. He crumpled limp to the ground, unable to hold himself up. "Don't leave me . . . I need you . . ." He tried to wave his arms, but they hung useless at his side. The man began sobbing.

She hurried away, taking her mother's hand. I could hear her sobs, but she never once looked back.

Father turned to me. "This mountain removes all human dignity. It's a grave for our souls."

* * *

There was only thick, tall grass ahead of us. I deliberately mirrored Father's steps, placing each footstep where his foot was last, wary of walking out of bounds by so much as an inch.

The air itself was wrong, carrying the stench of rotting flesh minced by the humid heat. Twisted forms lay across the ground. Entrails were strewn over the path and the woods. Mutilated, twisted corpses strained with open mouths, their final agony still imprinted on their faces. Children torn limb from limb. An entire graveyard of rot and decay.

The rotten, damp, burning smell invaded my nose, into my clothes. The flies, like spreading flames, nested on open eyes and mouths; wounds and detached body parts bubbled with millions of them, gorging on the rotting flesh. These were the remains of people desperate enough to run through landmines. We were left with only one choice: we had to walk through the dismembered bodies. We followed the dead to avoid dying.

I peered over the corpses and saw some were covered in gray refugee blankets with red stripes near the ends. I wondered if any of these were my family. I looked behind and did not see any signs of Choa and Sihong. I was too far down the trail to go back for them.

After no more than several hundred feet, the entire line stalled to the painful pace of a single step every fifteen minutes. Crumpled bodies were crammed in small heaps on each side of us, their sickening stench thick in the air. It threatened to suffocate me. My lungs strained. I could no longer get enough air into my chest. I folded the neck of my shirt over my mouth, forcing in thin, trembling breaths. It did little to block the evil smell. The muscles and nerves at the back of my throat screamed and my lungs burned, devouring what was left of me. The dead had their arms wrapped on my neck. My stomach twisted and my head spun, blurring my vision. I could not see the sky or ground, and I lost all sense of direction.

The line halted. There were so many refugees ahead of me, carrying their frail loved ones and pressing to seek the end no matter the costs. We crouched down for hours. A thick blanket of gritty black flies the size of bumblebees swarmed over what remained of the cadavers. There was only the sound of frantic buzzing. As I breathed in the air, the flies flocked, aggressive as hornets—they knocked into my cheeks, crawled into my ears, my mouth, and my nose, trying to follow the stench of death into my lungs.

When people rose to move again, all seemed to go quiet. "Don't even breathe," they whispered among themselves, or the sudden movements could trigger a bomb. We stayed stooped, crawling one inch at a time.

After seven hours, we reached open air for the first time in two weeks. A chill wind blew through the wisps of grass and made the hairs on the back of my neck stand up.

Chapter 21

Castaways

When I crawled out of the jungle, low-hung pale clouds blotted the skies, heavy and thick. We passed into an open field and I was elated to see several Vietnamese soldiers standing there. Everyone seemed to understand we were now on safe ground; people began to peel off in different directions instead of keeping in one line. It was a mad rush to get as far away from Preah Vihear as possible.

The Vietnamese soldiers shouted warnings and gesticulated, pointing directly behind me. We were the last batch of refugees, so the soldiers had come forward with discus-shaped mines cradled between their hands. They deposited them into the pits they had dug them from.

But Father cried out to them, "My daughter and son are still up there!" He began frantically asking the refugees around him if they had seen his children come out. They silently hurried past him.

Now Father and I were the last two there.

The Vietnamese soldiers hauled over a base plate and a bipod attached to a barrel. They assembled three mortars in a line and loaded their explosives. The mortars fired simultaneously with a hellish wail, climbed high in the air, and then landed and erupted on the mountain.

"What are they doing?" Father screamed. He turned to me. "Your sister and brother are getting killed!" The Vietnamese reloaded and fired twice more into the mountains. More violent explosions. Smoke rolled up from the tree banks. The soldiers retrieved their artillery equipment and ran away.

Black and white clouds gathered now, strangling any rays of light. The sky grew darker, its intensity stealing over the world like it was turning midnight. A lightning bolt silently arched over the tree line, and a moment later came a roll of rumblings and a tremendous clap of thunder. Just as it subsided, bright sparks flashed out of the mountainside, and for a moment I thought it too was lightning. But then came the distinct sound of gunfire.

I realized the Thai were shooting back, firing in our direction.

I immediately threw myself at Father and knocked him down to the ground and rolled. I tumbled over with my chin falling on the cold, rough earth. Right then, the sky cracked with a white splinter. Another bolt struck much closer, a brilliant red-and-orange strobe. The darkness that followed was total.

A giant dumping of rain fell and the heavens trembled and broke, no longer able to hold any more water. The rain crashed down so hard it pinched my skin, attacking my back, my shoulders, arms, and neck like a shower of hot bullets from the Thai soldiers.

The darkness and the rain enfolded me; I could not see a thing. I had no idea where Father was in this darkness. I blindly sought him, shouting over the din around us.

"Ba! Ba!!! Are you there? Do you hear me?!"

No answer.

But then lightning struck close by, and in the flash, I saw Father slumped on the ground. *Was he hit by a bullet?* I could not think straight. He wasn't moving. He just lay there, motionless, like another of the dead bodies.

Another bolt flashed and I saw him again, a shadow-like presence. I fumbled my way through the silt, and held him firm in my grasp, determined not to lose him in the middle of the jungle. I was never going to let him go, forsaken like the rest of the people on the mountain. Not after we'd come this far.

I looked to find my way out, but it was completely dark. I shouted my brother's name through the dark void.

"Tai!!! Where are you?!!!" I screamed more loudly than ever, perhaps in a need to assure myself of my own existence. Then I waited to be heard. Only thunderclaps responded. I cried out again.

This time my shouts yielded a faint reply, but there was no telling where it came from. Another thunderclap boomed.

"Tai! Wait for me! I'm coming!" I shouted through the rumble.

I scoured the dark emptiness for a path to get out. I could see nothing. Then my eyes turned just in time to see a lightning flash reveal deep footprints gouged into the mud, left by the refugees. Thousands of them.

I staggered with Father in my arms, slipping in the clumps of heavy, wet clay. He felt so weak, almost a deadweight. Streaks of lightning veined across the skies, but soon it was gone and the world was dark again. I just kept on walking, fearing we would blindly fall off the trail or that it would lead us to a minefield. It was far too dark to see bodies on the ground and take warning before one of us stepped on a mine.

I called out to my brother Tai again, telling him to wait for me. I could hear his voice getting closer. I continued to call him, all the way through the heavy rains and winds, waiting for him to respond louder. I followed the sound of his voice. Finally, I heard him right in front of me, even though I couldn't see his face in the darkness.

"Good, you are here!" Tai shouted. Blinding flashes lit up his face and the rest of the family behind him. The flash snapped off, and then they vanished like transient ghosts, swimming in my vision long after they were gone.

"How is Ba?!" Tai yelled.

"He can't move anymore," I hollered back. "We must find dry ground and rest for the night." A bolt streaked, and we could see each other's hollow faces again. Then utter darkness. Another two bolts pulsed, giving us two more quick glimpses of the terrain, in our search for a path to follow.

The rain plunged straight down. The water rose, calf-deep, and we splashed through it, searching for any dry spot. Another thunderbolt zigzagged out in the distant plains, revealing the crest of what looked like a long, stark burial mound. We beelined toward it, believing the spirits were generous and would see it was not our intention to plunder their resting place.

But when we neared it, we found it was not a grave, but an abandoned termite hill, old and hollow. We crammed together on the mound, pulling our knees tight to our chests and holding a plastic tarp over our heads. Rain spilled over the sides. We only had this one sheet for the seven of us. Beneath the plastic, I felt the close warmth, each of us breathing tensely. Thunderclaps shook the air. For the moment, on this splotch of land, it felt as if we were the only ones on the face of the earth.

We weren't though. We felt something pinching the bottoms of our feet. Vipers, foxes, eels, or wild animals might be searching for dry land, or giant creeping serpents crawling up the termite hill. At any other time, it would be enough to send people running off, screaming. In the midst of all this, we just stomped and kicked at whatever was below. The pinching ceased.

At last the rains tapered off; lightning forked over the distant hills and a deep rumble of thunder rolled across the prairie.

Images of Sihong and Choa snapped into my mind. *Where are they now? Did they get struck by the bombs?* I had to know if they were still alive, because I was certain the wounded, sick, and elderly would not make it through the night unless they found refuge. My heart went out to the hundreds, thousands of people swallowed up by the mountain.

While we sat with our sinking thoughts, a woman began screaming somewhere in the darkness. The screams penetrated to my bones. I could feel my skin shrinking while the terrible sound brought me back to the terrors on the mountain. I feared that the Khmer Rouge would follow her voice and find us, bringing certain death. I strained my eyes to look for the woman, somewhere out there lying on the ground and enduring an agonizing death.

The haunting screams lasted late into the night, then stopped. The rain continued to beat on the plastic drape, and now it was the only sound. I was unaccustomed to the silence.

* * *

A calm morning arrived with blue skies. Tall trees dripped raindrops, and patches of mist hovered over the ground until sunlight carried it away, revealing the surrounding woods and foothills. In the distance, I saw remnants of the refugee trail. It was the only path visible, and there was not a soul in sight.

"We have to hurry and catch up with everyone," I said to Tai.

But his youngest began crying with hunger. His wife pulled a packet of dried noodles from her pouch; she broke it and gave each of us a thumb-sized piece. Thirst drove us to drink rainwater from puddles.

Once we started walking, I began to warm up. We followed the path across the gray, wet fields into the jungle. Abruptly, Father asked, "Where are we?"

It was a good question. We had no idea what part of Cambodia we were in. Even with a map, I wouldn't have been able to pinpoint where we were. I was never taught geography in school, nor did I study about Preah Vihear. It was impossible to tell if we were moving east or west, or going around in circles.

"I don't know, Ba. All we have to go by is the refugee path."

"Can we take a rest?"

"No, Ba, we can't stop. We need to catch up. Otherwise we'll be lost out here."

We drew close to a river, and the sounds of flowing water cut through the woods. The river was swollen with the night's rainfall, and was now a powerful surge through the jungle.

And the path vanished at the riverside. We saw nothing to tell us how the others got across.

We paused there, and Tai made a fire while I scouted upstream along the muddy bank. The farther I traveled along the shore, the harder the waters appeared to be rushing. Along the muddy bank the sloppy foot tracks left by the refugees had been washed out by the swelling waters.

But when I swung back around downstream, I could see the river widening and gradually losing strength. I came to a heavy tree that had fallen above the rapids and landed with its leafless treetop perched on the opposite bank. I realized this was the bridge they must have used. The bark had been stripped away by the countless scratches and scuffs left behind by the refugees traveling over it.

I went back to get the family. Tai cautiously crossed over the beam first to drop his bundles and return for his wife and children. After them, I slung my sandals over my shoulder and gathered my nylon sack and the rest of my brother's possessions: his pots, cooking tools, mosquito net, and the scant handfuls of rice.

Navigating the nine-foot beam was made more difficult by the rushing waters below. It was dizzying. I reached the middle in three strides, and the unstable beam began to rattle beneath me. I took the next steps with jerky, wobbly movements, afraid of falling. One false slip and I'd tumble down and be swept away.

I regained my balance and steadily walked to the other side. After I put down the gear, I stood on the shore and called to Father. I went back for him, but he said, "Go. Go. You go first." He leaned on his walking stick, using the other hand to wave me off. I was afraid he had given up and that he was going to turn back. He had long since lost the will to go on.

Father stretched out the hand that held his cane and used it to weakly lift himself onto the trunk. He began to move in rigid, deliberate motions, stabbing the tree with his cane.

"Keep your eyes on the tree!" I shouted to him. "One step at a time." When Father reached the middle, the tree shook as it had done with me. He stopped to balance himself and tried once more, his every movement tentative, his whole body trembling. The beam narrowed near the end of the tree. Father labored to get close to me and lifted his quivering cane for me to grab. I held on to the end and steadied him forward.

After we brought Father down from the tree bridge, we gathered up our belongings to move forward. But Father stood unmoving beside the fallen treetop. I saw him staring hard at the sky, and I followed his gaze until I caught sight of a column of smoke rising from the mountain. The smoke trail was small in the distance, but Preah Vihear Mountain rose majestically before us.

The summit of Preah Vihear was bathed in the afterglow of the sun. High up, crowning the summit of the green mantle, ancient pointed roofs jutted out of the trees. I could see a rust-colored sandstone building. It looked like temple ruins tucked deep in the jungles. *Were there any monks up there?* I gazed at Preah Vihear and felt sad, as though I was parting with something. I was parting with my family. Even so, my spirit was crying out for me to leave this place, without knowing their fate. I reached out and held Father firmly by the shoulders.

"They are going to be fine," I told him. "Now we have to worry about ourselves."

Chapter 22

Ghost Mountain

Back up on the mountain, behind us, the rest of the family was still making their way down to the lowland. At the brow of a deep mountain glen, Sihong, Choa, and their families came upon a crowd gathered around the soothsayer we had encountered before. The crowd asked her where the other refugees were.

"We must go back as quickly as possible," she told them. "Back to the mountain where we can be rescued. Soon someone will come and save us there."

"Where is the passage the rest have taken?" a man in the front of the crowd interrupted. "I cannot believe that all the thousands of people just disappeared. How can we get to their destination?"

"We must go back!" the soothsayer cried. "If you go forward, you will put yourself in danger's way."

"What do you mean?" someone else asked. "Where have they gone?

What will we do here in the middle of nowhere? We can't stay here much longer."

"We were told we could go back to Cambodia!" others bawled. "Why mustn't we go with the others?"

"Yes! Tell us where they are!" another voice shouted from the throng. "We need to know the fate of our families at least!"

"They are down there." She pointed off to an area in the distance. What looked like heaps of human shapes—heads and limbs—lay sunken in the deep grass.

"Do not go," she warned. "These people were misled. The spirits have told me many people perished on the crossover. Even if they do make it through, they will have more hardships in Cambodia. It won't be the end of their woes and bitterness. It is better if you stay here."

It had only been two hours since Sihong and Choa had become separated from Tai, Father, and me. They began to retreat back the way they came. Of the tens of thousands of refugees who were originally sent to Preah Vihear, nearly a thousand of them remained behind. The refugees still listened to the soothsayer, in spite of her past mistakes.

However, not long afterward, three boys announced to the other refugees that they were planning on escaping to an American embassy. They promised if they made it out, they would get help from the United Nations and get the rest of them out. Money and supplies were pooled for the boys. Surviving on the few rations they had left and some wild fruits growing on trees, the other refugees stayed put.

A few days later, a refugee brought news of the boys. One of the boys had detonated a landmine not far away. The refugee found the boy screaming for help before he died. There was no sign of the two others.

On the sixteenth day on Preah Vihear, a group of refugees watched the soothsayer invoke the spirits of the forests and fall into a trance.

Possessed by the spirit, her voice changed into an inhuman utterance. The spirit spoke through her in hoarse and garbled words that no one could comprehend. The people asked her questions and the message became clear:

"Tomorrow. Thursday at eleven o'clock, you must all go to the top of the mountain. Walk to the road where the Thai soldiers are. There you must ask them to accept you into the refugee camp. The leader now has compassion for you all and will take you back."

The woman came out of the trance. She was exhausted and didn't recollect a thing she had said during her fugue state. The others, unable to keep her prediction to themselves, quickly spread the story around.

But it was an omen, not a fact.

It was a hope, not reality.

In one great line, a throbbing aisle of refugees marched back up the cleared path to the soldiers' outpost at the summit. When they arrived at the top of the ridge, they were met by two Thai soldiers. The soldiers signaled them to stay in place while they called in their supervisor via walkie-talkie. Having caught up with the people at the front of the line, our family waited with the soldiers while other refugees pressed around.

Fifteen minutes passed, then a pair of army trucks arrived and parked on the paved road. Soldiers sprung out with a clatter of boots and walked toward the refugees. They opened fire, shooting at the feet of the stunned crowd. Lumps of mud flew up and slapped their faces; pebbles blinded some of them. The people at the front of the firing line tried to retreat backward, but their legs were cut out from under them by the bullets and they fell shrieking to the ground, mowed down by the gunfire.

People screamed, pushed back, and tried to run, but there wasn't even enough room to turn their bodies around. Sihong, shielded by the crowd, pushed her kids behind her, trying to shelter them with her body.

"Run!" Sihong screamed to her children. The people stampeded downhill, frantically searching for an escape route. The soldiers pursued them, firing into the crowd, shot after shot.

Amid the cover of the throbbing masses, Sihong and her children escaped the bullets. They were able get away from the intense staccato gunfire and back to their campsite safely.

* * *

A week had passed since our group had escaped from the mountain. The refugees who remained understood there was nothing left for them. No one was going to get them out. Extensive searching and scavenging in the forests yielded only bamboo shoots, wild potatoes, edible yucca roots, and wild insects. No amount of scouring streams brought any rewards. Desperate, some men made a daring attempt to sneak uphill on their own and find someone to trade with far from where the soldiers were stationed. After a day, they returned with a handful of dried foodstuffs for their families—proof of the existence of a village.

More refugees made attempts to find the village. They each returned with the same promising results, having traded for rice and eggs.

Suspicion grew among the Thai soldiers. Two armed men tramped down to the refugees and harassed them with questions. "Did you go to the market?"

They shook their heads no. The soldiers moved to the group where Sihong and Choa were talking with some friends. One soldier, who smelled of whiskey, asked the same question again. "Did you go to the market?" He came in close and blew a cloud of cigarette smoke at the circle of people.

Choa remembered the soldier from a week prior, when the man came down and asked the refugees if they wanted any rice, saying, "Give me money and I will go to the market and buy it for you."

Choa answered, "No, we did not go to the market, but you promised us last week that you would buy rice for us if we gave you money. We gave you the money, where is our rice?" The question angered the soldier. He drew his cigarette toward his mouth, and missed. It dropped to the ground.

A man next to Choa crawled over to pick up the cigarette. He politely ducked his head forward and raised the cigarette in his palms for the soldier. The Thai soldier kicked the man, knocking him off his feet, then drew his weapon and fired at the man's chest. The man instantly fell back, dead.

Choa looked up and saw the soldier standing at the rim of the circle, pointing the gun at him. The soldier kicked Choa in the chest, pitching him backward. Choa rolled in the weeds and came up again, and at that moment dashed off. The drunk soldier pursued him, but was too unsteady to line up a shot.

"Bury the body!" the other soldier ordered Haileng, Sihong's son. Then he went to find his drunken comrade.

The dead man lay in a blossoming pool of blood, with a pin-sized entry wound in his chest and a fist-sized hole in his back. Haileng and Sihong dragged the dead man by his ankles and left the body hidden in a heap of leaves.

Choa, having fled the soldiers, returned to his wife and daughters, where he leaped into a hammock slung between two trees and pulled the covers tight over his head. Choa heard brisk footsteps closing in on him, and the sounds of his wife and children crying. The muzzle of the rifle slid beneath the hammock cover, pointed at his chest.

"Get out!" the soldier shouted.

Choa's quivering fingers pulled back the hammock cover and he slid out, then bent on his knees and held his hands in a respectful sampeah, begging for pardon from the soldier who had found him. It was a wasted effort.

The drunken soldier kicked him in the stomach and he fell to the ground in pain. Gasping on all fours, Choa touched his forehead to the ground at the drunken soldier's feet, but the vicious kicks continued. Then he raised his rifle and took aim at Choa.

Choa's wife rushed to the other soldier and knelt, clutching at his pants and pleading: "Please, honorable sir. Can you do something? He will kill my husband! Please be merciful!"

The soldier holding his gun on Choa pulled on the trigger. *Bang!*

The shot went off in the air over Choa's head.

Choa opened his eyes and saw the soldier's gun barrel raised, pointing upward. His partner stood next to him. He had used his index finger to push the barrel skyward and ruin the shot.

At the last moment the sober soldier had saved Choa from the drunk. He dragged the drunken man away. The two argued until the drunk soldier broke out of his comrade's grip and trotted with difficulty downhill toward more of the refugees. He was now on a merciless rampage. Several more shots reported, precisely aimed at other refugees.

* * *

Over the following days, many of the refugees stopped making village trips. There was no more source of food; the land had been plucked of every nourishment. They starved, bellies pained with hunger. Children cried, but there was nothing to be done for them.

Eventually a band of refugees decided to sneak over to that nearby village again. Sihong's sons, Sen and Haileng, joined them from behind.

They traversed up the slope and made it toward a crag of rugged rocks when they saw five figures fleeing downhill, running toward them.

"Go back! It is too dangerous to attempt to cross! We just ran into the Thai soldiers near the road! They captured two of our men already!"

Everyone headed back to camp. On the next day, the same refugees made another attempt, using a different dangerous passage near the steep mountain cliffside. Before they departed, a widowed mother asked Haileng and Sen, "Would you watch over my son?"

She told her ten-year-old boy, "Follow the other people. Try to get some food for your brother and sister." She sent him off with three hundred Thai baht.

This time it was a group of twelve refugees marching from the jungle toward the edge of the cliffs. Clambering out on the hilly bank, they slowed their pace as they encountered tall grass. It reached to the cliff's edge, where steep ridges dropped far below. As they treaded away from the sheer cliffside, two hidden Thai soldiers suddenly lunged up out of the grasses and ordered the refugees to stop.

When one soldier saw the three hundred baht in the boy's hands, he made an offer: their last package of dry noodles in exchange for all the boy's money. The boy refused.

"Give me that!" The Thai soldier snatched the money out of his hands. The boy cried out in protest, but another refugee squeezed his shoulder and told the boy to take the box of noodles. It was no use trying to get his money back. They had to leave now.

The refugees turned to go, except for the boy. He cried, crowding and pestering the Thai soldier for his money, demanding for its return in pleading screams.

Haileng never saw the soldier extend his leg and trip the boy at the edge of the cliff. He turned just in time to see the boy fall.

It was an eighty-foot drop.

* * *

When the defeated expedition returned to the others, they encountered a black-clad Khmer Rouge soldier wearing a red scarf, asking questions of the refugees. Few dared to answer. They were paralyzed by fear.

"How many people are down there?" he demanded. "I need to know how many people and families are here. Someone will have to take down everyone's name."

Some of the people refused to give their names, some pretended not to understand Khmer, and others used an alias, afraid they would get conscripted into the Khmer army. It was strange that they did not take their frustrations out on this group by opening fire like the Thai soldiers. After no cooperation, they gave up and disappeared up the mountain.

* * *

Three days later, Sihong found a small young banana tree bearing dwarfish green shoots. It was like striking gold. She took it apart and readied some water to boil and soften the firm, gluey flesh inside. As Sihong sliced the bananas ever so thinly, a Cambodian man appeared with a photographer. The photographer snapped pictures of Sihong cutting the banana.

Sihong stared. She recognized the man, with his Cambodian features of round brown eyes and a wide nose. But the clothes were different. This, she realized, was the Khmer Rouge soldier from days prior, yet at this moment he was wearing a dress shirt, like a diplomat's, with sleeves rolled up to his elbows.

"Next Thursday there is going to be food to help you guys," the Cambodian man said in Khmer. "You will have to retrieve it at the top of the mountain. Someone will give it to you." The photographer was visibly upset by what he was seeing here, and after he snapped enough pictures, they took off.

When Thursday came, the refugees trekked up the mountain and found many trucks arriving. Most of the Thai soldiers had evacuated the area, leaving a few to distribute stockpiles of rice and turnips. The refugees were allowed to take as much as they could carry back. They were left with a message: Within four to five days, someone would return to take them back to safety for good. The refugees cheered, elated. Though everyone was unsure who exactly had sent the man originally dressed in black to help. Choa was convinced it was the two boys, proving they had made it successfully to an American embassy.

* * *

The appointed day for departure arrived with falling rain. It was eleven in the morning on July 12, 1979, when the buses came and parked to wait, while rain clunked on the metal roofs. The refugees quickly vacated their campsite, leaving their garments, soup bowls, and tiny tin saucepans. As Haileng plodded up the jungle trail for the last time, he peered at the slope that met the dirt road above. Someone's daughter was crying at the summit for her father and brother.

"Ba! Brother Sear! Where are you?! The buses are here to pick us up now!"

She rushed down the mountain to search for them one last time, screaming their names. "Ba! Ba! Brother Sear!"

Soon the daughter came running up again, exclaiming to the upward-climbing refugees, "My father and brother are alive! I found them. Someone come help me." She jumped up and down, pointing downhill.

Some members of the group dropped their loads and followed the girl darting away down the trail. Her father and brother had set off a landmine. Although wounded and in convulsions, the father and son crawled along the ground and met the others, where the men could retrieve them. Six men pulled the two out, injured beyond recognition. Their eyes were swollen shut, their purple faces lacerated by gashes from jagged shrapnel tearing into their flesh. After they were hauled up from the jungle, someone brought a small car forward and they were rushed to the nearest hospital.

The refugees never saw the two injured men again.

Aboard the bus, Haileng gazed blankly out the window, staring beyond the spatter of droplets. The downpour was steady and chilled the air, making the jungle seem dark and cold.

As they were leaving, Haileng spotted a white Western man handing out money to each of the buses' drivers. Haileng wondered if that was the man who helped save them. So much of the cruelty and kindness they had encountered came from sources unseen to them, and for reasons that would remain unknown for a long time.

* * *

The drive to Mae Surin Refugee Camp took all day. When they arrived, the bus lined up behind a series of other rumbling buses, each spitting black exhaust fumes, waiting for the gate to open. A civilian stood at the side, speaking with the refugees in the bus.

It was Gengdi! The unexpectedness of fate was overwhelming.

Sihong opened the window and called out to him. He hurried over to her and asked if any of them had seen Ming's sisters and brother. Sihong told him she hadn't seen them since they were dumped on the mountain. Gengdi thanked her and graciously gave her five hundred baht, and then left to speak with the other buses.

The gate lifted.

They had been on Preah Vihear Mountain for twenty-nine days. It would only be two weeks before they would arrive at their next destination. The third foreign country:

America.

Chapter 23

A Sudden Illness

Tall unyielding sralao and chrey trees stretched solemnly upward, the tops taking root in the bright blue skies. Escaping death has a way of making me see things differently. A pair of cicadas slowly called out to each other, their whereabouts unclear. After drifting on the mud path for several hundred yards, we came upon an intersecting road. It was cut so straight through the red ochre dirt, it appeared to have been plowed by a tractor.

The cleared surface eased our burden by allowing us to move unencumbered by trees, thick brush, and mud. We trekked for about two miles, then encountered a pack of refugees surrounding a small unit of Vietnamese soldiers, who were handing out scoops of raw barley. I found my sister Sihun at the end of the waiting line, talking to another person. When she saw us, she broke into a gleeful smile and so did I. We danced with joy, crying in each other's arms.

"Where are Sihong and Choa?" she asked.

"We have not seen them since we left the mountain," Father answered. "They are stuck on Preah Vihear."

"We won't be able to continue, ourselves," Sihun stated. "Our food supply is low and the soldiers will soon run out of grain. We have to find somewhere we can trade for supplies. I heard people say there is a village three hours east of here."

Wensun and I agreed to go, while the rest of the family remained behind. Since we had to have something of value to barter, Sihong told Wensun to take her only sarong and a couple of items of their girls' clothing. Father told me to take his extra shirt and pants to exchange. They were meager goods and possibly of no value in exchange. So Father added, "Take your mother's diamond ring, in case they don't want any clothes." I had carefully kept it from the hands of thieves, but now it appeared to be time to let it go.

Before we left, Wensun took the little statue of Buddha he had somehow kept in his possession by taking it everywhere he went and never letting it out of his sight. Now he placed it on the ground and then lit several bamboo sticks.

He prayed powerfully, shaking the incense in the air and muttering chants. Whatever Wensun desired to do, he always first asked for Buddha's blessings and poured his soul into his prayers. He kept it up until the candles burned away and he was convinced he had been granted permission. Then he wrapped the statue in a blue blanket and carried it with him.

We started east for an outcrop of woods, heading for the sun beyond the trees, but without a clue where the village was located. There were very few tracks to follow, and the sparse woodland had enough long, skinny trees to conceal our location. I grew nervous, unsure if we were headed in the right direction.

Shortly, three young men came our way with sacks of rice slung over their shoulders. One carried a live rooster by the feet. They told us, "Follow east and you will get to the rice field. There you will find a dirt path. Follow it, and it will bring you to the village."

Before departing, they cautioned us that the villagers did not want jewelry or gold. Those possessions meant little to their survival out in the wilderness. All they wanted was garments and medicine. It was good news; they might want our items of clothing and we would not have to part with the ring.

After a couple of hours of walking, we saw an open field through the edge of the forest. Somewhere over that scrubby stretch of land, I spotted a thatched hut. A huge weight was lifted from my shoulders.

A dog lounged near the hut entrance, staring at us. It was scrawny with a smooth, short coat. Then it snapped to its feet, barking. The owner came out and yelled at the dog to be quiet.

"What do you want?" he called out.

"I want to exchange for rice and a chicken."

"Chicken was not born yet," he replied.

Wensun took out his sarong, which was new and never worn, and handed it to the man. The man held it for a moment and then passed it to his wife. Without hesitation she unfolded it and wrapped it around her waist, eyes beaming. This was the opening Wensun needed.

"I want a sack of rice and a dog for that sarong."

"You can have two sacks of rice, but no dog."

But Wensun held his ground. "No, I want the dog in exchange for the sarong."

The owner looked at his wife. Fortunately for us, she was already in love with the sarong. "I want it," she told her husband. They conversed back and forth in Khmer, blending in Kuy forms of speech. Finally, he agreed to exchange the rice and dog for the sarong.

I was also able to barter Father's clothes for half a sack of rice. It turned out to be a profitable trip.

The owner approached the dog with a rope in hand, but the dog growled, trembling. The man tied the rope around the dog's neck and yanked on the leash, trying to make the canine sit.

The dog clearly feared its owner, but still did not want to go into the unknown. It dug its feet into the dirt, pulling backward against the rope.

Wensun spoke to the dog in a soothing tone of voice, and soon won over the animal enough that the dog willingly followed him. We walked away, with Wensun balancing the sack of rice on his shoulders and pulling the dog behind him.

As Wensun walked the dog across the field, his face slowly changed. "I'm tired," he admitted. "I don't feel good right now."

I had not noticed he was feeling ill, but now I could see it. He was sweating, his forehead was shining wet, and his eyes were dry and dull.

"The dog is so spooked, it's going to slow you down," I told him. "We're not going to make it back before the daylight is gone."

To make the load easier, we hog-tied the dog with the rest of the leash. Four legs all together. Wensun found a bamboo stick and balanced the sack of rice on one side and the dog on the other, and lifted it on his shoulder. As he walked, the bound dog helplessly wiggled, shaking at the end of the bamboo pole.

* * *

It took four hours for us to get back. Wensun loosened the knots on the dog and tied it to a tree. The younger children ran to the dog and began petting it. Exhausted, Wensun dragged himself back to his family, pulled out his straw mat, and collapsed into sleep.

The older children surrounded him and asked, "Are we going to kill the dog to eat?" Wensun never gave an answer and just lay there, eyes closed.

* * *

The next morning the dog was missing. The rope was found lying on the ground, the ends chewed off. Sihun was upset. "How could you let that dog get away? You traded the best item for nothing."

At first Wensun showed regret for not killing the dog the day before. But then he retreated. "Maybe it's a good thing that my curse is spared."

I understood what he meant. Before the Communists, it had long been a ritual among Buddhists to liberate animals who were destined to be killed. Releasing the animals was an act of compassion. And according to Buddhist tradition, doing so would purge Wensun of his sins.

We decided maybe the dog's escape was for the best: Give the little beast a chance to lessen its own suffering in a state of freedom. In that sense, the escape was good for both of them.

"Get up. Get up," Sihun told him. "We must get going."

Now that we were restocked with rice, everyone was ready to leave. But Wensun had fallen into a fever. He lay on his mat, unresponsive. She pushed him again.

"It's time to go, Wensun. The children are waiting."

At that, he took a shuddering breath and willed himself to his feet, eyelids drooping. He swayed over to his family's rucksacks and picked them up.

* * *

Once the journey resumed on that red dirt road, Wensun groaned that he was burning up and took off his shirt. The weather was warm, but not hot enough to give us any discomfort. But for Wensun the sun seemed cruel, merciless. We could see the heat was too intense for him. He was quickly covered in a sheen of sweat and he walked tiredly behind us.

Sometime around midday, we reached a point where a heavy rain-water stream ran alongside the road. Wensun dropped his rucksacks and broke for the ravine. He charged like a thirsty water buffalo. He plunged into the river, up to his neck at first, and then submerged his whole head before bouncing back up, shaking water off his face with a grateful grin.

"Oh, it's so good. It feels so good," he kept saying.

Sihun tried calling her husband out. "What are you doing?" she scolded from her position on dry land. "You are crazy!"

"If you don't want to come in, you go ahead. I will stay here. But you should come in! It feels so good."

"You're crazy. We don't have time for that." An angry tension was growing in Sihun's voice. But he ignored her and continued to wallow in the water.

That did it. "Get out!" she insisted. "We have to go."

I did not doubt her intentions. She rightfully feared falling behind the others. At least they were a collection of people she knew, people she could perhaps trust.

But as soon as Wensun made the effort to pick himself up and stand straight, he wobbled and fell into a trance-like state. He seemed to be losing his grip on reality. He looked in her direction, but with a distant gaze he seemed to be staring at something somewhere else.

"We're going to be left behind," my sister said again. "We have to get going."

"Where are we going?" Wensun asked slowly.

"We have to follow everyone back to Cambodia."

Wensun picked up his bundles and walked with us for half a mile, striding on toward nothing. His body seemed to move on its own. He trudged on in silence for a time, then he shuddered in his tracks, dropping his things. He stood stock still and looked at us with a wild gaze for just a moment. Then his expression dissolved into impassive features and absent eyes. It was blank and unreadable.

"Why are you stopping?" Sihun asked him.

Wensun remained silent. His unblinking eyes were dark coals, pits of cold. And yet, when my sister touched his forehead, she declared, "He is burning."

He had a crazy look in his eyes, one of terrible confusion. Sihun realized he was no longer capable of carrying the bundles, so she had her oldest son, Heng, aged seven, carry one of the large bags. It contained the family's clothes and plastic tent. Heng cried as he lifted the large, heavy sack over his emaciated frame. Wensun stared blankly at his crying child, losing sense of himself, his wife, and his children. I took it upon myself to help my sister and picked up one of the bags containing their bed mats.

Sihun had to pick up the last bundles. She placed her four-year-old, Guihui, on the ground, despite his efforts to stay in his mother's arms, and then threw the rest of their items over her shoulders—the rice, the water bucket, and the cooking pans. She extended her arm and pushed against Wensun's back. "Keep moving."

"I don't want to go," Wensun objected. "I want to go home."

"We have no home!" Tears came to Sihun's eyes.

Wensun raised his finger, pointing down the road. "Our home is there . . . I want to go back home . . ." At a shadowy distance, a golden mist hung over Preah Vihear Mountain, smothering the trees, hills, and horizon. It was many days' walk away.

"That is the mountain the Thai dumped us on." Her voice stammered to keep steady. "Do you remember? It's not our home. Our home is back on this road, heading toward Cambodia."

"I don't want to go. I don't want to go. I don't want to go there. I am frightened. I am frightened." He kept repeating himself like a child. His five children began crying, watching their father degenerating before them. He scanned his children's faces, still struggling to remember who they were.

"It's okay," Sihun said. "Your children need you."

Once Wensun heard those words, the spell seemed to ease its hold on him.

"My children need me—" He bolted upright and attempted to walk away with us, but after only a few wobbly steps, he stopped, panting.

"I can't see the children!" he cried out. "I can't see the children! All I see is black. The blackness is there. I'm scared! I don't want to go forward. It's dark there—"

Then he began repeating in Khmer, "ងងឹតសូន្យសុង. ងងឹតសូន្យសុង. ងងឹតសូន្យសុង."—"It's the place of zero. It's the place of zero. It's the place of zero."

With bundles in one arm, Sihun put her hand on Wensun's back, piloting him forward. His head drooped and wobbled, and his body gave the impression of a lifeless puppet.

"Can we find a place to stay tonight?" Sihun asked. "Wensun is in no shape to continue."

The group kept moving. The terrible truth was, it made no difference if one of us fell behind; the others ahead of us were in a desperate bid for survival themselves.

We pushed on for another two miles down the road.

We were all feeling desperate for rest when we encountered a wooden bungalow, perched on high stilts.

Sihun went to the front and called inside. "My husband is very ill. Can we stay under the bungalow?"

"No," the owner yelled out. "You cannot stay here."

"Please," my sister pleaded. "I have five small children. You see my husband cannot walk. I can't leave him behind. Just for one night? I beg of you."

"No." The reply was blunt. "You have to leave."

"Sihun . . ." Wensun muttered under his breath. He was resting on her shoulder for support, languishing in and out of consciousness.

"Offer . . . my statue . . . to let . . . us . . . stay." His words came out in short, tortured gasps. I don't think he knew what he was saying. He never let that statue out of his sight. Wensun loved the statue so much that he would give up his life for it.

Sihun quickly reached into the bundles Heng was carrying and pulled out the brass statue. The owner saw the statue and exclaimed, "Oh my god! Oh my god! You put god into that bag with your dirty clothes! Oh my god! That's why he's sick. Give me the statue. All right! You can stay!"

He took the statue right away and immediately shined it with a cloth. "I will pray to god to forgive you. And that you will get better." The man then took it inside the hut and put it on a shelf. He kneeled down and worshipped it.

That night we rested on the side of the house under the overhanging straw canopy of the roof. We could hear a babbling stream behind the property, and Sihun retrieved water and sponged Wensun's hot skin with a cloth. Wensun's mouth hung open in wordless moans. She rinsed the cloth in the bowl and again wet Wensun's forehead. Throughout the night he moaned, his breathing harsh and uneven.

The next day, he had a turn for the worse.

A bleak, grating wheeze leaked from his open mouth, his lungs seemingly punctured. Whenever his name was called, he lay still a long while before opening an eyelid with a fixed stare at the ceiling. Wensun's long face remained unchanged; he never looked at us. His glazed eyes were vacant. Everything human had spilled from them.

* * *

On the dirt road, a Kuy man strolled up to us pulling a black dog. He spoke of desiring to exchange it. Sihun stepped up to him and said, "I don't have anything more to exchange. All I have is a lighter. Would you take this lighter?"

She extracted the lighter out of her pocket and pressed the plunger. The short, trembling flame popped up and the man gazed into it, mesmerized. We could tell he rarely encountered gadgets like these. He agreed to exchange the black dog for the lighter.

My sister brought the mangy dog over to me. "Wensun was afraid to kill the first dog," she said. "He is quite a dog lover. Back in the old days he used to raise them as a hobby. I don't think he had the heart to kill that dog. But we need food on the road. Would you take care of this for me?"

I asked Tai to come with me and dragged the dog by its leash down the inclined slope behind the hut. The dog obediently followed without a struggle, its red tongue lolling out. This dog was much larger than the one that escaped. This might be difficult. Beyond a small trail in the foliage, we reached the wide and brawling creek.

On the rocky shore, the dog began drinking water from the creek. We cut a heavy forked branch and stripped it bare of all its leaves. I was afraid to hit the dog, so we tied it and carried it to the deepest part of the creek to the point where the water was above my knees. I hooked its neck with the forked branch and dunked its head into the water. When I held it, air bubbles rose to the surface, breaths expelling from its lungs. The whole stick was shaking. Not because of the dog, but because of me. After that the bubbles ceased to trickle upward.

All of a sudden, the dog flew out of the water, its teeth bared, snarling, chomping jaws wide open. With the sudden movement, I flinched backward, then out of panic, I hit the dog twice on its head, hard, and it rolled back into the water. I kept hitting it not because I wanted it dead, but because I was afraid the dog would attack me.

The dog charged me again—a flash of black with a red ribbon of blood streaking from its head. It jumped on me, its pale gray eyes glassy with rage, barking and growling. My fear turned into uncontrollable anger, a powerful emotion that had been pent up inside me all these years. It was the same exact fear that I had of the Khmer Rouge. The distinctions were blurred: the same murderous set of eyes, the crooked teeth, the black uniform coat, the blood-thirst for red, the violent hatred for me. All of a sudden, my blood boiled, curdling through my veins, feeling thick and heavy. I lifted both arms into the air, high above my head, and used all my strength to smash the back of its skull. It crumpled like a thin wet rag. I smashed its temple. I smashed its neck. I struck at it again. A hard, popping fleshy sound. And again. The dog. The Khmer Rouge. The dog again.

The dog flopped, then reared up again, wavering to get in a position to breathe. Its resistance stirred my anger even more. Right then, I was not going to have remorse. Water splashed in all directions. I kept hitting the dog or the water. I couldn't tell. I couldn't stop. This dog had inflicted so much pain on us. I yearned to hurt where it had hurt the most. It was like the Khmer Rouge. Holding us back. Threatening us from living on.

I hit until there was no more pain, no more strength to hurt, until my fingers wearied, my arms grew fatigued. I stopped. I discovered my chest was furiously heaving. I was gasping for breaths. Tai came closer and he clutched the limp dog by its neck. The dog's mouth turned up, exposing threads of blood running on its teeth.

Cold air fell on my shoulders and radiated through my body. Behind the trees, someone was running down the slope. It was our niece, Bai. She was soon close enough to call out her news. "My father is dead," she announced without emotion.

We were so numb, so devoid of feelings and emotions, we never turned to her. No light could penetrate our darkened condition. I stared at the dog, hanging with its mouth agape. It must have been a coincidence, that Wensun and this dog died together.

Emptiness filled my heart. Perhaps this was for the better. Now he was in peace.

When I went to see him, there was already a Buddhist villager chanting in front of his body, which lay on a low bench. The chanting sounded melancholy and lonely as we wrapped him in a straw mat and tied both ends, sealing in both his head and feet. It was a casket, of sorts. There was nothing else to put between the body and the earth. Wensun's body was still warm when we put it in the ground and covered it by pushing the cold, crumbling dirt into the grave.

My sister showed little emotion. She had run out of tears. We had cried until we could cry no more. It was meaningless to shed tears, to mourn, to offer rage. What change would it bring?

The dead never feel the pain of separation. What good would it be to keep him? What wounds would it heal? He was parting with nothing. Living brought not a thing for him. There was little difference between life and death.

Except . . . Here. We were in the middle of the road between the two fates: neither living nor dying. It was a place that would be never-ending.

Chapter 24

Tarnished Gold

The land was vast and inexhaustible. After long days of ill-walking, we spent our nights out under the stars watching the pallid crescent moon appear from the twilight. It waxed into a new shining moon, round and smooth. More days passed, and the moon wasted away. A month went by. Then two.

Dawn broke on the eastern horizon. The journey resumed, another hot and empty day. I asked Father to travel onward along the dirt road while I helped my brother take down the tents. We could easily catch up with him later. He did not reply, but moved away in a slow walk, grimly fighting his exhaustion.

After an hour of packing, we went in search of him. Half a mile away, we spotted him seated against a tree trunk at the side of the road. He had fallen into a high fever.

"Find help!" I told Tai. "Ask anybody if they know how to get his fever down, or if they have medicine to exchange."

I sat with Father by the roadside and asked the same questions of all the hard faces that passed. Most people gave us a sorrowful shake of the head. Where would I find help? I had no idea.

Tai found a woman resting with her mother along the road who told him, "I was a nurse. I have an antidote to help him. It's a shot. But it will be a quarter ounce of gold for the shot."

"Are you sure the shot will help him?" Tai questioned her.

"Certainly. All it will take is one shot to bring down his fever." She reached into her bag and pulled out a dirty syringe with a barrel that was opaquely yellow and green. The dingy lines and numbers were fading. The needle, two inches of steel, was partly rusted at the end.

Tai led the woman to Father. The woman plunged the syringe into a vial and drew a milky substance into the syringe. She tried several times to jam it into Father. The dull needle would not go in easily. He winced and grimaced in pain. Finally, she stretched his arm straight, wiggled the needle in, and quickly depressed the plunger. After the shot, Tai promptly paid the woman and she departed on the road again.

By Father's side, I watched his face turn suddenly bloodless, sweat building on his forehead. His chest rose and fell, hard asthmatic rasping wheezed from his lungs. "I can't breathe," he said.

My brother and I looked at each other. "What did she give him?"

Storm clouds were gathering. As we examined Father, the shadows deepened on his face from clouds capping the whole sky. We heard thunderclaps far away. A flash storm was approaching, fast. The sky was turning to lead.

"Get up, get up," we told Father. Even when he tried to speak, his mouth did not cooperate. He was seemingly paralyzed. We lifted him up by his armpits and hoisted his arms over our shoulders and headed up the road, where a squat thatched roof jutted alone above the thin slice of the horizon.

When we reached the hut, a Cambodian lady was in the doorway. Tai said, "My father is very sick and the rain is coming. Would you give us shelter from the storm? We need a place to stay for the night."

"No, I can't. I have to ask my husband first," she replied. "Wait until my husband comes back from working in the rice fields."

"Please," my brother pleaded. "He can't walk. We have no place to go. Let us stay."

Tai's wife begged the woman with an offering of her white gown. "Just let us stay for one night."

She took mercy on us and accepted the gown, so we carried Father beneath the house, just in time. The storm unleashed and sheets of water poured down.

We settled in, holding Father up because he could no longer sit upright. In the deluge outside, the hoarse crashing rain swept across the road. Then a man traveled up, whipping an ox. He screamed through the thrashing rain. "Faster! Faster!" The whip cracked the back of the ox, over and over. He pulled the ox toward the house and saw us huddled underneath.

"What are you people doing under my house?" he yelled.

The wife ran down the stairs. "They need a place to stay for a night. Please let them stay."

"No! Get out of my house. You people don't belong here. Get out!" He took the ox and walked it to a shed that sat a short distance behind and tied the animal to a post inside. He returned with a long, threatening knife in his hand.

"Get out of my house!! Get out now!"

"Please . . . until the rain stops," Tai said. "My father is very sick."

"No!" He raised his knife in the air. "Get out now before I kill all of you!" The frightened children screamed and cried. I saw his face, hatred burning in his eyes. We picked up Father and left the under-house. It poured—stinging curtains of rain pelting sideways against us.

We headed to the ox shed, believing he would let us stay there since it was not his house. We fought the descending torrents, carrying Father to the shed, and sat him down against a post just as his knees gave way. He gave a faint groan and a shiver ran through his body. Like all of us, he was soaked. He breathed in hard gasps.

The man walked to the shed. "I told you to get out of my property. You're not allowed to stay with my cow."

The wife hurried through the pouring rain into the shed to defend us. "The man is very sick; the children are small. They need a place to stay out of the rain for just the night."

"I don't care," he said. "Not on my property." The man pointed out-side. Tai and I picked up Father, and we moved again out into the rain.

"Where are we going?" I asked my brother.

"I don't know," he said in angry frustration.

Up the road not far from the ox shed, we spotted a wooden pigpen. Rotten hay lay scattered inside, stained with dark patches of manure and filth. The seven pigs inside it were coated in grime.

"We are all going to stay here," Tai said.

"How? It's filthy. Besides, he might come after us again," I replied.

Tai screamed in frustration, "Where are we supposed to go?! There is no place to go. It's raining. It's dark! You tell *me* where we should go!"

Tai forcefully pulled Father into the pigpen and lifted him inside, stepping over the wooden side-rails. The air smelled of watery dung. The pigs shrieked, squirming into one corner to avoid the invaders.

We strung a hammock to the pillars holding up the roof and gently laid Father in it. His burning fever had abated, but his breathing was labored and thick, and he shivered uncontrollably. A cold sweat ran down his forehead. Tai gave me a dry shirt and I wiped his cheeks and brow.

"Ba. Are you okay?" I asked.

His eyes clouded over. "Why does this happen to us? . . . I've helped a lot of people when they came to me in need. I always had the heart to hide the Vietnamese from the Lon Nol government when their lives were in danger. I gave them money and arranged for their safety into Vietnam. I always did good things for others. Everyone. Always what I could. But when we're in dire need, nobody helps us. They turn away. There is no mercy for us."

He then stared blankly into the sky, silent and expressionless. The rain had slowly begun to taper off, and a hint of light showed through the overcast.

"Why . . . Why have the Heavens turned their backs on us?"

I held both his hands firmly with mine. There was nothing I could say to comfort him. I felt the same way. All we had wanted was to stay underneath the house.

Everywhere we went it was the same. We were pushed away from their homes. Uprooted from their lands. Banished from their country. Erased from their presence.

We were lucky to have a pigpen for shelter.

Rainwater leaked in through gaping holes in the roof. The rest of the family occupied a dry corner of the pen away from the pigs, who were now at ease in their own corner. The only room left for me to sit was on the wet ground, propped against the side railings.

A host of black flies and mosquitos descended on me, biting my face and legs. I made weak attempts to slap at them, only to agitate them into attacking me even more.

Chapter 25

The Long Wanderer

I woke early the next morning, broken. My hair was soaked, my body felt feverish.

With rigid motions, I tried to get Father up before dawn appeared, afraid the man would come after us again. However, Father was too weak and immobile, so we took the hammock down and tied the ends to a bamboo stick. With Tai's help I carried Father down the road.

Later, the hot afternoon light pierced the treetops. The farther we walked, the slower the journey became. My surroundings blended together. It seemed the same huddle of trees we idly passed had become the next. Tai and I carried Father for two strenuous miles before Sihun took my brother's place.

As Sihun strained to raise the hammock, I noticed for the first time how emaciated and sickly she was. The sunlight showed the hollowed angles of her haggard face. Her thin arms trembled, yet she was determined to carry Father. *How long could she go?*

"Stop. Put me down." Father strained to speak, feeling guilty seeing my sister struggle. "You have five young children to care for. I can walk." He gathered the last of his willpower to rise out of the hammock and walk. We followed alongside him closely. After a few feet, Father's breathing became labored. He shook with weakness and anxiety.

Tai and I placed Father back in the hammock and slowly hauled him. We finally reached the Stung Sen River, where there was already a mass of people waiting for a ferry to cross. The rapids of the wide, murky river were turbulent. Nevertheless, some of the strong swimmers jumped into the churning water and managed to swim across to the other side. The opposite shore was barely visible. Although it seemed far away, I was happy because I knew somewhere across the water there would be a town or city where Father could get medical attention.

* * *

At daybreak the next day, we crossed the river on the ferry and then carried Father on the wide clay road that continued just as it had left off from the other side of the river. It went on far into the distance and ran straight through spurts of jungle.

A mile along the road, we came across a Vietnamese motor truck parked on the side. We put Father down and ran toward it. We communicated with the men inside it using Khmer and sign language to beg for a ride. We told them Father was very sick and could not walk. The Vietnamese driver looked behind the two of us and saw Father wrapped in the hammock down the road. He nodded his head.

Tai's wife and children climbed in, while we ran back and retrieved Father, but when we got back the truck was already full. People clambered in, elbowing for the last seat. Other refugees must have heard our conversation. Tai and I pushed Father above the other passengers' heads and then forced ourselves inside. Compressed side by side, tight against each other, there was no room for Father to lie down or even stand. It was so cramped that Tai and I quickly roped the hammock across the high grid railings so he could stretch out.

* * *

The truck sped off, bowling down the bumpy dirt road, throwing up spirals of dust in its wake. Dozens of refugees ran after the truck even as it drove away. The truck rumbled on along the dusty, unpaved road.

The wind raised thick layers of red dust. It stuck to my sweaty skin and clothes, coating my lips and tongue. When the truck jerked to avoid refugees on the road, I clutched the hammock, trying to limit its swaying against the guard rails. Everyone frequently fell on each other. I feared I would be crushed to death.

The day was getting hotter. I could barely fill my lungs in the scorching wind. I asked Father how he was doing, but he could not hear me. The hammock was closed tight like a black cocoon. When I opened it to see if he was still breathing, Father gasped for air and his eyes squinted tight against the blowing sand. His face was colorless.

The truck drove for two hours, until it finally stopped at a Vietnamese checkpoint and dropped us off at the end of its zone of permission. We were getting close to Kampong Thom province, the end destination that we had heard other refugees talk about.

The sun had just turned west, signaling the afternoon heat, when we started again on the bone-dry road. With our scrawny bodies and limited strength, Tai, Sihun, and I picked up Father together this time.

He was so heavy. We made little progress. This was the slowest we had ever traveled on this journey, marching strictly by force of habit, conscious solely of the stumbling, bare thud of our feet. The intense heat clung to my back and the hot sand stung my heels. My legs became unsteady and I felt my own fever was worsening.

We dropped the hammock to the ground in sheer spirit-breaking exhaustion. We halted. The road continued to go on, but there was no point in walking into more uncertainty and hunger. The day had sapped the rest of our strength, and we were parched and trembling from fatigue. We could not go any farther. Father was ill; I was sick; we had eight small children with no more food. Complete despair descended on us.

For more than half an hour we sat there, abandoned in the middle of nowhere. For a long time, I trained my eyes on the distance before I glimpsed a man riding a silver bicycle down the road. The rider stopped each time he saw a refugee to ask them a question and moved on. I knew if there was a bicycle here, we may not have to travel that much farther. The biker pedaled toward us. I thought the man looked like Chiv and I asked my family if they thought so too.

The bicycle drew closer. A glad cry broke from my sister. "It *is* Chiv!" The children excitedly ran for him.

Tears sprung from his eyes. Chiv told us he had been riding for days looking for us. His bladder had begun to bleed from dehydration, but he had continued on. He carried more than a hundred pounds of rice sacks and dried fish on the back of his bicycle. When Chiv saw the state Father was in, he told us to remain where we were and eat while he went to get help. He said to give him a day to return.

* * *

The day after, Tai, my eldest brother, shoved off. He told us he was going to carry on and attempt another escape out of Cambodia, this time traveling east through Vietnam. He felt we were safe now that Chiv was going to bring aid. He took his entire family and said a simple goodbye.

Later in the day, an oxcart arrived that Chiv had sent to retrieve us. I rested Father on his back and pulled myself up into the cart. The last of my strength ebbed away. My mind slipped, yielding to the fatigue. I did not have the energy to utter any words. I could only surrender into this immense wave of relief.

The cart jerked into motion and the wheels creaked. Never in my life had I valued so greatly something as simple as an oxcart. The wooden boards carried me as driftwood on waves—clouds on land. It moved at a slow pace, but that didn't matter as long as it was moving toward somewhere better.

In front of us, refugees still carried their babies and possessions balanced over their heads. Silhouettes of heads and shoulders bobbed, vying to keep up with the oxcart. They seemed determined not to let it get out of their sight, as if it promised an end. They could tell it was very close—this felt like the end of the journey.

Soon the dirt road intersected with the paved National Highway 6, and evening gloom spread above us. A convoy of canvas-covered Vietnamese trucks passed by on the heavy road. We slept that night alongside the highway in the floodwater ditches. Father was stricken with a deathly hack of a cough. He was growing weaker, his lips thin and purple.

I asked myself what I would do if he died. For two and a half months, we had roamed almost one hundred fifty miles from Preah Vihear Mountain into the heart of Cambodia. It was a distance that could have killed a man half his age.

I lifted my eyes to see refugees meandering on the highway. Many people had walked to and from great distances. The long roads had not broken their spirits. They had places to go, and places to return to. They had not lost all.

I had a sense that life might prosper again. If all the beauty had been lost, it would be rediscovered. Like a dry pond that swelled with rainwater and leaping fish. This was the beginning of peace and plenty and potential.

That night, sheltered under the eaves of a traditional Cambodian wood house that Chiv rented in the village of Damdek, we began to recuperate from the treacherous months and years of our long suffering.

Chapter 26

The Forked Road

Behind the house there was a huge rice field fanning out in all directions, green as far as I could see. Each day before sunset, I walked out there and sat beneath the shade of a palm tree. The sun was low and red in the west, sinking beneath the mountain horizon. It brought sadness. I did not want to stare out at rice fields and dull brown huts for the rest of my life. I wanted to be where the people were, to see them in colorful clothing, dancing, playing music, and laughing. Traveling by car instead of water buffalo. I wanted to drink Coca-Cola out of a glass bottle, instead of water from bamboo cups. I wanted to see buildings, electricity, construction, markets, city faces among open shops and restaurants. I wished to experience the ordinary once again. I became fed up with the heat in my face, caked mud between my toes, and blisters on my hands.

But a defined period in my life had closed. I could not dwell in the other lands. My best efforts were not good enough to carry me through another two and a half months. I hoped fate would allow me to settle here with Father. There was enough in this small town to start anew once more: a house, my family, food.

However, life was still dangerous and difficult in Cambodia. The country always seemed to face war and strife. I was young, and if I stayed, there was a real possibility conflict would break out again and I would be drafted into a war I did not believe in.

* * *

On the fifth day in Damdek, it was dark when Tai and his family arrived at the door and broke the quiet. Tai carried his heavy bundles, disappointed. He was gaunt—his brown eyes sunk into his skull and his sun-beaten cheeks hung slack. Inky shadows lay beneath his blood-shot eyes. Disappointment had left a desire that burned at the back of his throat. Yet he was surprisingly emotionless when he uttered, "I'm not giving up. I want to escape again to Thailand."

All of us yearned for freedom.

I slept with Father on a straw mat in a corner on the small, second-floor balcony. That night, he spoke in a worn and wretched voice: "I want you to leave with your brother Tai."

"What about you?"

"I can't do it anymore. There is no need to worry about me," he replied, without any obvious sadness or regret. "I will be with your brother Chiv, here. You are young and have a future ahead of you. There is none here. With your age they will constantly try to draft you to be a soldier. This is not your country anymore."

Sihun heard us talking from below. "Please take my son," she spoke, in a flat restrained tone, as if she had learned to swallow her grief. "If you make it, I will have one child who will have a future. I cannot support five children by myself. Help me to spare one of my children."

Necessity was breaking apart our family.

In the morning, Tai came up and said goodbye to Father, then went back outside to wait for me. I did not want to leave. I looked at him. With his wrinkles as deep as gashes and pallid cracked lips, he appeared so weak and old. He stretched his hands across my head. He held me close, his bony fingers brushing my hair gently back and forth.

"If you make it. If one day you have the opportunity, find your cousins in China. You have six of them in China. Tell them all about us." Father's eyes were empty and solemn. "You are so young. Why has this happened to your life? To mine? I have nothing to give you." Then he said something I never forgot. He asked me to remember him in my heart.

Words stuck in my throat, which squeezed tight with despair. I could only manage to say, weakly, "None of this is your fault. I can still stay here with you."

"You're not going to do any good staying here. You will only be in trouble. It won't help anything. Just go!" His voice died away. He did not speak again. He just fixed his gaze on me. My chest burned.

"Ba . . ."

He did not answer. His eyes flooded with tears.

"Ba!" I repeated. "Ba!"

I tried to shake him. He did not return a word, keeping his eyes from me. I tried to catch his eye, but he looked away. I could not move. He would not glance at me again. I stood in front of him, not knowing what to do. In the past, I had always looked into his eyes for answers. Now there were none.

I had to let go.

Nothing more was said. I had become blank. My memory dug a hole to bury the hurt, the madness. I shoveled the truth into this hole, blocking out the terrible pain of that moment. I knew then, in my heart, I was not going to return and he was never going to come. I could not wait for the grim realities he feared to come true.

That was the way I remembered saying farewell to my father. I left him without saying goodbye.

PART III

Unbroken Threads

PART III — UNBROKEN THREADS

A   Damdek   **5**   National Highway 5

B   Sisophon   **6**   National Highway 6

C   007

D   ▲ Buriram Refugee Camp

Chapter 27

Farewell Cambodia

Sihun hugged her son Heng and cried, "Listen and obey your uncle and be a good boy. I will always love you."

"Why do I have to go?" he asked.

"Mother can't take care of you right now. This way you can go to school." Tears rimmed her eyes. He could not understand the troubles that could possibly bring a mother to give up her son. Was any reason good enough in a child's eyes? As he tried to bravely make sense of it, I grabbed his hand and walked out with him. I could see the sadness in his eyes. Heng withheld any further protest, afraid to make his mother cry more. As a child, this is how he protected his mother.

Saddled with Father's fervent wish, I took to the road. I had survived this far through some combination of luck and resilience. We had escaped and cheated death. But with all that, I still feared my very existence could be denied again if events turned against us, and we could be hurled back to Preah Vihear Mountain.

We had no choice but to risk death again to return to Thailand, even if it posed catastrophe once more. I had to find a way to create a new fate for myself, and the result would either be blissful freedom or scornful graves. We prayed to the Heavens and the spirits to keep watch and lead us.

Our best hope was to return to Sisophon, where we could get information for our escape.

* * *

The marketplaces had already closed for the night when we arrived in Sisophon, after more than eighty miles of walking. Paper litter and trash choked the alleys. A number of people were sleeping in a small street of fruit and vegetable stalls. In the vacant corner of a market stage, we sat to rest our bony backs against the wall and fell into an exhausted sleep.

I awoke to the sounds of footsteps crunching on the sandy dirt. People carried boxes of goods and produce into tents. A buzz of voices emerged in the markets. Noodle grills and cooking woks fired up. The sidewalk concessions soon came to life.

Kiosks and cart vendors vied for space on the walkways. Thoughts of my past life in Poipet flooded my mind while I wandered through the city crowds. I found many people had lugged in goods from Thailand: cigarettes, Mama-branded dried noodles, sugar, fake jewelry and watches, MSG, canned sardines, fruits, fishing line, and clothes. I had thought we would never see this again. When I asked a shopkeeper where the products came from, he said they were brought in by Cambodian smugglers who traveled here every day. They convened to buy the goods on the Thai border.

At this, an idea came upon Tai like a seed in the winds. Along with the prospect of earning money through the trading routes, he said, we might find information on how to elude the Thai authorities at the border. A feeling of hope came over me like a sweet sickness. Surely, somewhere out there, we were bound to find the right help.

We sought to hear what the people in Sisophon had to say about getting to the border. They told us we had to quickly traverse a wide swath of many miles of forest during the day because the Khmer Rouge still occupied it at night. So while the rest of the family remained behind, Tai and I set off early the next morning, making arrangements with a group of smugglers to lead us through the forest.

The smugglers brought us to a well-traveled path that had been worn through the dense woods to Thai soil. At the edge of the border, in a circle of dead grasses and trampled bushes, we found gatherings of Cambodians and Thais that tried to trade with each other in sign language. More and more people were coming in. It was an unorganized auction, with hands going up in flailing gestures.

Cambodia now had many demands: fishing hooks, tire tubes, used bicycles, oversize beaten-up radios, medicines, mosquito nets; anything to restore the country. People who made purchases bumped and jostled each other, trying to make off with their items while dozens more clamored around the Thai vendors. The people had not lost their entrepreneurial spirit.

Using the last bits of gold I had left, I bought a carton of Thai cigarettes. In that moment, I observed the struggles the Cambodians were having following the Thais' demands. The difficulty in communicating left some of them empty-handed. Since I could speak Thai, I quickly brokered deals with the Thais to buy a bulk quantity of cigarette cartons for cheap, then I immediately sold these off to the Cambodians right there at a higher price. I did it again and again. The Cambodians came flocking to me. I quickly doubled and tripled my wages! It didn't matter what price I charged because they all bought the cigarettes. I had long forgotten the triumph, the unspeakable thrill of buying, selling, and interfacing with Thai people.

Those who purchased my cigarettes immediately opened the boxes and smoked right there. A man asked if I wanted one. "What the hell," I said. "Why not? What could it hurt?" The man lit it—my first cigarette. Copying the other smokers, I sucked on the stick, but after a few drags I coughed it up.

As time passed, more people flooded in. Amid the crowds, I saw a woman I thought I recognized, selling sarongs and MSG out of baskets. It was Jie-Ya from Aranyaprathet! She was so happy to see us. But it was the words she said that I will never forget. Sweeter than any water.

"I have good news for you. Your brother and sister were saved. They are now in America!"

I could not believe my ears. She extracted a torn envelope from her pocket and gave it to us. "I can't believe I found you," she told us. "I've been holding this letter, coming here every single day looking for you."

It was like a message from beyond the grave. Choa had sent the letter to her, and he wrote that he had been rescued from the mountain and was now living in America. He described America as if living in Heaven. If we were alive and received the letter, Choa instructed us to escape as soon as possible, so he could sponsor us.

Written at the bottom was an American address and phone number. An American address and phone number.

* * *

My spirit soared to heights I thought I would never reach. I wanted to laugh, dance, and scream like a madman. Suddenly the links to a new and better life were right there. The vague search for freedom was over.

We hurriedly bought supplies, especially water, and crammed our rucksacks full. After discovering that Sihong and Choa had been miraculously saved, we were eager and anxious to have such fortune find its way to us.

When we arrived back at Sisophon, someone I thought was a stranger sat in the home where my family was staying, conversing with Tai's wife. She was old, with a red krama scarf wrapped around her head. Her face was bony and weathered, and she had coarse red hands with long prickly veins along her arms.

It was our old Cambodian nanny, Yeay Sek! I failed to recognize her because she looked so different after the years of deprivation. Yet before I could utter a word, she flung her thin arms around us in delight and cried, "I was looking for you guys for six months!"

She told us after the Vietnamese liberated the country, she had gone off on her own, searching for us. It was a strange stroke of luck that Tai's wife was shopping in the Sisophon markets and found Yeay Sek with a woven basket of rice balanced on top of her head.

We asked her what happened to her son. She answered in an angry voice and cursed. "He tricked me to go live with him! And now he has abandoned me! When the Vietnamese came, he picked up and left. He is not my son or part of my life anymore. You all have always been my family. I've been wondering how you have been doing these last four years. Where is the rest of the family?"

A glow of sheer excitement passed over us as we told the family the good news that Sihong and Choa were now living in America. "Where is America?" asked Yeay Sek. To her, the whole world was Asia, and that was the only region that mattered. We laughed. We didn't know either.

But we knew it existed somewhere out there.

To make sure we were quick and nimble on foot for the journey into a border area of Thailand we had never been, we culled our possessions. We sold most items to the merchants and gave the rest to Yeay Sek, who decided to stay behind because she missed Father very much and wanted to find him to help take care of him. She and Father were both born the same year, the Year of the Dragon, and she had always held great reverence for him. Tai gave her medicine to take to him and asked her to pass along the news that his children were now bound for America.

* * *

We awoke three hours before dawn. It was still black as pitch when we set off in the obscurity of darkness before anyone could see us leave. Desperation made people do unpredictable things, and we did not want other frightened people to demand that we take them with us, when we still did not know just how we would accomplish reaching our destination.

Jie-Ya had already arranged for a man named Liang to help sneak us into another Thai camp that had housed refugees prior to their expulsion to Preah Vihear. We had to meet him just over the border before evening of the next day, near a military encampment known as 007. This was the best route because it was the least populated by roving bandits and less prone to guerrilla attacks.

Upon returning to the same forest that the smugglers had guided us through before, we encountered on the narrow path smugglers heading in the opposite direction, toward Cambodia. One weary man shouldered bails of goods harnessed at each side. We asked him how the conditions were ahead of us.

"Walk fast and pass the Khmer Rouge zone before sunset. Once you get to the border crossing, you must be careful of the Khmer Serei. The Khmer Serei are not organized by any government, they just call themselves soldiers. Many of them are ex–Khmer Rouge. Watch out for a man they call Don. Everyone is afraid of him. He is a high-ranking soldier who controls the rest of them. He has been known to rape, loot, and kill people."

At the mention of Don, I was flooded with a cold panic. I asked the man to describe what Don looked like, but he replied that he had never seen him. All he knew was the name. "He is a Khmer Rouge like the rest of them."

I could not believe it was the Don I knew. I grew scared.

* * *

Darkness had fallen at the border when we arrived. The sparse land leading to the crossing point was littered with plastic bags and dirty paper wrappings. Masses of people had already staked out places to camp for the night, populating the area with campfires and blue plastic tarps slung between narrow teak trees.

We made a shelter among some trees a few paces off from the crowds. It was an abandoned spot where the grass was already flat, trampled by someone else. I kept a quiet lookout for Don. I didn't tell the family I knew him. It would only trouble them more.

All night, my mind was fettered by Don's tautly stretched smile.

* * *

In order to disguise ourselves among the smugglers, we dumped our last belongings except for empty gunny sacks. For a quarter of a mile, pockets of smugglers traveled back and forth between the border crossing. Thai tradesmen were heading to Cambodia, while we were heading to Thailand.

I was so afraid Don might appear and recognize me and call out, "Hello, Bean Brother," that I made myself half a head shorter than the rest. I trailed behind a pair of old men and covered my face with one of the gunny sacks to protect me from Don if he appeared.

We reached a military outpost, where loud Cambodian music came from inside a thatched tent. Empty beer bottles and plastic crates cluttered the area, giving the impression of soldiers who spent more time partying than protecting the borders.

On the far side of the outpost, a stocky man walked along with four Khmer Serei trailing him. He reminded me of Don, with his broad shoulders and a sidearm harness on his leg. But I was afraid to even look in his direction. I crept in the middle of the family and turned my head away while the men passed us.

We followed the smugglers for a bit more before they led us to a border market just within the Cambodian border. The place was abuzz, teeming with people scurrying about in all directions carrying bags of merchandise in their hands. Tai began speaking to different merchants in search of the best way to cross the border.

Long green spears of grass grew behind the market. When nobody was looking, Tai snuck into the tall grasses and hunkered down there, while we waited beside a busy market stall. Tai looked back toward us, surveying for any sight of guards.

At last he raised his hand. His wife ran to him with her youngest boy tight in her arms, then the other children followed behind. I watched with my nerves building inside me. Tai took another look around and gave me a reassuring nod.

I joined them all in the shrubbery and we made a beeline for the thin forest. Every now and then, I heard the stir of leaves and snap of fallen twigs. Each noise sent a shiver of fear through me.

The spikes of dusty sunlight in the forests dimmed. The faded light made us feel even more vulnerable. This territory was now into Thailand, the same country I thought we had left behind.

After staggering through the hushed surroundings for several minutes, we came to a clearing with stubby grass covering the soil like a poorly shaved beard. In the still air, we could just barely catch the rumble of engines and the hum of tires from rushing traffic.

"We need to follow that sound," Tai said. After holding still for one more cautious moment, we started forward and broke into the scrub clearing.

"Stop! Don't move!"

An angry voice yelled in Thai from behind us. "Put your hands above your heads and kneel down." The Thai soldier came up from behind and stood, his gun raised at us.

"Please don't shoot," we pleaded in Thai, shaking feverishly.

"Get up with your hands over your heads, turn around and go back, before I shoot!" We would not get up. We would not go back. I could hear the cars rushing. Beyond the line of trees ahead was the highway, and there Liang was waiting for us. We were so close.

"Please don't send us back." My sister-in-law spoke, her voice wracking with sobs. "We are refugees that were sent to the mountain. We lost a loved one. Now the Cambodian government is after us, looking to arrest and throw us in jail. Please don't make us go back. Have mercy on us." She took out five hundred baht and held it for him. Her quivering voice begged him to take it. The soldier did not want it.

She crawled out to him with her face down on the ground, and at full length her hands nearly touched his feet. The soldier pointed the gun at her. "I beg you. Please let us go," she cried. Ignoring his threats, she clawed over him, sobbing wretchedly into his shirt. She stuffed the money in his top shirt pocket. Shocked, the soldier pulled his rifle to his shoulder and snatched the Thai baht out of his pocket. He tried to give the money back to her, but she crawled backward from him and stayed bowed on the ground, trembling with cries.

He pocketed the money again but spoke without a vestige of sympathy. "All right, hurry up. There are other soldiers over there." He pointed off in the direction of safety. "If you get caught again, don't say you saw me."

"Yes sir. Yes sir." We groveled and thanked the man.

* * *

At dusk, we neared the intersection of a highway. Liang was waiting there on foot when he saw us. "Why did it take you guys so long?" he said with urgency. "Stay put in the bush there. I'm going to get the truck."

We hid in the bushes by the road. A few cars rushed by. Liang soon reappeared with a white delivery truck with twin exhausts. He got out of the truck and looked around, then waved his hands and called out, "Hurry! Get on!"

We dashed to the truck and clambered into the back. Once we entered, his workers pulled the roll-up doors down, enclosing us in darkness. Car doors slammed. The truck rumbled, honking twice, lurching down the road.

Inside, I could not see anyone's face. The air in back was thick with the musty smell of urine and rotten fish, mingled with diesel fumes and old leaking oil. Fortunately, we did not have to stay in the truck for long. We entered thick Thai traffic, surrounded by whistles and horns, and before long the truck edged up a street, crunching over gritty asphalt.

The truck engine dropped to an idle and the roll-up doors slid up. "There is a checkpoint ahead," Liang said. "My workers will take you guys through a detour around the checkpoint. Stay quiet. Don't talk, just follow them. I will meet you on the other side." He watched for any cars, then gave us the go-ahead. "Now! Go! Go!"

We jumped out of the truck and followed two of his workers into the forest. They immediately took us down a rabbit path that was so faint it was not apparent to our eyes. As we picked our way through, the path grew wilder and fainter.

Until it completely vanished.

* * *

"We are close," one worker reassured me. Using a machete, he swiped to clear a path through the woods. But his confidence seemed to diminish with each hack that caught in the thick tangle.

At about midnight we came to where the forest met agricultural land. I peered out from the woods and saw glistening rice paddies and glassy water shimmering in the milky half-moon. In the distance, white lights dotted the blackened horizon, but we did not know what they were. We asked the guides if we were lost. They did not answer. They both talked to each other, pointing in different directions.

"It is late now. We will take you guys directly to the camp."

The workers had us clamber over the four-foot-wide levees into the marshy rice paddies. I stood deep in the paddies, the air releasing smells of churned earth and swamp grass. The feathery rice stalks were up to our hips as we plodded heavily; the deep, sticky mud released our feet with a sucking sound.

We climbed onto another dry hunk of land, into another stretch of rice fields, another lagoon. We moved like trench soldiers. Holding one of the little ones in my right arm, I windmilled the other arm, pushing through the tall clusters of waving grass and towering rice plants. We were merely thin silhouettes blending into the land. Everything was dark and wet and swirling. There was nothing to see but endless swampland.

* * *

It was still predawn, around five in the morning, as the guides stared out at the shrinking darkness and debated the best route. One sighed in defeat, tired of the aimless wandering.

"That's as far as I go." He pointed at the distant lights, which looked to be coming from a cluster of buildings.

"You walk toward that light," he told us. "There is a refugee camp there. It will be able to save you. You must get there before sunrise." He tried to mask the nervous tension in his voice, perhaps shame at their failure. With their shoulders hunched and heads hung low, they walked back in the direction of our thinned, churned tracks and left us on our own once again. Nothing more could be done. We kept moving.

As we waded knee-deep in the heavy clods of swamp mud, the partial sun straddled the skyline: rays slowly spread and our shadows formed beneath. I saw a highway crossing the length of the fields and a car go by. Another truck drove in the opposite direction, fouling the air with black exhaust.

We crawled forward to the edge of the highway embankment and crouched at the bottom of the hill, peering out from the screen of grass. On the other side of the road was a strip of grass and then a high fence. The fence had wooden posts driven firmly into the ground and was topped with wicked coils of barbed wire. It ran around a community of corrugated-tin and plywood roofs, rusting in many rows.

Joy overwhelmed me. This is what we had crossed a never-ending jungle to find.

Tai wiggled himself three feet up the embankment and ran across first. I looked at both ends of the road and saw no cars. Tai then gave the signal to run no matter what came our way. Pulling the hands of the children behind me, we all vaulted over the embankment and sprinted across the highway as quickly as their little legs could carry them. We slid down the hill and ran across the deadened yellow grass right up to the barbed wire fence.

Tai pulled up the bottom wire, and I got down on my hands and knees to worm my way under. It was more difficult than I expected, and it was several minutes before I was on the inner side. I staggered to my feet, wet and smeared with clay and dirt, and took stock of my surroundings. There was nothing I could do to hide myself. But with the wind in my hair, the dawn in my eyes, I felt human for once.

Beams of sun broke across the earth, bathing the land in orange.

Chapter 28

The Haven

We ducked into the first sleeping quarters to blend in with the other refugees. A Cambodian man stood at the door opening while the other refugees slept on wooden beds.

"Can you help us please? Can you find a place to hide us?" we begged him in Khmer.

"I can try, but this camp is for refugees who escaped before 1975," he explained. "All the new refugees who arrived were sent back."

"Stop! Don't take another step!!!" a Thai guard shouted and ran toward us. I froze in the doorway. We were already caught; nobody could save us now.

At the same time, an unsettling sound from outside the camp: a low strumming, rising and easing. It turned into a prolonged howl, and a vehicle edged into the refugee camp.

"I'm going to get you guys help," the Cambodian man said. And with a glint of an idea in his eyes, he disappeared into the long sleeping quarters.

Two men stepped up. One had a long rifle, with a face cut to the bone and a pronounced pointy jaw. The other was chubby, with military stripes on his arm and a pistol strapped to his leggings.

When we saw them approaching, we kneeled to the bare, compacted earth of the shelter.

"Have mercy on us. Don't send us back," Tai said.

"How did you get in?" the thin-faced guard asked. "Someone must have brought you here." We remained silent.

"Tell the truth before we beat you," the stout supervisor yelled, red-faced. "Who brought you here?" He towered over us with a baton, shaking and threatening us with it.

"No one brought us here, sir. We came ourselves, sir," Tai said.

"You liars! If no one brought you here, you must be spies to find your way into here." He then told the guard, "Take the men to the room. Bring the rope. Beat them and we will get the answer."

They led us toward the front of the camp, where a watchtower stood. There was a night watchman on the roof. Somehow we had not seen the watchtower when we sneaked in, but the man inside it had spotted us.

The supervisor flung the door wide open. A cloud of cigarette smoke veiled the inside. The murky room had a single table, three chairs, and a staircase leading to the roof. I paused at the threshold. Before I could move, a strong hand pushed me in. Then one of the men grabbed me and tossed me into a sharp-edged chair.

The supervisor sat in the desk seat and lit a cigarette, tusking the smoke out of his nostrils. The guard by the window held a whip in his hands. Tai's wife and children were left outside.

A loud crash came down on the desk. "Who brought you here?! Where are you from?" screamed the supervisor.

He lifted his fist from the table to lean over and scream in my face. I could see his black-stained teeth. Again, he yelled, "Who brought you here?! There is no way you got here yourself." We still did not answer back. I didn't dare move. These guys were going to lash us. My throat and chest compressed in fear until it was difficult to breathe. He looked at me with cold eyes. "Tell me! There is no way you guys came here alone! You must have had someone bring you here! Tell me where you were going. Tell me now!"

Suddenly, right behind the guard, I saw the faces of two white Western men outside the windows. They were talking to Tai's wife and she urgently pointed to the room where I was being held. One of the Western men peeked inside, sending the Thai guards into a fit of rage.

The man entered the room. He exchanged a few words with the soldiers. Immediately, they erupted into shouts at the Western man, throwing their hands up in aggravation.

The Cambodian man from the sleeping quarters came in from behind, gasping from running. When he spoke to us, he whispered so as not to be overheard by the guards. "You are very lucky! These Western men drove in today of all days. This just happened. Get out. You can go. Hurry!" He eagerly motioned for the front door. "You are getting saved!"

We got off our seats and we were met by the other Western man. He saw the fright on our faces as we pleaded, "Don't let them send us back again. We are refugees of the mountain." The Cambodian man translated our frantic words for us.

The Western man with his sharply pointed nose nodded and spoke. The Cambodian man translated back, "Don't worry. You are safe with us." My chest lightened at his promise. We followed the Western man to the entry gates of the camp. Behind us I could still hear the other one arguing with the Thai guards. He was trying to hold the guards back.

At the entry gates stood a mini-bus with Western words emblazoned in big letters on the side-front doors. I could not read it. The Western man opened the door and sitting inside were four other refugees. They were in much better shape, and they stared with pity at our torn clothes and muddy hair.

Something froze my feet to the ground. I knew the importance of this escape, that it meant our freedom. But somehow my feet wouldn't budge. It was as if my muscles and bones could not understand that this was real.

The Western man had to shoo me aboard out of concern over the approaching Thai guards. Once inside the mini-bus, I sat by a window and I cried. It was over, but it was not over.

I was saved. But Father was not.

Chapter 29

The Letter

I saw Father one last time. He appeared to me at night.

It was at the end of a long November day in Buriram Refugee Camp. We had received a letter from Chiv telling us that a week after we departed, Father became gravely ill. Chiv and Sihun sat Father against a post and coined him, rubbing his skin to remove the illness from his body. Father had said to them, "It is of no use. The hour is here. My soul has already walked away. I shall go before the sun arrives."

To ready for the moment, they prepared his possessions to take with him. They filled his pockets with gold, Thai baht, and Mother's ring, then dressed him in many clothes, in all of his shirts, so not a piece of his skin showed except for his head. But Father requested they remove the gold and money, and cut the pockets from his shirt and pants to ensure he would not take his children's prosperity with him. He asked Sihun to make sure the diamond ring was passed on to me.

Father's final desire was to leave the world before sunrise, thus preserving the next day's meal for the children. He hoped that in this manner his last sacrifice would be deemed worthy to put his family right with the Heavens again, opening the way for the many stolen blessings to be restored to them and to the ones yet to come. "I wish you and all your children have the most that fortune can offer," he told them.

Chiv and Sihun sat beside him throughout the night. When Yeay Sek found them the next day, arriving with medicine, it was too late.

Tai's hand trembled as he held the yellowing paper. I was so emptied by the news, I ran off alone, away from my brother, nieces, and nephews.

I could not see anything at all. All I could do was follow Father's voice in my mind. My thoughts raced while images of Father arose: waiting at the train station, at play with his grandchildren, giving me his last sweet potato, in pure joy of reaching new land, his smile asking me what country I wanted to go to. I remembered carrying him downhill, on my back, holding his arm. I wished I could have helped carry him once more on the second escape. But it was not to be. He would not have made it. What more could I have done?

I retreated to a quiet pavilion at the center of the camp. The hurt was overwhelming. Father had not even received the news that we made it out. I wanted him to know we were all safe and sound. Had he known we were going to America, he could have died in happiness instead of despair.

For a long time, I remained in the pavilion. A patch of silver light fell from the faint moon. I stared up at the white stars over the Cambodian country skies. Over that land, where Father's spirit rose, I longed for the stars to somehow reconnect me to him.

But Father had passed away a month ago. The only place I could see him was in my dreams.

* * *

Late that night, I saw the hills, lush green, and a bridge and river surrounding his tiny new home. Heavenly tones rung the air. He was haloed in the splendor of a Chinese suit, gleaming in silver, glowing fierce like the sun. Father was holding Mother's hand, and she was dressed in glittering red.

His voice was healthy and bright as I remembered. "I am fine now and with your mother. Do not worry about me, my son. It is your life now. Move on. Go on and find your brother and sister."

He smiled tenderly and they turned, heading in a shining aura for their home on the hills.

Chapter 30

America, America

On the day we left for America, I wore blue jeans, a blue button-up shirt, and a white Dancing Fever cap purchased at the Thai flea market. The only thing I carried in my hands was a brown duffle bag made of imitation leather. In the afternoon, a bus picked us up with other refugees and departed for Bangkok's Mueang International Airport. Tai did not come with Heng and me to America, but he was fine because he had been sponsored by his brother-in-law to immigrate to France.

When I entered the airport, I saw refugees sprawled all over the terminal floor. Women were breastfeeding their babies. A lone shriek echoed from a child wildly running down the long departure hall. And all of it was so beautiful: the neat rows of chairs, the shiny orange ceramic floor tiles, the long stretches of ticket counters. Everyone seemed to be brimming in smiles. Here at the airport, it already felt like a welcoming foreign land.

The resettlement workers came to distribute a white laminated bag to each of us, with our documents inside. They told us to always have our identification numbers on the front, displayed at all times. "If you lose it, they will never find you." One by one, they called us and then led us to an airport gate.

As we stood at the bottom of the boarding stairs, the plane of shining aluminum and glass looked gigantic, larger than the freight trains to Battambang. The evening air throbbed with intense heat, but when we boarded the plane, I felt a fresh blast of cool air hit my face.

I could not believe it. The cockpit was right there for me to behold. In front of the pilot seats was a dizzying array of panels with flashing buttons, circuits, levers, switches, and clocks of different shapes and sizes. The exhilarating whir inside the plane was strange and new and wonderful: the air buffer, the swooshing sounds outside the hatches, all of it together flooded my mind with thoughts of the past.

It stuck me, then: After all the years and the endless trips through the countryside, forsaken, I had found my Apollo.

I may as well have been climbing aboard Apollo 11.

Seeing the awe on my face, the flight attendant smiled and spoke to me in English. I immediately held up my bag. She looked inside and pulled out the United Airlines ticket with our seat number, and she led us to our seats at the back.

Heng took the window seat. Then it sounded as if the voice of an angel spoke. I looked up to see a tall blond flight attendant trying to explain to all the passengers how to use the seat belt and slip on the safety oxygen bags. Not one of us had a clue what she was doing. Her passengers stared back at her, dumbfounded.

The angelic woman walked down the aisle, helping the refugees fasten their belts, one by one, slamming shut the overhead compartments. The pitch of the engine rose higher. I also felt it in the center of me.

Peering at the dark sky outside, I felt lightheaded with the emerging reality of freedom. We were soon to cross the mountains, the seas, the clouds, the skies themselves. The passengers were equally excited, and I could feel their rising energy.

The plane taxied, then at last took off and soared away. Heng pressed against the window. He pointed outside, bursting with joy. "Look! Look! It's getting smaller. Everything is getting smaller!" It was all new to him, enough to make him forget, for a moment, all he was leaving behind. I leaned over and saw the city lights shrinking below. I felt Father's spirit there, at the center of it all, as real to me as the lights themselves.

As soon as the seat belt sign went off, the aisles flooded with refugees waiting for the bathroom. They took a long time trying to figure out how to use Western toilets. Plus, since it was the first time on a plane for many of them, maybe all of them, the refugees were having air sickness. In our depleted condition, even something as simple as a fast car ride would make some of us nauseous. There were plenty of air sickness bags, but nobody knew how to use them.

After two hours of flight time, the plane made a quick refueling stop. It was dark and we could not see the country where we landed, but I knew it was Hong Kong from the language of the cleaning crew. Two maintenance crew workers entered the plane, and one of them opened the bathroom door. He shouted in disgust and covered his mouth with his white-gloved hand.

He spoke Cantonese, which I could only understand a little bit. The worker tried to enter the bathroom once more, only to jump back, cursing and screaming. The other worker also unsuccessfully attempted an entry. They steeled themselves for a third try and managed to clean whatever was in there, then stomped down the aisle, peppering their angry Cantonese with curses.

The plane flew from Hong Kong to Alaska and then to San Francisco. The blue water of San Francisco Bay sprawled beneath us. From our altitude, everything was so small, the buildings like boxes and the cars like toys.

And oh, there were so many, many cars. I could only think there were more cars than all the bicycles in Cambodia. I took note of each unfamiliar shape and object, mentally hearing all the sounds of Cambodia: the train on the way from Battambang, the energetic rings of speeding rickshaw horns, the glee of children playing soccer, the calls of women selling fruit drinks and tea in the markets, fishermen singing songs by the lakes, men clamoring over a chicken fight. In that illusory moment, I thought about my life in Cambodia; I had not really left it behind. Even if I were back there at that moment, those things would still be far away.

* * *

When we got out of the Apollo 11 airplane, I saw American passengers heading toward public telephones on the walls and putting quarters into the machines. I had my brother's number, but had no money and didn't know how to use the phone. So I quietly stood in the terminal hall and held my laminated bag close to my chest, making sure the people walking by could see the numbers.

People arrived, left, and were replaced. Distorted loudspeakers echoed the long terminal halls, announcing things that made some of the travelers run. As the airport swallowed them up, no one gave notice of me. We had slipped into America quietly and without fanfare. The flight was monotonous and uneventful, and yet for us, everything here was foreign and new. The air was different, as were the food smells and the Western style of clothing.

However, some things never change, and I needed to relieve myself.

I saw some overwrought travelers jostle into the bathrooms. "The men are going into this one," I told Heng. "It must be for us."

A man standing at a urinal had just finished, and I heard a loud *whishhh* as he turned to leave. Heng and I went over to the walls and tried to mimic the man. Heng finished first without flushing. I reminded him he must follow what the others did and use the lever. I pressed down on it, and water cascaded down. So much water. It seemed as if it would never stop. Panicking in my ignorance of Western life, I thought the handle had to be pressed again to turn the water off. I pulled the lever once more, and more water gushed loudly into the basin. "We broke it!" I told Heng in panic. "Hurry up and run!" I grabbed his hand and we ran out.

Fortunately, no toilet police showed up and no arrests were made.

The resettlement workers arrived with a translator. "You still have to fly to New York. That is your final destination. We are going to take you to a place to stay."

So after flying for two whole days, I still had not arrived at Choa's home. I had expected him to pick me up here, not realizing America was so big. Before we exited and braved the windy weather outside, the resettlement workers gave us beautiful brown polyester winter jackets with a beige stripe across the chest. It was cold until I put on the jacket, and then it immediately filled me with warmth. *How can foreign strangers love us like this?* I wondered, touched by their affection. In this way our arrival in America was warm, amid the loving protection of total strangers.

* * *

After two nights, the resettlement workers drove us back to the airport and put us on a plane to New York City. As I boarded the plane and walked through the aisle, unable to find my seat, I looked around and had no idea what the passengers were saying. For this flight, the plane was full of Americans, and from what I took in, we were the only two refugees. They were all so strange and different. They smelled of meat. Their faces looked funny with their long-bridged noses, and their blond and brown hair color looked to me like the spotted coat on Cambodian oxen. In Cambodia, I only saw foreigners who took boat trips on the Mekong River, photographing the little children playing in the waters. I had not encountered so many white Americans before.

"Hi. I'm Barbara," a flight attendant said to me with a smile.

"Hel-lo Baarber," I replied, my own smile nervously wavering. She helped me to my seat on the right side. I sat by the window, Heng in the middle, and a young American man with big glasses by the aisle. Barbara then held up my documentation bag in her hand, urging me to hold it tight so I would not get lost.

The plane sped forward and kicked off the black blurring runway. Heng leaned nearly into my lap to get closer to the window. The morning city was getting smaller, soon obscured by lapping shrouds of clouds. I closed my eyes, floating in the engine's thrum. With the bag hugged close to my chest, the light from the airplane window was warm on my eyelids and my breathing softened, relaxing away.

I arrived in New York City on April 25, 1980, exactly five years after the Khmer Rouge expelled us from Poipet. We waited outside the terminal, where I continued to hold my bag tight in my hands. The airport was busy, exhaling and inhaling people. Impatient travelers leaped into waiting taxis and rushed off for their next destination. People drove up and found their families, hugged them, and turned for home.

More people came and went. But nobody came for us.

Heng and I waited for two hours. I didn't see any signs of Choa, and I was too timid to ask for help in making a phone call. I feared he was lost.

After a long while, a black man with a uniform and cap approached me. Using gestures and English words I did not understand, he persuaded us to follow him. Without any other options, we did. He turned out to be a limo service driver and took us to his car. It was a taxi station wagon. He told us to get in.

In the back were three other Cambodians.

"Do you know where we are going?" I asked in Khmer.

They shook their heads. The taxi drove away.

I gazed at the tall buildings: glass, metal, and concrete soaring toward the sky. Fast cars with shiny bumpers and hubcapped wheels, long highways and bridges. We drove on without stopping for what seemed to be hours, long after the buildings shrank into the background.

The streets became more spacious, lined with more trees. But there was nothing relaxing about any of it. The ride was really taking a long time. *When am I finally going to meet my brother?*

It was not to be, yet. Day turned to evening; the streetlights flickered orange.

At last we arrived at an abandoned church. It turned out to be a safe spot. A refugee aid organization was using the place to house new arrivals.

The organization that temporarily managed the refugees, and my sponsor, the International Institute of Connecticut, called my brother Choa. He quickly came to meet us.

When I saw him, my throat seized up. *Choa! How was he still alive?* The sight was overwhelming, as if he had returned from the dead. I relived it all in an instant: the time it took for us to get here, the miles, the long separation between us, the efforts of many. Now we were finally together again.

I was so caught up in the turbulent memories of the past five years, I felt deeply connected to Father. There was a part of him in both my brother and me, and always would be. Something inside of me began to thaw.

We looked at each other for a long moment. Choa smiled and broke the silence with two words.

"Welcome home."

* THE END *

Epilogue

As my father's long story of survival to America concludes, this leaves me with the responsibility to give the rest of the scoop. I began helping my father write his story when I was nineteen, nearly the same age as when he lived through his ordeals. Years after we began, he told me he had expected me to give up before finishing the book, because I knew nothing about the life of a refugee. He was convinced that one had to live that life to understand, and since nobody wants to do that, he could not believe I would relate to his story. The only meaningful response I could make to those concerns was to keep going.

And so I diligently typed and recorded every word, down to precise details. The story was so difficult for him to tell, to relive; he had to close his eyes and put himself back in that place and experience the emotions all over again. My questions summoned demons he thought had been vanquished.

The stories he told in daylight returned to him at night. He would wake up in his bed with dreadful night terrors. After thirty-some years of distance from the experiences themselves, the attacks returned and repeated themselves to him, night after night. It was all harder to bear, the second time around, since the story had taken place for a young man in his prime. Now Father's heart was older and his aging body was tired.

The nightmares faded for him minutes after awakening, so all he knew for certain was they were terrifying. To calm his heart, he would remind himself he was at home. "I'm in bed in the United States, not Cambodia. I am somewhere safe."

Sometimes he would stay up for the rest of the night to avoid the nightmares. Several times his PTSD grew so grave he asked to stop telling his story and abandon the project. I gave in each time, trusting that somehow we would be able to pick it back up again at some point. Each time, he found a way to rise to the occasion and the storytelling continued. His courage and determination brought this gift to us.

* * *

My father, Mae, remained in Bridgeport, Connecticut. Mae was his childhood nickname, and when in America he at first went by his more formal name, Bunseng. After taking factory assembly jobs at General Electric and U.S. Surgical, his entrepreneurial roots as a tradesman took hold again in a similar fashion in America. When he was thirty he started his own home painting business and selected the nickname Ben when his clients found it too difficult to pronounce his name. Due to pronunciation differences, the last name Chen had been changed to Taing in the Buriram Refugee Camp. He would meet my mother, Cambodian-born herself, at a wedding in Philadelphia, and they would go on to have two children, myself as the eldest.

Sihong, her husband, and all of her children except Kip were able to resettle in Connecticut. Choa's family also arrived in America with Sihong's family, and both families remained in Connecticut for many decades. They were the first of our family to arrive in America because they had been rescued at Preah Vihear, under terms that resulted from negotiations involving compassionate American officials. The family and the thousand refugees with them were allowed by Thailand to stay only a very short time in the Mae Surin Refugee Camp, before moving to the United States as promptly as possible.

After the landmine accident, Sihong's son Kip was hospitalized at the Vietnamese military camp in Sisophon. Chiv found him, and once Kip recovered, they fled over the border to Khao-I-Dang Refugee Camp. Sihong's boy, Liam, was never found, even with the assistance of a few people searching in Cambodia.

Sihun, her family, and Yeay Sek also followed Chiv and Kip in their final escape into Thailand. They all resettled in Bridgeport, Connecticut. Tai and his family originally planned to resettle in France, but as fortune would have it, a quicker sponsorship came through from America first. He joined the rest of the family in 1980.

Dangdi didn't run far before he was captured by the Khmer Rouge. He was sent to a different concentration camp and was finally freed when the Vietnamese liberated the country. Today he lives in the Los Angeles area and works in the restaurant business.

Ming and Sudian stayed married and resettled in Paris, France. They had three children together. Today it is unknown what happened to Ming's three other siblings.

In the early 2000s, the bones of Mae's father, my grandfather, were retrieved from Damdek and reburied in Roka Kaong.

There has never been an attempt to find Wensun's body. He is survived by his five children.

Mother's diamond ring is still part of the family's keepsakes.

LOOKING BACK ON HISTORY

The Preah Vihear Temple is an imposing eighth-century masterpiece that looms hundreds of feet over the site where my father and other Cambodian refugees were repatriated. The landmark ruins have had an impact on me, personifying two opposing chapters of the Killing Fields. One represents a former symbol of glory and another of neglect. It is a place that embodies both beauty and horror. It represents my adoration for Cambodia's marvelous ancient past, and at the same time reminds me of those who mercilessly suffered from the Khmer Rouge's tragic attempt to recapture the achievements of those same ancestors.

As of today, nearly lost and invisible in the kingdom of the jungles are the discarded clothes, U.N. blankets, and burlap bags. Shattered ceramic and porcelain objects lie among the wreckage, all covering the graves of thousands of refugees who lost their lives there.

Even after forty years, countless thousands of landmines still riddle the area. The border soldiers have named the site Ghost Mountain. The ghosts of those who died there await the ghosts of those foolish enough to walk the mined fields.

It is unknown exactly how many refugees were lost at Preah Vihear. The current estimate by the CIA reports that out of the forty-two thousand refugees sent there, roughly ten thousand lost their lives or went missing; nearly one in four innocent people.[1]

The forced push of Cambodians down Preah Vihear Mountain remains one of the worst incidents of refugee repatriation in international history.

The question remains as to Thailand's reasons for so ruthlessly rejecting Cambodian refugees. Thailand had become increasingly

---

1   Thompson, Larry Clinton. *Refugee Workers in the Indochina Exodus,* 1975–1982. Jefferson, NC: McFarland & Co, 2010; 175, 178.

fearful of the Vietnamese encroaching on their borders, fearing the Vietnamese would purposely allow Cambodian refugees to flood into Thailand and destabilize the country. The past decade had given credibility to this concern, since each of their neighbors to the east— South Vietnam, Laos, and Cambodia—had fallen to Communism. Given the deteriorating border climate, Thailand was not set up to deal with the humanitarian emergency, and at that time the international community showed no interest in helping them.

The legacy of the United States in Cambodia has also taken on twin narratives. On one hand is a failure in foreign policy that justified bombing neutral Cambodia in the name of peacekeeping. The illegal and ineffectual bombardments were not only responsible for the deaths of thousands, but also created the terror and civil disruptions that enabled the Khmer Rouge to gain power. The ramification of this failure in foreign policy still lingers today, as seen when the U.S. has conducted other bombing strikes without Congressional approval in the years since.

The other legacy has been mostly forgotten, but should be remembered because of its uplifting nature. It took countless unsung heroes to manage the humanitarian crisis. These were maverick aid workers who defiantly risked their careers and often their own safety. That motley collection of people came from every spectrum, bringing an unprecedented response of rescue and relief. Washington, D.C., had awakened to the need to clean up the war mess after Vietnam, and ever since, the United States has been a leader, proving the merits of human rescue to the public.

No other country but America has ever shown this type of legacy. And it is one the American public should admire and honor. It prevented greater human catastrophe, demonstrating how to deal with conflicts and disaster going forward. When Cold War fighting engulfed one country after another in Southeast Asia, further violence was averted not by bombs and bullets, as has been so common in past policy, but by aid, relief, and compassionate rescue.

Their courage to right wrongs brought redemption to an otherwise terrible and difficult period in American history. Thus this story of my father is not so much a Cambodian one—but an American one. Their noble acts of mercy and kindness were immeasurable achievements of duty, virtue, and heroism that our country can remember with pride. That message of upholding human dignity and rights, especially when they are in jeopardy, will always be vital to our world's needs.

In tribute, I have them to thank for a freedom and a country that are now mine.

—J.T.

Acknowledgments

For her invaluable contribution we'd like to thank Jenny Taing. From reading early drafts to giving us time at the most inconvenient hour for advice on the cover. Thank you for caring about this book. She was as important to the birth of this book as anybody.

Our gratitude to Sokcheat and Sothea Heng for helping with the translation of words and the names of people, towns, and cities.

The biggest thanks to Virginia Lynch Dean and William Douglass for believing in this story and helping to share it with others. It has been your support that has been the most encouraging. Also, heartfelt gratefulness to Dianne Wildman, Aaron Clar, Amy Kalafa, and Ian Holden.

Thanks to everyone on the Greenleaf team who helped us so much. Special thanks to the lead project manager, Lindsay Bohls, our lead editor, Erin Brown, and the talented art director, Neil Gonzalez. It was a privilege to work with Anthony Flacco to blast away at the earlier draft to arrive at a more developed book. Much appreciation to Peter Smith and Heather Zavod for taking a look through those early manuscripts. And thank you to our editors, Karen Cakebread and Stephanie Bouchard.

Many warm thanks to Joshua Lin for your printer, which was important in more ways than one through the many various drafts.

Gratitude to all those who have been a part of us getting here: Katie Allen, Colin Ambrose, Charles L. Atwood, Drummond Bell, George Biddle, Roy Brosler, Karen M. Castaldi, Christy Cerio, Kuong H. Chaing, David Chang, Arn Chorn-Pond, Sam and Vathana Chhiv, Everett Cook, Jay Cross, Isabel Duke, John Duke, Jodie Eastman, John Erdmann, R. Bradford and Barbara Evans, Terry Flatley, Joan M. Frost and Jeremy Frost, Richard Furlaud, Ludwell Gaines, Andrew and Christine Hall, Celia Hegyi, Dean Herbert, Jerry Ing, Russ Janisch, John Kazickas, George Kellner, Seng Kim, Cristie Krauss, Darcy Kuzmier, Jarrett Lilien, Mike Lowrey, Jake and LeeLee Ma, Mitchell S. Marcus, Terry Marsh, Georgiana and David Mellgard, Albert Messina, Charles Miner, Chris and Sandra Neubert, Kate Parenteau, James Pool, Whitney Quillen, Christina Robert, Aron Rose, Robert S. Salomon, Idoline Scheerer, Russ Schif, Richard G. Schneidman, Derek Vance Schuster, Stephen Siegel, Mary Streep, Katie Taing, Tim Taylor, Beth Tiedemann, Patricia Toole, Edward S. Trippe, Peter Turino, Kathleen L. S. Turner, Johnathan M. Wainwright, Thaddeus Walkowicz, David and Cynthia Whitehouse, Elaine Yip, and Brandon Yu.

Lastly, unmeasurable thanks to the exceptional leaders (among so many others) for their relief work and refugee rescue in Southeast Asia: Lionel Rosenblatt—U.S. State Department Lead Refugee Officer, Morton Abramowitz—U.S. Ambassador to Thailand, Lord Mark Malloch Brown—U.N. High Commissioner for Refugees in Thailand, Sheryl Keller—Head Nurse at Khao-I-Dang Refugee Camp, and to the late MacAlan Thompson—U.S. State Department Deputy Officer and Robert P. DeVecchi—President Emeritus of the International Rescue Committee. A president once remarked after the fall of Saigon that, "History will judge whether we [Americans] could have done better."

Undoubtedly, that judge in history could only wish that more was made today of your selfless charity and lionhearted compassion. And it shall here. Thank you for following your heart and instinct by putting "humanity ahead of politics." You are legends.

About the Authors

MAE BUNSENG TAING is a survivor of the Khmer Rouge genocide in Cambodia. His story and that of his family inspired the documentary *Ghost Mountain*, released in 2019 and directed by his son, James, and Virginia Dean. Mae Bunseng lives in Connecticut with his wife, where they raised their children and where he has run a full-time home painting business for more than thirty years. This is his first book.

JAMES TAING is the son of Mae Bunseng. Over a decade ago, he began interviewing refugees before codirecting the HAAPI Film Festival award-winning documentary *Ghost Mountain*. He is the founder of the Preah Vihear Foundation, a nonprofit that advocates for preserving the history of refugee rescue in Cambodia and the greater French Indochina region in the 1970s. He also works in risk and finance in the metro New York area.